KU-135-903

PUBLICATIONS

OF THE

NAVY RECORDS SOCIETY

VOL. 110

THE SAUMAREZ PAPERS
THE BALTIC
1808–1812

THE NAVY RECORDS SOCIETY was established in 1893 for the purpose of printing rare or unpublished works of naval interest.

Any person wishing to become a Member of the Society is requested to apply to the Hon. Secretary, Royal Naval College, Greenwich, S.E.10, who will submit his name to the Council. The Annual subscription is Two Guineas, the payment of which entitles the Member to receive one copy of each work issued by the Society for that year, and to purchase back volumes at reduced prices. The Subscription for those under the age of 30 is One Guinea.

MEMBERS requiring copies of any volume should apply to the Hon. Secretary.

Subscriptions should be sent to the Hon. Treasurer, 81 Bromley Road, Shortlands, Kent.

THE COUNCIL of the NAVY RECORDS SOCIETY wish it to be clearly understood that they are not answerable for any opinions or observations that may appear in the Society's publications. For these the responsibility rests entirely with the Editors of the several works.

ADMIRAL JAMES, 1st BARON DE SAUMAREZ
(1757–1836)
reproduced by kind permission of the Trustees of the National Maritime Museum (Greenwich Hospital Collection), from a copy by Edwin Williams after the original painting by
THOMAS PHILLIPS, R.A. (1770–1845)
the original being in the possession of the Saumarez family and painted in 1810.

THE
SAUMAREZ PAPERS

SELECTIONS FROM THE
BALTIC CORRESPONDENCE
OF
VICE-ADMIRAL
SIR JAMES SAUMAREZ
1808–1812

Edited by

A. N. RYAN, M.A.

Senior Lecturer in Modern History in the University of Liverpool

PRINTED FOR THE NAVY RECORDS SOCIETY
1968

©

Navy Records Society

1968

122112

DA 25. N12

QUEEN MARY
COLLEGE
LIBRARY

PRINTED IN GREAT BRITAIN BY
SPOTTISWOODE, BALLANTYNE AND CO. LTD.
LONDON AND COLCHESTER

THE COUNCIL
OF THE
NAVY RECORDS SOCIETY
1967–68

———◆———

PATRON
H.R.H. THE PRINCE PHILIP, DUKE OF EDINBURGH, K.G., F.R.S.

PRESIDENT
THE RT. HON. LORD CARRINGTON, P.C., K.C.M.G., M.C.

VICE-PRESIDENTS
JOHN EHRMAN, F.S.A., M.A.
LIEUT. COMMANDER PETER K. KEMP, O.B.E., R.N., F.S.A.
THE REV. J. R. POWELL, M.A.

COUNCILLORS

A. J. L. BARNES, M.A.
DANIEL A. BAUGH, M.A., Ph.D.
NICHOLAS R. BOMFORD, M.A.
CHRISTOPHER DOWLING, M.A., Ph.D.
PROFESSOR GERALD S. GRAHAM, M.A., Ph.D.
VICE-ADMIRAL SIR PETER GRETTON, K.C.B., D.S.O., O.B.E., D.S.C.
VICE-ADMIRAL SIR ARTHUR HEZLET, K.B.E., C.B., D.S.O., D.S.C.
SIR JOHN LANG, G.C.B.
PROFESSOR M. A. LEWIS, C.B.E., Litt.D., F.S.A.
PROFESSOR CHRISTOPHER LLOYD, M.A.
E. W. R. LUMBY, M.A.

R. F. MACKAY, M.A.
PIERS MACKESY, M.A.
RICHARD OLLARD, M.A.
COMMANDER J. H. OWEN, R.N.
A. W. H. PEARSALL, M.A.
PROFESSOR A. TEMPLE PATTERSON, M.A.
PROFESSOR B. McL. RANFT, M.A., D.Phil.
CAPTAIN S. W. ROSKILL, D.S.C., R.N., M.A.
ANTHONY N. RYAN, M.A.
JONATHAN STEINBERG, M.A., Ph.D.
E. K. TIMINGS, F.S.A., M.A.
OLIVER WARNER, M.A.

HON. SECRETARY
THE HON. DAVID ERSKINE, M.A.

HON. TREASURER
BERNARD POOL, C.B., C.B.E.

IN MEMORY

OF

CHRISTOPHER STEPHEN RYAN

AND

MARTHA ELIZABETH RYAN

PREFACE

The Saumarez papers were deposited in the Ipswich and East Suffolk Record Office in 1963 by the Hon. James V. B. Saumarez to whom the society and the editor are deeply indebted for his ready consent to the preparation of a volume based on a selection therefrom and his interest in its progress. The papers consist of a vast collection of unbound documents and letter books relating to the Baltic command of Vice-Admiral Sir James Saumarez, later Admiral Lord de Saumarez, in the period 1808–12. The editor owes an immense dept of gratitude to Mr. Derek Charman and the staff of the Ipswich and East Suffolk Record Office for their most attentive and efficient service. Material from the Keats papers and Yorke papers is printed by kind permission of the director and trustees of the National Maritime Museum, Greenwich. The editor is pleased to acknowledge the prompt and unfailing assistance of Mr. A. W. H. Pearsall and the staff of the Students' Room at Greenwich. The selection also includes crown copyright material from the admiralty correspondence in the Public Record Office, which is published by permission of the controller of H.M. Stationery Office, and material from the Martin papers in the British Museum. The editor's thanks are due to the staffs of the Public Record Office and the British Museum for their assistance over many years. A few documents already in print are reproduced here. They are taken from Sir John Ross's rare biography of Saumarez which was published as long ago as 1838 and has not yet been supplanted.

When he began to study the Baltic campaigns the editor was privileged to enjoy the encouragement and guidance of the late Professor Mark Thomson. He is highly conscious of what he owes to many colleagues and friends. In limiting his acknowledgements to those who helped with specific problems in the preparation of this volume, he is nonetheless mindful of others who have kindly advised and encouraged him. Professor David Quinn of the department of Modern History in the University of Liverpool readily discussed editorial problems whenever requested to do so. Professor Nadejda Gorodetzky of the department of Russian and Mr. Donald Barker of the department of German, both in the University of Liverpool, gave generously of their time to answer questions which baffled the editor. Mr. Brian Morgan read several versions of the general introduction and found ways of improving each one of them. Miss Rosemary De Sausmarez, to whom the editor was unknown, graciously supplied him with much valuable information about the Saumarez family and related families in Guernsey and Jersey. Mr. Douglas Birch, the photographer to the Faculty of Arts in the University of Liverpool, laboured for many hours over the maps. The kindness and helpfulness of the society's honorary secretary the Hon. David Erskine were a constant source of encouragement.

The editor has failed to invent a simple rule governing the spelling of place-names. Modern English and foreign usage is observed except where the name of a place has been fundamentally altered by modern political changes. In these cases the contemporary name and spelling is preserved in the text: e.g., St. Petersburg, not Leningrad; Christiania, not Oslo. Furthermore the manner of spelling certain place-names was so much a part of the contemporary vocabulary of the British navy that it too has been preserved, with the modern spelling given on the first occasion in square brackets. Nobody who has read the official and unofficial correspondence of Saumarez and his colleagues could possibly substitute Vingå Sund for Wingo Sound or Sprogø for Sproe.

The portrait of Lord de Saumarez is reproduced by kind permission of the director and trustees of the National Maritime Museum, Greenwich.

The Council of the Society is once again pleased to acknowledge the generous financial support of The British Academy in the production of this volume.

CONTENTS

LIST OF ABBREVIATIONS

Add. Mss.	Additional Manuscripts preserved in the British Museum.
Adm.	Admiralty Papers preserved in the Public Record Office.
F.O.	Foreign Office Papers preserved in the Public Record Office.
Kea.	Keats Mss. preserved in the National Maritime Museum.
R.A.	Riksarkivet, Stockholm.
Rockingham.	*The Rockingham and Hull Weekly Advertiser.*
Ross.	Sir John Ross, *Memoirs and Correspondence of Admiral Lord De Saumarez*, 2 vols. (1838).
Yor.	Yorke Mss. preserved in the National Maritime Museum.
877.	Saumarez Mss. (Ha. 93.877) preserved in the Ipswich and East Suffolk Record Office.

ILLUSTRATIONS AND MAPS

GENERAL INTRODUCTION

James Saumarez was born at Saint Peter Port in the island of Guernsey on 11 March 1757. He was the third son of Matthew Saumarez, a member of the medical profession, and his second wife Carteret Le Marchant. The Saumarez family was of Norman extraction, the family estates in the Channel Islands having been held originally in fief from the dukes of Normandy. Saumarez, the anglicized version of the name De Sausmarez, only came into use as late as the first half of the eighteenth century. Matthew Saumarez, born on 10 October 1718, was a son of Matthew de Sausmarez and Anne Durell, daughter of John Durell the lieutenant-bailiff of Jersey. He was one of several sons, two of whom, Philip and Thomas Saumarez, were naval officers. The profession of his uncles had a decisive influence upon the life of James Saumarez.

The officer corps of the Royal Navy in the eighteenth century had many characteristics of a club, the members of which were linked, in spite of the fierce and frequent feuds, by bonds of blood, friendship and professional solidarity. Membership was open to men of courage and talent whatever their social origin, but it was conferred most readily upon those who numbered among their relations or friends a serving member prepared to introduce them. In the case of the Saumarez family the initial naval connection came through the Durells. Philip Saumarez was born in 1710 and entered the navy under the auspices of his uncle Captain Thomas Durell in 1726, being followed at a later date by his brother Thomas born in 1720. Neither Philip nor Thomas lived to reach the top of the profession. Philip, a survivor of Anson's circumnavigation, was posted captain in 1743 and appointed to the command of the *Nottingham* (60) in 1746. He was killed in Hawke's battle off Finisterre on 14 October 1747. Thomas, widely regarded as a post-captain of great promise, died prematurely, possibly from a disease contracted in the West Indies, in 1766. The deaths of Philip and Thomas did not sever the naval connection. Matthew Saumarez was able without difficulty to place his son inside the quarter-deck circle; firstly by having his name entered in the books of the *Solebay* (28) commanded by Captain Lucius O'Brien in 1767 and secondly by obtaining a position for him on board the *Montreal* (32) commanded by Captain James Alms, a friend of the brothers

Saumarez, in 1770. From this ship James Saumarez was soon transferred for a short period to the *Pembroke* (64) commanded by Captain Philip Durell.[1]

The advantages of a naval connection were shared by Saumarez with the great majority of entrants into the profession. While they may help to explain his ultimate rise to high rank, they certainly do not explain his attainment of a high reputation. Saumarez was commissioned in 1776. A bald summary of his career thereafter reads like a list of great naval occasions. As second lieutenant of the *Fortitude* (74), flagship of Vice-Admiral Sir Hyde Parker the elder, he won the approbation of his chief at the battle of the Dogger Bank in August 1781. A few months later, having in the meanwhile been promoted commander of the *Tisiphone* fireship, he sailed off Brest under the orders of Rear-Admiral Richard Kempenfelt and 'had the good fortune to be the first who discovered the enemy's fleet consisting of nineteen sail-of-line escorting a numerous convoy from Brest'.[2] Several of the latter were captured; and the object of the expedition, the reinforcement of the French forces in the West Indies, was frustrated. He was thereupon detached to the West Indies with intelligence of this event, was posted captain shortly after arrival there and appointed to command the *Russell* (74), in which ship he fought with credit in Rodney's victory over de Grasse at the Saints on 12 April 1782.

His first appointment in the war with revolutionary France was the command of the *Crescent* frigate. In October 1793 he took the enemy frigate *Réunion* off Cherbourg, the reward being a knighthood. In 1795 Saumarez was removed at his own request into a ship-of-the-line, the *Orion* (74), and took part in Bridport's battle of the Ile de Groix on 23 June of this year. At the end of 1796 the *Orion* was ordered to the Mediterranean. Within a week of joining the Mediterranean fleet Saumarez fought in the battle of Cape St. Vincent on 14 February 1797. Subsequent to this engagement he was employed in the blockade of Cadiz, where his conduct was highly approved by the commander-in-chief, Vice-Admiral John Jervis, earl of St. Vincent. Saumarez was by now a senior and highly experienced post-captain. He was selected as second-in-command of the squadron sent up the Mediterranean in the spring of 1798 under Nelson, with whom his relations were not always easy, to hunt out and bring to battle the Toulon armament: a hunt which ended in the discovery and destruction of the enemy fleet in Aboukir Bay on 1 August. In 1799 Saumarez was attached to the Channel fleet of which St.

---

[1] This account is based on material in 877/119; Ross, vol. i, pp. 7 ff.; J. Marshall, *Royal Naval Biography*, vol. i (1823), pp. 174 ff.; information privately communicated by Miss Rosemary De Sausmarez.

[2] Adm. 1/10, Statement of the services of Vice-Admiral Sir James Saumarez, dated 4 June 1810.

Vincent assumed command in the following year, when he was put in charge of the newly created inshore squadron of six sail-of-the-line employed in the close blockade of Brest. He served on this hazardous station from August to December 1800 and again from March to May 1801. Early in 1801 he received his flag; and in July he commanded a squadron in battle on two occasions. The first was a tussle in confined waters beneath the batteries of Algeçiras which was remarkable for the loss to the enemy of a British ship-of-the-line, the *Hannibal* (74): a unique event in the wars of 1793–1815. Three days later on 9 July, though outnumbered by nine to five, he shattered a Franco-Spanish squadron off Cadiz. This was his last battle engagement with the enemy. He missed Trafalgar being at the time on the Channel Islands station; and after a spell as second-in-command of the Channel fleet in 1806–07 was again serving as commander-in-chief Channel Islands, when he received the first lord's invitation, dated 20 February 1808, to accept the command of a fleet about to be sent to the Baltic (doc. 3).

Saumarez was now within a few weeks of his fifty-first birthday and had not yet tasted the responsibility of high command in a major theatre of war. The Channel Islands command had been of local importance during the period of the French invasion threat, but with the passing of the threat, the holder of this post could look forward to neither glory nor distinction. The truth was that Saumarez had still to establish himself as a fleet commander. So far he had given every proof of being, to quote Mahan's assessment, 'the accomplished and resolute division or corps commander'.[1] This assessment is very near to that made by Saumarez of himself. When scouring the Mediterranean with Nelson for the vanished Toulon armament in 1798, he wrote frankly of his own misgivings:

'Some time must now elapse before we can be relieved from our cruel suspence; and if, at the end of our journey, we find we are upon the wrong scent, our embarrassment will be great indeed. Fortunately I only act here *en second*; but did the chief responsibility rest with me, I fear it would be more than my too irritable nerves would bear. They have already been put to the trial in two or three instances this voyage.'[2]

The sense of relief experienced by Saumarez then aged forty-one at not having the burden of the chief responsibility must surely exclude him from any list of heaven-born commanders. To leave it at that would be judge his professional merit by the most high, and at the same time most arbitrary, standard. There is also the fact that in an age of strenuous professional competition he outshone most of his contemporaries.

[1] A. T. Mahan, *Types of Naval Officers Drawn from the History of the British Navy* (1902), p. 409.
[2] Ross, vol. i, p. 210.

Saumarez belonged to that select group of officers, including Horatio Nelson and the gifted Thomas Troubridge, who may be counted as the *protegés* of that most exacting master in the naval hierarchy, the earl of St. Vincent. The earl may not have esteemed him as highly as he did Nelson and Troubridge, but when in 1800 he decided in the teeth of a great deal of professional opposition to institute a close and continuous blockade of Brest it was Saumarez he chose to command the inshore squadron. 'Really and truly', he wrote, 'after Sir Jno. Warren, who neither knows nor fears dangers of any kind, Thornborough and Saumarez are the only men within reach I dare confide that post to'.[1] The strain of commanding a squadron off the Black Rocks in the Bay of Brest was a trial for the 'too irritable nerves'. Those who met him in the late autumn of 1800 spoke of his being 'as thin as a shotten herring'.[2] Yet he clung to the post, hitherto considered tenable only by frigates in the autumn and winter, until December and resumed the watch in March of the next year. In February 1801 St. Vincent became first lord of the admiralty. His satisfaction with Saumarez's conduct was such that he appointed him on 7 June commander of a squadron ordered to go off Cadiz. Before sailing he was created a baronet. This mark of distinction had, significantly enough, been solicited for him almost twelve months earlier by St. Vincent, who urged it not only on the ground of past services but also because 'nothing can gratify me more than that officers, who have signalized themselves under my auspices, should be amply rewarded'.[3] The powerful backing of St. Vincent brought Saumarez to the threshold of high command. He accepted the invitation to step over it on 27 February 1808 (doc. 4). For the next five summers his flagship H.M.S. *Victory* rode the Baltic, at once a man-of-war and a floating embassy; and Saumarez himself was an armed diplomat.

The creation of the Baltic command was a consequence of the Franco-Russian treaty of peace and alliance signed at Tilsit on 7 July 1807. The significance of the treaty as it affected northern Europe was that Russia agreed to make common cause with France in enforcing the commercial, military and political exclusion of Britain from the continent, her responsibility being the closure of the Baltic to British merchantmen and warships. The policy of exclusion was a function of French imperialism in Europe and a condition of its success. Each one of Napoleon's victories of 1805–07 was followed by an enlargement of the area from which the British were banned. A declaration of intent to make the ban effective from one end of the continent to the other was implicit in the Berlin decree against British trade

[1] St. Vincent to Spencer, 5 Aug. 1800, H. W. Richmond (ed.), *Private Papers of George, second Earl Spencer*, vol. iv (Navy Records Society, vol. lix, 1924), p. 8.
[2] St. Vincent to Spencer, 29 Oct. 1800, H. W. Richmond, *op. cit.*, p. 19.
[3] St. Vincent to Spencer, 26 July 1800, Ross, vol. i, p. 335.

published on 21 November 1806, five weeks after the destruction of Prussian power at Jena. The realization of the intent had, however, to wait upon a change in Russian policy. This necessary change was achieved by the French victory over the Russians at Friedland on 14 June 1807. Tsar Alexander I, dissatisfied as he already was with the inadequacy and tardiness of the British contribution to the continental war, was rapidly convinced that an alliance with France might be more rewarding than the one with Britain had been. The price of the alliance was a pledge of Russian collaboration against the British.

Alexander agreed to compel Denmark, a neutral state, and Sweden, a member of the now almost defunct anti-French coalition, to close their ports to the British flag and to expel British diplomats and subjects from their territories unless Britain accepted his mediation by 1 November. Here was a direct threat to freedom of navigation in the Sound and Great Belt, the narrow entrances to the Baltic, which flowed through Danish territory. The hint of such a threat was enough at any time to alert Britain whose naval arsenals were in great part stocked with flax, hemp and timber from the Baltic region. In the existing circumstances the government, alarmed by rumours concerning the Tilsit negotiations which revived memories of the hostile Northern Confederation of 1801 created by Napoleon and Tsar Paul and agitated by morbid suspicions of Danish policy which owed something to the part played by Denmark in the said confederation, launched without warning a combined assault upon the city and naval base of Copenhagen in August 1807.[1] The objects thereof were the seizure of the Danish fleet and the terrorization of the northern powers. The policy of terror misfired. It alienated both the Danes and the Russians without doing anything to remove the impression formed in the war of the third coalition that Britain had neither the will nor the means to support effectively continental states that resisted the power of France. Denmark instead of capitulating as she had done following Nelson's bombardment of Copenhagen in 1801 declared war against Britain and concluded an alliance with Napoleon. Russia, affronted by the violation of a state of which she was the traditional protector, followed suit with a declaration of war. Prussia, suspended in isolation between France and Russia, had no choice but to adhere to the anti-British line. The attack upon Copenhagen had decisive consequences quite apart from its political repercussions. The seizure of the fleet deprived Denmark of the means to close the Sound and Great Belt. Though the passage through them of merchantmen could still be impeded and inconvenienced, the British fleet was able to intervene at will in the Baltic Sea, where its chief function was to

---

[1] A. N. Ryan, 'The Causes of the British Attack upon Copenhagen in 1807', *English Historical Review*, vol. lxviii (1953), pp. 37–55.

brush aside by force and persuasion the obstacles to British commercial and political activity in northern Europe.

The post-Tilsit alignment of the northern powers did not include Sweden whose ruler Gustavus IV Adolphus was convinced that the war against Napoleon was a war for the survival of legitimate government. The element of reality in this view was, however, warped by his obsession that Napoleon was the Beast of the Apocalypse.[1] Gustavus's apocalyptic daydreams rendered him unfit to guide Sweden through the dangers which confronted her following the Russian *volte-face* at Tilsit, for they dimmed his appreciation of the facts of power. He rejected the Russian request that Sweden should abandon the war against France and subscribe to a declaration that the Baltic was a closed sea to foreign warships.[2] He ignored the broadest of hints from London that the British government would not regard it *per se* as an unfriendly act should he seek an accommodation with France and her allies in order to extricate Sweden from the danger of war with Denmark and Russia.[3] He thus wrecked the slight possibility which, despite the hostile declarations, existed at the end of 1807 that the state of formal war between the Baltic powers and Britain might not necessarily result in belligerent action: a solution acceptable enough to Russia whose hopes of expansion were fixed upon the territories of the Ottoman Empire[4] and equally acceptable to Britain whose attitude towards the Russian declaration was tempered by the hope that the alliance with France was an aberration, incompatible in the long run with Russia's true interests as those interests were understood in Whitehall (doc. 45). But the obdurate refusal of Gustavus to deviate from his set course left the Russians and Danes without any clear alternative to the use of force against him. The Russian army invaded Finland on 21 February 1808; the Danes began to prepare an invasion across the Sound into southern Sweden to be led by the French marshal Bernadotte who had under his command in northern Germany a polyglot army made up of Belgian, Dutch and Spanish contingents.

The invasion from Denmark never materialized. Preparations were arrested by the appearance off Zealand in mid-March of a detachment from the North Sea fleet commanded by Captain George Parker of the *Stately* (64) (docs. 1, 2, 5, 8) and brought to a final halt through the destruction of the *Prins Christian Fredrik* (64), Denmark's last operational line-of-battle

[1] S. Carlsson, *Gustaf IV Adolf: En Biografi* (Stockholm, 1946), pp. 152 ff.
[2] S. Clason, *Gustaf IV Adolf och den Europeiska Krisen under Napoleon* (Stockholm, 1913), pp. 104 ff.; A. Grade, *Sverige och Tilsit-Alliansen, 1807–1810* (Lund, 1913), pp. 108 ff., 138 ff.
[3] R.A., Diplomatica Anglica, Adlerberg to Wetterstedt, 4 Dec. 1807; F.O. 73/45, Canning to Thornton, 15 Jan. 1808.
[4] P. Tommila, *La Finlande dans la Politique Européenne en 1809–1815* (Helsinki, 1962), p. 17.

ship, by the *Stately* and *Nassau* (64) on 22 March. Bernadotte's army was ruined as an offensive force early in August when 9,000 of the Spanish officers and men under his orders, who were stationed in Jutland and the Danish islands, mutinied on receiving intelligence through various channels of the anti-Napoleonic rising in Spain and succeeded in making their escape to the British warships cruising in the Great Belt (docs. 30, 36, 39, 40).

These events eased the pressure on Sweden, but they did not alleviate the anxiety of responsible Swedes concerning the likely outcome of the king's adventurous policy. Pessimism was widespread in official and military circles. The army in Finland was deeply infected by it with the result that ground was yielded to the Russians at a rate which precluded any chance of recovery. The great coastal fortress of Sveaborg, near Helsinki, was surrendered after only a token resistance early in May, largely because of the despondency, not as was supposed at the time the disloyalty (doc. 12), of its commandant Carl Olof Cronstedt, though disaffection among Finnish born officers on his staff cannot be ruled out as a contributory factor.[1] Swedes were not alone in questioning the capacity of Gustavus. Lieutenant-General Sir John Moore, leader of an expeditionary force ill-advisedly sent by the British government to aid Sweden (docs. 11, 15, 22, 25), came away from Stockholm after fruitless discussions concerning its employment, which ended in his virtually being placed under house arrest, determined on no account to commit the force to the king's direction.[2] Retribution for the royal errors came in March 1809, when a revolutionary movement initiated by Colonel Georg Adlersparre and a section of the western army (doc. 58) and continued by aristocratic officials in Stockholm deposed Gustavus and replaced him by his uncle Duke Charles with the title of Charles XIII (docs. 63, 92).

Saumarez, therefore, was faced from the moment of his first arrival off Gothenburg on 7 May 1808 with a deteriorating situation, over which he did not have complete control. The loss of Sveaborg and of one hundred craft of the oared flotilla, the *skärgårdsflottan*, which were stationed there tore a gap in the eastern maritime defences of Sweden that the British could not adequately fill; for the vessels of the *skärgårdsflottan* were the only species of naval force able to operate in the coastal channels running from Viborg to the Åland Islands inside the chain of rocks and islets which fringed the

---

[1] W. Odelberg, *Viceamiral Carl Olof Cronstedt* (Stockholm, 1954), pp. 338 ff., 366 ff., 469.
[2] For a discussion of Moore's expedition in the context of Anglo-Swedish relations, see R. Carr, 'Gustavus IV and the British Government, 1804–09', *English Historical Review*, vol. lx (1945), pp. 36–66.

Finnish coast.[1] Russian control of the channels sealed the fate of southern Finland and exposed Sweden itself to the danger of enemy raids. In these circumstances Hangö Udd, the south-western promontory of Finland, was a place of the utmost strategic significance, since in rounding it coastal shipping was forced to emerge from the inner leads thus exposing itself to the action of sailing ship men-of-war (doc. 12). It was the one point where British warships could intervene effectively in the Russo-Swedish war. On 25 August 1808 a battle fleet skirmish was fought in these waters between the Swedish fleet of eleven sail-of-the-line, most of them in a very sickly condition, reinforced by the British *Centaur* (74) and the *Implacable* (74) and the Russian fleet of nine sail-of-the-line. Had Saumarez not been detained in the Belt to rescue the Spaniards, he might well have been present on this occasion (docs. 38, 41). As it was, he joined on 30 August by which time the Russians had taken up a defensible position in Port Baltic on the southern side of the Gulf of Finland, where they were blockaded for what remained of the campaigning season (docs. 42, 44, 47, 50, 51). In 1809 a detachment of the fleet under the personal direction of Saumarez again cruised off Hangö and in the Gulf of Finland, where, in addition to harassing Russian coastal traffic (docs. 82, 85, 94), it ensured the immunity of a Swedish amphibious counter-attack in Västerbotten from interference by the enemy sea forces (docs. 87, 89, 93).

This counter-attack, undertaken in the vain hope of improving her negotiating position by a military success, was Sweden's last throw. The treaty of Frederikshamn signed in September 1809 registered the cession to Russia of Finland, the Åland Islands and part of Västerbotten. The heavy price which had to be paid for peace was all the harder to bear since the revolution of 1809 had been inspired in part by the assumption that Swedish interests would be well served by a reversal of Gustavus's policy towards France. But the revolutionary government's request to Napoleon that French influence be exerted at St. Petersburg in favour of the Russian evacuation of Finland was rejected as inopportune.[2] Knowing well that Alexander's war aim was no longer the coercion of Sweden but the possession of Finland, Napoleon was averse to any action calculated to weaken the Franco-Russian alliance at a moment when he stood on the brink of war with Austria. Contrary to its expectations then the new government discovered that an understanding with Britain was a means of escape from the perils of isolation. Of greater moment still for the future course of Anglo-Swedish relations was the conviction of an influential section of the regime that the best compensation for the loss of Finland would be the acquisition from Denmark of Norway. This,

[1] R. C. Anderson, *Oared Fighting Ships from Classical Times to the Coming of Steam* (1962), pp. 90 ff.; C. C. Lloyd and R. C. Anderson (eds.), *A Memoir of James Trevenen* (Navy Records Society, vol. ci, 1959), p. 101.

[2] A. Grade, *op. cit.*, pp. 327 ff.

it was realized, might be achieved in the future with the aid of British sea-power. Swedish diplomats, therefore, endeavoured during the negotiations for peace with Russia, Denmark and France to avoid an irrevocable break with Britain (doc. 98, 104). Sweden emerged from the negotiations pledged to adhere to the Continental System, but not formally bound to declare war. This was, however, only a temporary respite. In 1810 Napoleon determined to close by force, where necessary, the loopholes which had become manifest in the blockade against Britain. A consequence of this determination was a resolve that Sweden should abandon her non-belligerent status.

The enforcement of the Napoleonic decrees against British trade depended throughout their history upon the political and military state of the continent. At the beginning of 1808 the situation in the north of Europe seemed on balance to favour the policy of exclusion, all the Scandinavian and Baltic countries, except Sweden, being pledged to close their ports to the British flag and to sever their links with Britain. The hostility of Denmark-Norway was especially significant, for the Danes and Norwegians were active in the construction of brigs-of-war and oared gunboats and in the equipment of privateers with the grand design of sweeping from the seas all merchantmen suspected of being laden on British account. These raiders operated from bases on the coasts of the Skagerak, Kattegat, Sound and Great Belt; and within the Baltic from the islands of Bornholm and Ertholmene. In addition French privateers were fitted out along the southern coast of the Baltic, particularly at Danzig (docs. 60, 61, 62, 64), in the hope of picking up prizes in the vicinity of the ports. The trade was most vulnerable however in the restricted navigable channels of the Sound and Great Belt which were infested with regular and irregular commerce destroyers. It was here that a continuous battle had to be fought to prevent the closure of the Baltic to British trade.[1] The seriousness of the threat may be measured by the abandonment in 1809 of the use of the Sound (docs. 76, 82), hitherto regarded as the safer and more reliable route (doc. 26), and the re-routeing of convoys through the Great Belt which, though wider than the Sound, was much more tortuous and indirect. Here the British navy was forced to employ line-of-battle ships in defence of trade, for the Danish gunboats could outgun and outfight the brigs and sloops of the Royal Navy on windless days which were frequent in summer in the waters around the Danish islands. It was not just that line-of-battle ships were proof against enemy attack; their most important function was to act as floating gunboat bases, the boats of each ship being pressed into service as gunboats when a convoy came under fire (doc. 84). Despite occasional setbacks, such as the seizure of a convoy by

---

[1] A. N. Ryan, 'The Defence of British Trade with the Baltic, 1807–1813', *English Historical Review*, vol. lxxiv (1959), pp. 443–466.

a force of Norwegian brigs in the Skagerak in 1810 (doc. 129), the protection afforded by the well-tried system of cruisers and convoys gradually blunted the edge of the hostile attacks and exposed the authorities in the Baltic ports to the pressures of a British commercial offensive.

Britain's reply to Napoleon's policy of exclusion was a series of regulations principally enshrined in the orders in council of January and November 1807. Their ostensible intention was to impose a strict blockade upon all ports from which the British flag was excluded. In practice the purpose of the blockade was less retaliatory than remedial. It was to confront the merchants and shipowners of the blockaded ports with a choice between trade only with Britain and no trade at all. The importance to the producers, merchants and shipowners of the Baltic region of the traffic with western Europe in naval stores worked in Britain's favour. The inadequacy of land transport was such that the movement of these commodities in bulk was only possible by sea.[1] Britain commanded the sea routes in the summer months, when the Baltic ports were open, and could therefore either block or direct the trade as she willed. The interest on both sides of the North Sea in the survival of the trade was stronger than the political forces on the continent which worked for its abolition. There existed from the beginning the nucleus of a commercial resistance movement against the policy of Napoleon and his allies. The Baltic merchants of Britain were in many cases men of foreign origin. They had built up in the normal course of business a network of agents and correspondents in the Baltic ports. This was the machinery of resistance. Once convinced of Britain's will to preserve the trade and of her ability to protect it, the merchants and shipowners of the northern states, acting through the well-established commercial channels, took shelter beneath the umbrella provided by the Baltic fleet. The fleet was at once their protector and their controller; for the convoys which protected the merchantmen followed carefully prescribed courses.

This measure of rigid control over the movement of ships was a frank acknowledgement that the trade owed its survival to the practice of widespread fraud and deception. The ships employed in it had to be foreign, not British. They were furnished with false papers and certificates, the work of professional forgers, which served to demonstrate that their business was between places in amity with France; thus baffling the local authorities and French agents in the Baltic ports as well as the commanders of privateers at sea (doc. 114b). They were also furnished with a British licence, usually obtained in London (doc. 78), which conferred immunity from detention by British cruisers 'notwithstanding all the documents which accompany the

[1] B. de Jouvenel, *Napoléon et l'Economie Dirigée: Le Blocus Continental* (Paris, 1942), pp. 269 ff.

ship and cargo may represent the same to be destined to any other neutral or hostile port, or to whomsoever such property may belong'. The use on this scale of simulated papers made possible extensive evasions not only of the French but also of the British regulations. The remedy for this potential flaw in the British maritime system was insistence upon strict adherence to convoy within both the Baltic and North Seas. A licence for a vessel bound from a Baltic port to Britain was granted on condition that the said vessel, having joined convoy off the island of Hanö, 'shall proceed with such convoy and not desert the same till her arrival at the port of destination or as long as such convoy shall be instructed to protect her; and on further condition, that if the said vessel shall by accident or otherwise be separated from her said convoy she shall repair as directly as may be to the port of Leith and there put herself under fresh convoy and not desert the same till her arrival at the port of destination or as long as such convoy shall be instructed to protect her, unless the said vessel shall be bound for Ireland; in which case she shall sail north about'. Ships found to have strayed from convoy were automatically suspected of being bound to a forbidden port of destination. They were liable to be detained and, if the evidence were unfavourable, condemned.

Commercial transactions, directed by the fleet and disguised as something other than they were, kept the Baltic ports open to Britain. After a slow start in 1808 the volume of trade increased enormously, as confidence was built up, in 1809–10.[1] The Baltic ports were of vital importance as both the chief outlet from the continent of naval stores and the main gateway into the continent of British manufactured and colonial goods. There is no doubt that the breakthrough in 1809 was favoured by Napoleon's absorption in the Austrian war. Faced in 1810 with the evidence of what was happening, he decided upon the use of force as the answer to the durability of proscribed trading connections. The closing months of 1810 witnessed the French annexation of Holland, the Hanseatic towns and duchy of Oldenburg, the reinforcement of French garrisons in the Baltic ports of Germany and the exercise of relentless pressure upon the Prussian government to enforce the decrees of Berlin, Milan and Fontainebleau; which last, dated October 1810, ordered the seizure and destruction by fire of British property.[2] These draconian measures threw the trade into confusion (docs. 138, 142), led to wholesale confiscations in the Prussian ports and drove the insurance rates, quoted in London for the Baltic trade, up to unprecedented heights.[3] They

[1] F. Crouzet, *L'Economie Britannique et le Blocus Continental* (Paris, 1958), vol. ii, pp. 422 ff.
[2] F. Crouzet, *op. cit.*, pp. 589 ff.; E. F. Heckscher, *The Continental System: An Economic Interpretation* (Oxford, 1922), pp. 235 ff.
[3] C. Wright and C. Ernest Fayle, *A History of Lloyd's* (1928), pp. 187 ff.; J. T. Danson, *Our Next War in its Commercial Aspect; with some Account of the Premiums paid at Lloyd's from 1805 to 1816* (1894), pp. 33 ff. and 70 ff.

also alarmed the tsar, whose uneasiness was reflected in the ukase of 31 December 1810 permitting the import into Russia under neutral flags of colonial produce. This was the first open crack in the Tilsit agreement; a public avowal that if the enforcement of the continental system required the establishment of a great French military base in northern Germany, Russia wanted no part in the system. From this moment men began to anticipate the outbreak of war between France and Russia.

The steps taken by Napoleon to tighten his grip on northern Europe co-incided with the election of the French marshal Bernadotte as crown prince of Sweden and his arrival in that country; an event which was rapidly followed in October 1810 by a peremptory demand from Paris that Sweden should forthwith declare war against Britain. At this critical juncture Saumarez demonstrated the mature political judgement that carried him through the closing weeks of the 1810 campaign and the whole of the 1811 campaign. He refused to be hustled into drawing the obvious conclusion that Sweden must inevitably be forced into the French system. His forbearance was based upon the conviction that Swedish interests could not be reconciled with war against Britain in view of her dependence upon imports of salt and corn from abroad; that given her semi-insular position on the side of the sea opposite to the French troop concentrations she was more vulnerable to pressure from the British navy than from the French army. He also appreciated that, so long as the Franco-Russian alliance endured, Sweden must avoid at all costs a repetition of the experiences of 1808–09 and that she had therefore no option but to publish a declaration of war at the end of 1810, when the British fleet had, as was customary, to retire to its home ports with the onset of the Baltic winter. He staked his reputation upon this assessment and upon the private assurances of prominent Swedes that the declaration was purely formal (docs. 151, 152). He continued to insist in 1811, despite certain adverse evidence concerning the treatment of British property in Swedish ports (docs. 162, 163, 166, 167), that Swedish foreign policy under Bernadotte would be formulated in accord with Swedish, not French, interests.

Bernadotte's reported determination to pursue an independent Swedish policy was not, however, a guarantee that he would necessarily break with Napoleon. He owed his election as crown prince to the belief that a man of his stature would either recover Finland or obtain Norway as compensation. Swedish public opinion inclined towards the idea of a war of revenge against Russia in the event of a Franco-Russian conflict.[1] Bernadotte, though not fully convinced by the arguments for it, was undoubtedly interested in this scheme. He was at the same time attracted by the idea of a union with Nor-

[1] P. Tommila, *op. cit.*, pp. 62 ff., 114 ff.

way, envisaging the joint kingdom as a natural political unit territorially secure within a seagirt frontier. The attraction of this project was an argument in favour of restraint in the conduct of the war against Britain, for there was little prospect of winning Norway without, at the least, British acquiescence. This condition, added to Bernadotte's appreciation of Sweden's vulnerability to a British blockade, ensured the survival of an unwritten, and at times uneasy, truce in 1811; under which conditions Saumarez continued to make clandestine use of anchorages off the Swedish coast for commercial and naval purposes in much the same way as he had done in 1810.

As Bernadotte's Norwegian policy was taking shape in 1811, so were the chances of a Franco-Russian conflict in the fairly near future becoming more real. A serious obstacle to future Franco-Swedish co-operation now emerged. The possession of Norway could hardly be approved by Napoleon since it could only be achieved at the expense of Denmark, the steadfast ally of France.[1] The unpromising reception given by Napoleon to Swedish approaches on the subject compelled Bernadotte to re-orientate Swedish foreign policy by seeking from Russia what he could not obtain from France. The task of educating public opinion in Sweden was aided by the French occupation of Swedish Pomerania in January 1812 as a reprisal for continued commercial connections with Britain. This made it easier for Bernadotte to effect a treaty of alliance with Russia in April. The tsar, faced with the prospect of war with France, promised to support the Norwegian policy in return for an understanding that Sweden would remain at peace with Russia.[2] The conclusion of the treaty paved the way for a conference between Bernadotte and Alexander at Åbo in August, when the tsar promised the help of a Russian army in Sweden's projected attack upon Denmark with the object of forcing the latter to surrender Norway (docs. 230, 234).[3] Saumarez's policy of forbearance—a policy not always understood in London (doc. 172)—was therefore vindicated by events. By acting with restraint he allowed Bernadotte room for manoeuvre and gave him a credible alternative to the policy of alliance with France. His greatest asset in the crisis was his ability to estimate realistically the working of national interests and to use the power at his disposal accordingly. He also possessed the ability to distinguish exactly between the possible and the impossible, the exercise of which was influential in shaping his attitude towards Prussia in the autumn of 1811, when he carefully avoided encouraging the party of resistance there

---

[1] T. T. Hojer, *Carl XIV Johan: Kronprinstiden* (Stockholm, 1945), pp. 76 ff.; J. Weibull, *Carl Johan och Norge, 1810–1814: Unionsplanerna och deras Förverkligande* (Lund, 1957), pp. 52 ff.

[2] P. Tommila, *op. cit.*, p. 297.

[3] P. Tommila, *op. cit.*, pp. 352 ff.; J. Weibull, *op. cit.*, pp. 74 ff.

with promises likely to remain unfulfilled. By so doing he contributed
towards saving that country from a disastrously premature war with
Napoleon.

Saumarez arrived at the top of his profession at a time when the chance of
commanding the fleet in battle with the enemy was negligible. He was thus
denied the opportunity of associating his name with an annihilating victory.
Even in 1812, when men's eyes were focussed on the great contest in Russia,
his rôle in the conflict was essentially passive. True, a small detachment of the
fleet off Riga assisted in the defence of the city against the left wing of the
Grand Army; but the fleet was for the most part employed, as it had been
since 1808, in the defence and control of trade (docs. 201, 211, 212, 213, 216).
Saumarez was compelled to sit at his anchorage off Gothenburg and wait:
firstly, for the signing of peace by Britain with Sweden and Russia (docs.
205, 219, 221, 222); secondly, for the opening of the Franco-Russian war;
thirdly, for a decision concerning the employment of Sweden's armed forces
(docs. 222, 223, 226, 231, 236). Had the projected Swedish attack upon
Zealand materialized, he would of course have been at the heart of things.
But Bernadotte, too wary to commit Sweden to open war with France until
the probable outcome of the Russian campaign was clear, found plenty of
excuses to refrain from action (doc. 243). Owing to the sudden death of his
daughter Mary, Saumarez returned to Britain shortly before the end of the
campaign (doc. 245). By the time he came ashore the French army was fighting a desperate rearguard action to cover its retreat across the Beresina
(doc. 250). And the preparations, begun under his auspices, for the transfer
to Britain of the Russian fleet for its better security were nearing completion.
(docs. 239, 245, 246, 248). The wheel had come full circle since 1807. His
work in the Baltic was at an end.

The maritime war in the Baltic did not provide the setting for the emer-
gence of a national hero. It was a hidden, in some ways a secret, war. The
importance of the contemporary achievements of the duke of Wellington in
Spain was easily grasped. Those of Saumarez defied evaluation. He
governed a commercial and political underworld peopled by men whose
business was necessarily conducted in dark corners remote from the glare of
public events and whose furtive journeys across the Baltic were shrouded in
a fog of secrecy. Although there was plenty of hard fighting on the trade
routes, the guns of the great ships were curiously silent.[1] In the circumstances
of the time, their power was most effectively exercised when to all outward

---

[1] A. T. Mahan, *op. cit.*, pp. 421 ff. pays a brief tribute to the work of Saumarez in the
Baltic, but he also writes of the events of 1801 that 'in this blaze of triumph the story of
Saumarez fitly terminates. He was never again engaged in serious encounter with the
enemy'.

appearances it was not being exercised at all. The appearances were very different from the reality; but the reality has been long buried in many a dust-covered volume or bundle of correspondence in public and private archives. There is certainly no shortage of evidence; if anything there is too great an abundance of it. The publication of this selection will, it is hoped, shed new light on the war at sea, as well as upon European history, in the post-Trafalgar period of the Napoleonic war and upon the career of a distinguished officer whose unique contribution to the war was to keep open the gates of northern Europe after Napoleon had decreed that they be closed.

PART I

1808

PART I

INTRODUCTION

The two flag-officers appointed to serve under Saumarez in 1808 were Rear-Admirals Keats and Hood. They were later reinforced, at the commander-in-chief's request, by Rear-Admiral Bertie who commanded the squadron in the Sound (docs. 21, 24). The problem which weighed most heavily on Saumarez was that of co-operation with Sweden in the war against Denmark and Russia. The selection of documents has been proportioned accordingly. At the same time the problems of trade protection were ever present and grew more intense as the threat from the enemy raiders unfolded itself. Saumarez was requested by the admiralty to account for the losses sustained by the trade. His explanation (doc. 53a) satisfied their lordships that all had been done that could be done. In spite of the aid given by Britain, the year ended with Sweden plunged into a desperate situation. When the time came for the fleet to retire to its home ports, Keats was instructed to remain behind at Marstrand with a small detachment to be on hand to lend immediate assistance in the spring of 1809 (doc. 52). A disastrous note was struck by the almost total loss in the ice of the last homeward bound convoy (doc. 56); the first of the savage blows dealt the Baltic fleet by the northern winter. Saumarez's proceedings in a series of tense situations were approved by the admiralty, except for his private venture into the complicated politics of Anglo-Russian relations: his letter to the tsar of 17 September (doc. 53a).

The SOUND and GREAT BELT

1. Pole[1] to Russell[2]

2 Jan. 1808.

Sir, I am commanded by my Lords Commissioners of the Admiralty to signify their direction to you to order Captain Parker[3] of His Majesty's ship the *Stately* to take under his command the ships and sloop named in the margin, [*Nassau, Quebec, Lynx*], and receiving on board the *Stately* and *Nassau* the money[4] at present on board His Majesty's Ship *Amelia* proceed with the same, accompanied by the *Quebec* and *Lynx*, to Gothenburg and deliver it agreeably to its consignment.

On his arrival at Gothenburg you are to direct Captain Parker to make enquiry with as much privacy as possible what British merchantships there are at Carlshamn [Karlshamn] or any other ports of Sweden within the Baltic, and whether those ports are open and so far free from ice as to afford any expectation of the ships being brought out of thence. He is also to inform himself whether the passage of the Sound or of the Belt is clear of ice and can be navigated with safety to and from the Baltic; and if it should appear from good information that there are not less than eight British merchantships in the ports abovementioned and that they can be brought to sea, also that the Sound or Belt is open and navigable, he is to proceed with the *Stately* and *Nassau* into the Sound or Belt and assist the *Quebec* and *Lynx* in their passage by Copenhagen over the grounds or through the Belt, directing their commanders to make the best of their way to Carlshamn and such other ports as may be open, for the purpose of taking under his protection any British merchantships which may be at those ports, and returning with them either through the Sound or the Belt, as may be most advisable for the security of the king's ships and the trade; and on being joined by the said ships and sloop with the trade he is to use his best endeavours to conduct them in

[1] William Wellesley Pole (1763–1845), the second son of the 1st earl of Mornington, assumed the additional name of Pole on inheriting his cousin's estates in 1778. He was secretary to the admiralty, 1807–09; created Baron Maryborough, 1821; succeeded to the earldom of Mornington, 1842.
[2] Thomas Macnamara Russell (c. 1763–1824), the commander-in-chief of the North Sea fleet, was said to come of a respectable and once opulent Anglo-Irish family. He entered the navy from the merchant marine about 1766, was commissioned ten years later, posted captain in 1781 and advanced to flag rank in 1801. He directed the capture of Heligoland from the Danes in September 1807.
[3] George Parker (1767–1847) was a nephew of Admiral Sir Peter Parker. He was commissioned in 1782 and promoted to captain in 1795. He became rear-admiral in 1814 and rose through seniority to admiral in 1837. Parker, who never hoisted his flag, was created K.C.B. in 1837.
[4] The current instalment of subsidy to Sweden.

safety to Yarmouth, where he is to remain until he receives further orders. You will at the same time inform Captain Parker that he is at liberty to pass through into the Baltic with the *Stately* and *Nassau* or remain in the Sound or the Belt, as he may deem most expedient to effect the object of the service entrusted to him with the least risk of the safety of the whole.

If Captain Parker should receive certain information that the trade in the ports beforementioned cannot be brought out from thence, or that the passage through the Sound or the Belt is impracticable, he is in either case to return with the ships under his order to Yarmouth Roads.

And as information has been received that several British merchantships have been captured by the Danes and carried into the island of Eartholm[1] you are further to direct Captain Parker in the event of his going into the Sound or Belt to use his endeavours to retake and bring the said ships with him from thence to Yarmouth; but as the harbour in which the ships in question are said to be is defended by batteries, he is to use his discretion in making an attack upon them according to the intelligence he may receive of the state of the defences, I am etc.

2. *Pole to Russell*

2 Jan. 1808.

Sir, I am commanded by my Lords Commissioners of the Admiralty to signify their direction to you, in addition to the orders which by my letter of this day's date you are directed to give to Captain Parker of His Majesty's ship the *Stately*, to order him in case Mr. Thornton,[2] His Majesty's minister to the king of Sweden, should make any application to him for the continuance of all, or any part of, the force under his command at Gothenburg, to communicate freely with His Majesty's said minister upon the subject of such application; and if it should appear to him that the objects held out are of a nature that can be accomplished and that no hazard to the safety of His Majesty's ships will be incurred by his compliance therewith, you are to direct him to continue at Gothenburg accordingly notwithstanding the orders for his return to Yarmouth contained in my letter above referred to. I am etc.

---

[1] This resort of the Danish privateers was a cluster of rocky islets—Christiansø, Frederiksholm and Gräsholm—which formed an excellent natural harbour situated to the north-east of Bornholm; known by the collective name of Ertholmene. Their occupation for military and commercial purposes was frequently urged.

[2] Edward Thornton (1766–1852) was envoy extraordinary and minister plenipotentiary to Sweden in 1808 and 1812–17; minister to Brazil, 1819–21; to Portugal, 1823–24; G.C.B., 1822.

3. *Mulgrave[1] to Saumarez*

Admiralty Office,
20 Feb. 1808.

Dear Sir, I am in daily expectation of receiving accurate intelligence of the present state of the naval arsenal at Cronstadt. In the event of this information being as satisfactory as I have reason to hope, it is my intention to send a squadron into the Baltic, consisting of not less than twelve or thirteen sail-of-the-line. If your health should be such as to admit of your taking command of this fleet, I know of no arrangement which I can make that would be so satisfactory to myself as to entrust the important service of attempting to destroy the Russian fleet and of affording protection to His Majesty's firm and faithful ally, the king of Sweden,[2] to your direction. It will not be necessary that you should come immediately to England in the event of your undertaking the command as all the necessary preparations may be forwarded beforehand; and your coming immediately over might tend to excite suspicion of the object we have in view. I have not yet opened this project to any officer, but those on whom I have fixed my views to assist you are Rear-Admirals Sir Samuel Hood[3] and Keats,[4] who, besides their great professional merits, have the additional advantage of being well acquainted with the Baltic. I have etc.

4. *Saumarez to Mulgrave*

Guernsey,
27 Feb. 1808.

My Lord, I have had the honour to receive your lordship's private and

[1] Henry Phipps, 1st Baron Mulgrave of Mulgrave (1755–1831) entered politics, after service in the army during the war of the American revolution, as a follower of Pitt and became one of his chief military advisers. He was first lord of the admiralty, 1807–10; created 1st earl of Mulgrave and Viscount Normanby, 1812.

[2] Gustavus IV Adolphus (1778–1837) succeeded as king of Sweden after the murder of his father Gustavus III in 1792. Autocratic and unstable, he was dethroned in 1809 and became a stateless wanderer known variously as Count Gottorp and Colonel Gustafsson. He died at St. Gall.

[3] Sir Samuel Hood, bart. (1762–1814) was first cousin once removed to Admiral Lord Hood. A captain of 1788, Hood commanded the *Zealous* at the battle of the Nile. In 1805 he lost his right arm in an action off Rochefort, but recovered to serve at Copenhagen under Gambier. He was promoted rear-admiral in 1807 and vice-admiral in 1811, when he was appointed to the command of the East Indies squadron. Hood died of a fever at Madras.

[4] Richard Goodwin Keats (1757–1834) received his first commission in 1777 and his advancement to captain in 1789. He commanded the detached squadron which policed the Great Belt during the Copenhagen expedition of 1807, and became a rear-admiral in September of the same year. He was made a K.B. in 1808. His later appointments included the governorships of Newfoundland and of Greenwich hospital. He was promoted vice-admiral in 1811; admiral in 1825.

2

secret letter of the 20th. instant, and I feel most deeply impressed with the very obliging manner in which your lordship has been pleased to offer me the command of the squadron proposed to be sent to the Baltic. Although it is with great diffidence that I undertake a trust of so high and great importance, having ever made it the principle of my life to go upon any service where my exertions for my king and country would be deemed most useful, I cannot for a moment hesitate to comply with the commands of your lordship, and I shall hold myself in readiness to proceed from this station whenever called upon, requesting your lordship will have the goodness to allow me sufficient time to make such arrangements as may be required in London previous to my going upon the proposed service. The two officers selected to co-operate with me are possessed of the highest merit, and, of all others, those I should have been happy to apply for, had they not been previously appointed. I shall be obliged to your lordship to mention the ship intended for my flag, as also such further information as may be judged necessary for me to know, with the probable time that I may be required to go to London; all of which shall be held by me in the strictest confidence. I have etc.

5. *Pole to Russell*

7 March 1808.

Sir, I have received and laid before my Lords Commissioners of the Admiralty your letter of yesterday's date enclosing a letter from Captain Parker of the *Stately* with one referred to therein from Mr. Thornton, His Majesty's minister at Stockholm, stating that in consequence of the requisition of the latter he had determined to remain with the whole of his squadron in the Categat [Kattegat] and, as the season advances, to place his ships in such a manner as to accomplish all the objects held out by Mr. Thornton. And I have their lordships' commands to acquaint you that they are pleased to approve of Captain Parker's proceedings, and to signify their direction to you to order Captain Parker to co-operate to the utmost of his power with the force under his command with the Swedish government towards repelling any attack of the enemy that may be made from Holstein, Zealand or Norway, acquainting him at the same time that preparations are making to reinforce his squadron as soon as the season will permit. I am etc.

6. *Instructions by the Lords Commissioners of the Admiralty to Saumarez*

21 March 1808.

You are hereby required and directed to order Rear-Admiral Sir Samuel Hood to take under his command the ships named in the margin [*Implac-*

cable, Orion, Goliath, Dictator, Salsette, Daphne] and proceed in the *Centaur* with the said ships to Gothenburg; and on his arrival at that port to take also under his command such of His Majesty's ships and vessels as he may find there or cruising in its vicinity and use his best endeavours to co-operate with the naval force of the king of Sweden for the defence of His Swedish Majesty's dominions against the attack of His Majesty's enemies either from Zealand or any other quarter, communicating with the British envoy at Stockholm and complying with such requisitions as he may make relating to the service on which the rear-admiral is employed, as far as circumstances will permit.

You will also order the rear-admiral to use all the means in his power to obstruct the passage of any French troops from Holstein into Zealand by stationing a part of the ships and vessels under his orders in the Belt and to carry into execution the instructions under which Captain Parker of His Majesty's ship *Stately*, the senior officer of His Majesty's ships at Gothenburg, is at present acting for the protection of the trade of His Majesty's subjects in the Baltic. Given etc.

7. *Hood to Saumarez*

Deal,
25 March 1808.

My dear Sir James, I arrived here too late last night to send the post. From the moderate state of the weather yesterday and today I hope the *Centaur* may reach this [anchorage] by tomorrow, when I shall not loose a moment in proceeding on with her agreeable to my orders. The *Goliath* is the only ship at present in the *Downs* that *was* to have sailed under my orders. Captain Puget[1] says he hopes all her provisions will be on board this evening. He will then, when he gets his orders, have only to wait for 100 of her men that are not yet come round from Portsmouth. The *Charger*, one of the four gunbrigs, sailed yesterday, and the *Snipe* and *Exertion* will this afternoon. The [*Tickler*] is represented by the surgeon to have a severe fever on board. Admiral Campbell[2] has ordered a survey on her state which will of course be transmitted to the admiralty.

On enquiry respecting pilots for the Baltic here, I find that there are now collected and borne on board the *Princess of Orange only* three for the North Sea and *Baltic*, three for the North Sea, Cattegat and Belt, and six for the North Sea *only*. I believe most of the pilots are at Yarmouth, so think it

---

[1] Peter Puget, lieutenant, 1790; sailed with Vancouver and gave his name to Puget Sound; captain 1797; commanded the *Goliath* (74) at Copenhagen in 1807; C.B., 1819; rear-admiral, 1821; died, 1822.

[2] Rear-Admiral George Campbell (1761–1821), the commander-in-chief in the Downs.

requisite for the ships that cannot get pilots here to call off Yarmouth unless some other method is adopted for obtaining them.

I have taken the liberty of mentioning these circumstances to you, should you not be informed of them, as I shall anything I may judge useful to you while I remain here and on all occasions. I am etc.

8. *Saumarez to Hood*

London,
26 March 1808.

My dear Sir Samuel, I hope the present weather will enable the *Centaur* coming to the Downs, as I well know your anxiety to [get to] the station. The accounts from thence are rather favourable. Five of the Swedish ships-of-the-line and some frigates have been enabled to clear the ice;[1] and it is ascertained that the French troops have not been able to cross from Holstein. Our ships were expected to be cleared before the 18th.,[2] so that I trust we shall be in time to render important service. The king of Denmark,[3] I have just been told, is dead, and Bernadotte[4] is at Copenhagen. I have been to the Admiralty respecting the charts which, I am sorry to find, are not yet ready. They are expected by Monday. The pilots, besides those in the Downs, are at the Nore and Yarmouth. The *Dictator* is ordered to receive a bower anchor and cable for the *Vanguard* and a main topmast for the *Stately*. No arrangement has yet been made with regard to Keats, but I think it very probable he will have the *Pompée*. I am impatient to get from Town, but see no prospect of it till after the wind changes. With my best wishes for your health and every success, I remain etc.

9. *Castlereagh[5] to Mulgrave*

6 April 1808.

My Lord, I transmit to you enclosed the copy of a paper which I have received respecting the islands of Bornholm and Eartholm, stating the

---

[1] The first division of the Swedish battle fleet did not in fact sail from Karlskrona until the end of March, though smaller warships were at sea earlier.

[2] Parker's squadron was at sea by 19 March. On 22 March the *Stately* and *Nassau* destroyed Denmark's only operational line-of-battle ship, the *Prins Christian Frederik* (64), off the north Zealand coast.

[3] Christian VII (1749–1808) died on 15 March.

[4] Jean Baptiste Jules Bernadotte, prince of Ponte-Corvo, later Charles XIV John of Sweden, (1763–1844) was at this stage of his long and remarkable life governor of the Hanseatic towns and commander of the army in northern Germany which was under orders from Napoleon to co-operate with Denmark in the war against Sweden.

[5] Robert Stewart, Viscount Castlereagh (1769–1822) was secretary of state for war and the colonies in the Portland ministry from March 1807 to October 1809.

advantages which would arise from the possession of those islands by this country. As I think it adviseable to obtain further information on this subject, I shall be obliged to you to give directions to the naval officer commanding in the Baltic to report his opinion on the value of these islands either as commercial or naval stations, and on their means of defence and subsistence.

Enclosure:

9a. *Paper on Bornholm and Eartholm*

It has been recommended by several merchants in the Baltic, and it is also our opinion, that this government should take possession of the islands of Bornholm and Eartholm as considerable trade may be carried on from those islands to the ports of Mecklenburg, Prussia and Russia. The Eartholms are slightly fortified and have a good harbour. A few months ago there was only a small garrison and, it is presumed, not capable of making any great resistance; but, if well provisioned and in our hands, it might easily be rendered impregnable. The island is barren and contains but few inhabitants. Bornholm, which is close adjoining, is a large fruitful island incapable of resistance. The privateers of the enemy have carried away many valuable prizes into Eartholm, which may all be retaken with their cargoes consisting principally of hemp and other naval stores. The island is a receptacle for privateers from whence they can annoy our trade to the Baltic more than from any other place. In our hands it would be of the greatest utility as it may be made the rendezvous for all our vessels bound to and from the ports in the Baltic. A great smuggling trade may also be carried on with the ports under the control of the French. The French generals, after some short residence, are in the habit of giving permission to the merchants to import goods from England, but it is the policy of Bonaparte to change the generals very often, by which means the permission granted is of little avail on account of the length of the voyage to and from Britain. If we were in possession of these islands, this inconvenience would be remedied as the merchants would suffer the vessels to remain there until they could go into port with safety.

10. *Instructions by the Lords Commissioners of the Admiralty to Saumarez*
16 April 1808.

The close alliance which subsists between His Majesty and the king of Sweden having determined His Majesty to send a squadron into the Baltic for the protection of His Swedish Majesty's dominions, to the command of which squadron we have thought fit to appoint you, and the right honourable

Lord Castlereagh, one of His Majesty's principal secretaries of state, having by his letter of the 12th. instant signified to us the king's pleasure with regard to the instructions which are to be given to you for the regulation of your conduct on the above service, we do in pursuance of His Majesty's pleasure signified to us as aforesaid hereby require and direct you immediately on your arrival in the Baltic to communicate with His Majesty's minister at the court of Stockholm, and to concert through him such a system of co-operation with the Swedish marine as may best combine the united efforts of the two powers against the common enemy, and at all times to keep up the most confidential intercourse with His Majesty's said minister and to attend as far as possible to his suggestions.

Your own experience and ability will suggest to you on the spot the arrangement and disposition of your force best calculated to protect the dominions of His Majesty's ally against invasion, we do however require and direct you specially to direct your attention to the following objects:

1st. To prevent as far as possible the passage of troops from the continent across the Belt into Zealand and to interrupt supplies of all descriptions from being carried thither.

2nd. To discover where the enemy are assembling, or have assembled, vessels for the reception of troops, to watch those points, and to cover Sweden on the side of Scania and the Sound from any armament preparing either in Zealand or in the ports of the continent for its invasion.

3rd. To watch the ports of Jutland and to guard with the utmost vigilance against the passage of French troops into Norway, and to prevent as much as possible the introduction even of French officers into that country as their activity would probably immediately be directed to prevail upon the Norwegian army to undertake offensive operations against the Swedish frontier; and in order to discourage any attempt of this nature by attracting their attention to the defence of their own harbours and maritime frontier, you are to cause the coast of Norway to be menaced by the ships which may be stationed in the Cattegat as far as is consistent with a due attention to other important objects to be provided for.

With a view to the safe navigation of the Cattegat you are hereby required and directed to take measures for ascertaining whether the lighthouse on the island of Anholt may not be re-established and protected, and to take measures for so doing if it should be judged practicable and expedient. You are also to cause the islands of Bornholm and Eartholm to be examined with a view of ascertaining how far either of these islands, if occupied, would prove of advantage either as a commercial depot or naval station. The latter island has been represented as possessing a good harbour with a lighthouse and, from its very limited extent, capable of being held by a small force.

You are to cause the motions of the Russians in the higher parts of the Baltic to be observed. Should Åbo[1] have fallen into their hands, from its proximity to the Swedish capital it will deserve particular attention.

The amount of naval force which can under present circumstances be appropriated to service in the Baltic will not admit, consistently with the immediate protection of Sweden, of detaching on your first arrival an adequate force for the attack of the Russian arsenal at Cronstadt. You will, however, direct your earliest enquiries to the practicability of successfully approaching that and other ports in which the Russian fleet is lying with the view of acting offensively against them as soon as it may be possible to furnish you with adequate means for so doing without exposing Sweden in the absence of such naval force to invasion.

You are also to consider as one of the principal objects of the service on which you are employed the affording every protection in your power to the trade of His Majesty's subjects by granting convoy from time to time (as far as the force under your command will admit of your so doing) to the said trade to and from the different ports of the Baltic, and also to ships and vessels under neutral colours which may be furnished with licences from one of His Majesty's principal secretaries of state. And as it is of much importance that His Majesty's ships and vessels which may be sent from England with convoys to Gothenburg or into the Sound (as may be hereafter determined) should not be delayed beyond the time necessary to collect the trade at either of the abovementioned places, we do further require and direct you to order the commanders of His Majesty's ships and vessels so employed to put to sea in the execution of their orders the moment they have furnished the merchantships intended to proceed under their convoy with instructions, or at the period of sailing appointed by their orders, or as soon after as the wind and weather will permit. Given etc.

11. *Instructions by the Lords Commissioners of the Admiralty to Saumarez*

22 April 1808.

Whereas the right honourable Lord Castlereagh, one of His Majesty's principal secretaries of state, hath by his letter of the 21st instant acquainted us that His Majesty has been pleased to order a corps of his troops under the command of Lieutenant-General Sir John Moore[2] to proceed immediately

---

[1] The modern port of Turku in Finland.
[2] Sir John Moore (1761–1809) was a talented soldier with a good record of service in West Indian and Mediterranean theatres of war; he was also associated with the introduction of new training methods in the British army. In his diary he wrote, not unfairly, of this expedition that the government 'had no specific plan and had come to no determination beyond that of sending a force of 10,000 men to Gothenburg to be ready to act if occasion offered.' After returning from Sweden he was posted to Spain and to his death at Corunna.

to Sweden for the support of His Majesty's ally the king of Sweden, and that the said lieutenant-general has been instructed to co-operate with you in execution of the orders which you have received from us, so far as they relate to conjunct operations and as may be consistent with the immediate security of Sweden, you are hereby required and directed, in addition to our order of the 16th. instant, to keep in view the possibility of destroying any assemblage of vessels the enemy may have collected on the opposite coast with a view to the invasion of Sweden, an operation which, if successfully executed, will contribute in the most essential manner to the security of His Swedish Majesty's dominions. And from the efficient nature of the corps entrusted to Lieutenant-General Sir John Moore's command and the means it will possess of moving with celerity to any point where its services may be required, every facility will be afforded you in the execution of the enterprize hereby recommended to your particular attention. Given etc.

12. *Thornton to Hood*

Stockholm,
7 May 1808.

Sir, On the 3rd. of this month (the evening of the day on which I had the honour of addressing letters to you by the messenger Schaw), this government received the painful intelligence that the Swedish Admiral Cronstedt,[1] who commanded the fortress of Sveaborg and the flotilla of gunboats stationed there, had surrendered this important post, with everything appertaining to it, to the Russians. The enclosed newspaper contains the report of this officer and the convention of armistice by which it was to be surrendered on the 3rd. of this month in case of an effectual relief not arriving, which I am sorry I can only send to you in the original Swedish, the convention itself excepted. That document, however, bears sufficient testimony to the treacherous conspiracy by which this important post had been lost to Sweden.

It is not to you, sir, who are so well acquainted with every maritime port of the Baltic, that it is necessary to speak of the fatal and ruinous consequences of this loss which seals irrecoverably during the present war that of the province of Finland, and which opens up the whole coast of Sweden to the invasion of Russia by the coasting navigation of their gunboats among the rocks

---

[1] Carl Olof Cronstedt (1756–1820) served in both the sailing ship navy and the *skärgardsflottan*; lieutenant, 1774; captain, 1777; distinguished himself at the battle of Svenksund, 1790, and became an aide-de-camp to Gustavus III; rear-admiral, 1793; vice-admiral and commander-in-chief Karlskrona, 1801; commandant of Sveaborg, 1801. Lack of confidence in the king, despondency and the influence of Finnish born officers, who wished to see the Finnish-Swedish links broken, explain his conduct in 1808 better than does the contemporary charge of premeditated treachery.

and islands of Finland to the Gulf of Bothnia. The loss of the flotilla of Sveaborg, which constituted the principal part of that species of maritime force which Sweden possessed, is absolutely irreparable, and cannot be effectually supplied by any ship which Great Britain can at present furnish.

His Swedish Majesty, after having taken the counsel of his ministers, sent for me yesterday and urged me in the most earnest manner, not only to press upon His Majesty's government the necessity of the immediate appearance of all the squadron destined for these seas and of a considerable augmentation of it, but also desired me instantly to request you to detach into the Baltic whatever part of your squadron you could best spare to co-operate with that of Sweden in watching the coast of Finland and that of the south of the Baltic. His Majesty said that he should order two or three ships-of-war immediately to the station of Hangö Udd (S.W. promontory of Finland) for the purpose of arresting the movements along the coast of Finland of the Russian flotilla, and that it would be very important if we could co-operate with a ship or two in the same service, and particularly if we could watch the southern coast lest the Swedish ships stationed at Hangö Udd should be surprized by the Russian division from Revel or from Cronstadt. You are aware that in the last Russian war with Sweden some ships of the latter stationed at Hangö Udd stopped during the whole war the passage of the Russian flotilla.[1]

I assured His Majesty that I was so penetrated with the importance of the object that I had meant already, as was literally the case, to write to you to this effect; and I begged that he would order to be communicated to me in writing the dispositions and distributions of his own force, that you might judge with exactness what was best to be done with any force you could spare.

Last night I received, at a late hour, the enclosed *memoire* addressed to His Swedish Majesty by the Admiral de Rajalin,[2] which does not, however, give me at all the information I required, and which contains a plan that appears to be as little within my competence to recommend to you as it would be within yours, with your force and under the instructions by which you are guided, to act upon. It is, in fact, a plan rather to be submitted as a general system to government; but, as it contains ideas which may be useful to you, I take the liberty of annexing a copy to this dispatch. I was informed at the same time that His Majesty had ordered him to proceed immediately to Helsingborg [Hälsingborg] to concert with you a plan of operations. You

[1] The allusion is to the Russo-Swedish war of 1788–90.
[2] Salomon Mauritz, Baron von Rajalin (1757–1825) was naval aide-de-camp to the king of Sweden, 1801–09; he was also governor of St. Barthelemy, 1785–7; governor of Gotland, 1787–1811. Rajalin fought in the war of 1788–90. He became rear-admiral in 1791; vice-admiral, 1799; admiral, 1809.

will learn, therefore, from Admiral de Rajalin in person every essential information as to the distribution of the Swedish force; and I have only to request you, with real earnestness, to detach as many vessels, as you think you can spare without injuring the essential defence of the Belt and Sound, into the Baltic to sweep the coast of Germany and Livonia and to watch the entrance of the Gulf of Finland. It would be very presumptuous in me even to hint at any point from which this detachment could be made most safely.

The loss of Sveaborg and the danger from the Russian gunboats and small cruisers along the coast of Finland and in the Gulf of Bothnia renders the appointment of convoys to Stockholm itself more necessary than ever. In fact, till a cruising squadron of Great Britain or Sweden appears in these seas, Stockholm itself, it appears to me, is hardly secure from a *coup-de-main*.

I am told that in the Dvina, the river of Riga, all the vessels, corn laden, which came down after the breaking-up of the winter, are obliged to lie much below the town and the forts on account of the weight of the river, and may be easily taken or destroyed by an unexpected attack. This may be ascertained by your cruisers when they proceed up the Baltic.

Today a courier has arrived from the upper parts of Finland with the agreeable intelligence of a signal advantage gained by the Swedish army who have defeated the Russians in something like a regular battle, taken several pieces of cannon, two pair of colours, and made several hundred prisoners. I am etc.

13. *Saumarez to Mulgrave*

Victory, Flemish Road, off Gothenburg,

10 May 1808.

My dear Lord, I have the satisfaction to inform your lordship of my arrival at Gothenburgh last Saturday. An officer who had been ordered here by General d'Armfeldt[1] to wait the arrival of the troops from England accompanied the consul[2] the next morning on board the *Victory*. He informed me the general was particularly anxious for a diversion to be made by the English troops on the side of Christiania.[3] It appears that several

---

[1] Gustav Mauritz Armfelt (1757–1814) Swedish soldier and diplomat of Finnish birth; commander-in-chief in Pomerania, 1805–07; commander-in-chief on the Norwegian front, 1808; withdrew to Russia after the revolution of 1809; appointed president of the committee for the management of Finnish affairs, 1811; created a count of the Russian empire. He was dedicated to the anti-Napoleonic cause.

[2] John Smith was employed in a vice-consular capacity at Gothenburg from 1796, if not earlier. He acted as chargé d'affaires at Stockholm from February to October 1804. From 1804 until his death in 1813 he resided at Gothenburg continuously as consul and, during 1810–12, as an unofficial intermediary between the British and Swedish governments.

[3] The modern city of Oslo.

skirmishes had taken place on the frontiers of Norway which in general had proved favourable to the Swedish troops, but on the 5th. instant a detachment from General d'Armfeldt had sustained considerable loss, and obliged him to concentrate his force which left an extensive tract of country exposed to the Danish troops, who are reported to be more numerous than the Swedish Army. The badness of the roads, rendered almost impossible from the frozen snow and drifts of ice, give no cause for much apprehension at the present moment, but from what this officer stated General Armfeldt's position would be rendered critical when the season admits of more active operations and might oblige him to risk an action against superior numbers the result of which might even affect the safety of Gothenburg.

I am in daily expectation of seeing Sir John Moore with the troops under his orders, and if anything can be done consistent with the views of His Majesty's government not a moment shall be lost. I have etc.

14. *Hood to Saumarez*

Centaur, off Helsingborg,

11 May 1808.

Sir, I beg leave to enclose herewith letters I received since noon from Mr. Thornton, His Majesty's envoy at Stockholm. The messenger that brought them with the *memoire*[1] (and is his servant) I have thought right should proceed on to you the moment I have taken copies. I had come to the resolution as follows this morning early and long before his dispatch arrived and is:

'The *Goliath* having been detained so long and the wind breezing up out S.E., I have come to the determination to proceed in the *Centaur* up the Baltic taking with her the *Implacable* and the *Dictator* from the Belt leaving the *Euryalus* in her stead until you may be able to form further arrangements; having no more news from Gotland and the season advancing in which the Russian naval force can move which I hope you will approve. I shall leave Sir A. C. Dickson[2] with the command in the Sound, and I have directed him to open my orders or letters from you as well as others in service until you know of my moving from hence.

I will send something into Carlscrona, if I meet nothing through the Sound or off Bornholm, for any orders you may be desirous of forwarding,

[1] The memoir drawn up by Rajalin for Gustavus Adolphus proposing the entry into the Baltic of the British squadron and its appearance off Hangö Udd.

[2] Sir Archibald Collingwood Dickson, bart., the commander of the *Orion* (74), was the eldest son of Admiral William Dickson a relative by marriage of Admiral Lord Collingwood. He was commissioned in 1791; posted captain 1796; unemployed after 1818; rear-admiral, 1819.

and I will avail myself of forwarding also any occurrences or information of my proceedings to you.'

This is what I wrote before Mr. Thornton's dispatch came, but the wind failed. I hope now I shall get out and in following this course I hope I shall meet your approbation. Mr. Thornton's letter will be some guide to me. I have etc.

In the Sound:

Orion
Goliath
Vanguard
Charger
Centaur between the Koll and Helsingborg.

15. *Saumarez to Hood*

Victory, Flemish Road, off Gothenburg,

18 May 1808.

My dear Sir Samuel, I have the satisfaction to acquaint you that Keats arrived here with Sir John Moore and the ships attached to the expedition yesterday morning having been prevented entering the port for three days owing to the thick fogs, and we have not been able to ascertain from the blowing weather what transports are missing, although there is every reason to hope they are all safe. What is to be done with this force remains doubtful. Colonel Murray[1] who went up to Stockholm on my arrival is not yet returned. He is hourly expected, when I hope something will be arranged for employing so respectable a corps to the benefit of the country and for the security of Sweden. I cannot at the same time help knowing that it may be a great clog to our naval operations. They must inevitably draw a considerable part of our force that we can at this time so ill spare from other services.

The moment the wind will enable the *Tribune* to get out of this road I shall order her to proceed to the Sound from hence, after having sent Captain Baker[2] and the *Vanguard* to join you off Carlscrona and Bornholm; and I shall be glad you detach the cutter that conveys this with any intelligence you

[1] Leiutenant-Colonel George Murray was quartermaster-general in Moore's army. His sober assessment of the strength of the Swedish armed forces increased Moore's reluctance to undertake offensive operations. Murray afterwards served in Spain; K.C.B., 1813. His later appointments included the governorship of Sandhurst, 1819–24; the chief command in Ireland, 1825–8; the colonial secretaryship, 1828–30.

[2] Thomas Baker, lieutenant, 1792; captain, 1797; C.B., 1815; rear-admiral 1821; K.C.B., 1831; vice-admiral, 1837; died, 1845.

may have for me through the Sound where not finding me it will call here for my rendezvous. But I hope before that I shall be able to proceed to the Baltic. Believe me etc.

16. *Saumarez to Hood*

Victory, Flemish Road, off Gothenburg,

18 May 1808.

My dear Sir Samuel, Since my letter of this morning the Baron of Rajalin has been on board this ship to concert with me on the measures to be adopted for the defence of Sweden and for the operations of the naval forces of the respective countries. And, it having been decided that the Swedish squadron [commanded] by Vice-Admiral Cederström,[1] consisting of seven sail-of-the-line and four large frigates, shall occupy the station off Hangö Udd, I have directed the division of three sail-of-the-line and two frigates, with such other vessels as I may be enabled to spare, shall be stationed on the south side of the Baltic towards the enemy's ports and prevent any expedition that they may fit out from thence getting across the Baltic. I hope to have it in my power to augment your squadron, but, under present circumstances, I have no other vessels without taking them from other services of the greatest importance. I shall be obliged soon to order the *Euryalus* to Carlscrona to convoy the duke of Angoulême[2] from thence to Lisbon or any other port where he can be received in safety. I hope you will find opportunities of letting me hear from you. I shall endeavour to communicate with you off Rugen by one of the vessels stationed in the Belts. Believe me etc.

17. *Rajalin to Saumarez*

Karlskrona,

23 May 1808.

Sir, I hope Mr. Smith has made my excuse that I could not have the honour immediately to answer your excellency's letter of the 18th. this month. I was just then to set off for my further voyage. When I arrived here Rear-Admiral Baron Cederström arrived from Gotland, has retaken the island and left troops there for its defence. The Russian commander, Rear-Admiral

---

[1] Olof Rudolf, Baron, later Count, Cederström (1764–1833) entered the navy in 1779 and made his reputation in the war of 1788–90. He became rear-admiral in 1801 and assumed command of the Baltic squadron in 1808. He was promoted vice-admiral, 1809; naval aide-de-camp to the king, 1815–28; governor of Stockholm, 1816–18.

[2] Louis Antoine de Bourbon, duke of Angoulême (1775–1844) was the eldest son of the count of Artois afterwards Charles X of France.

Bodeskoy,[1] with the Russian troops to a number of 2,400 men, after laying down their arms, and all their arms, artillery and ammunition delivered to the Swedes, passed to Libau or the Prussian coast, according to the wind, upon the same vessels who carried them to Gotland with promise to do no service during a year.

Glad to has made your excellency's acquaintance and making use of your's offer to correspond, I take the liberty to let your excellency know that your dispatches to Rear-Admiral Sir Samuel Hood is sent to him, and that order is given to the Swedish fleet to go to the Gulf of Finland. I beg your excellency would be kind, when it will be in your power, to send four or five ships-of-the-line to the Gulf of Finland, because if the Russian fleet whose number is 10 or 13 should come out, all our ships must be employed to fight them, and then the Russian flotilla could profite of that opportunity to pass Hangö Udd, which is a principal object to prevent, and for our ships not be possible if by your means the forces not will be strengthened.

I hope I have explained me clear enough for your excellency that you will be good charge you to prevent an invasion on the coast of Sweden, and for that purpose have cruizers from Libau, for covering Gotland to the Sound and Ertholmarna with Bornholm; a frigatte at Hamrarna (passage between Bornholm and Sweden) is of the greatest importance. It will be necessary to think upon to take that island from the Danes.

Your excellency would be good to excuse the faults I comit in writing in a langage that I not possess in that perfection I wished; and with a man of your character I am sure that if I have forgot any courtial or due attention, it is entirely against my wishes, and against the sentiments of the highest consideration with which I have the honour etc.

P.S. If your excellency will honour me with further correspondence, please to send your letters addressed to Stockholm.

18. *Saumarez to Toll*[2]

Victory, off Gothenburg,

27 May 1808.

Sir, I have received the honour of your excellency's letter in which you are pleased to acquaint me with the recapture of the island of Gotland by the

---

[1] A hastily equipped Russian force of 1,800 men commanded by Rear-Admiral Bodisco landed on Gotland on 22 April with the object of occupying this strategically well-placed island. Swedish warships came to its relief on 11 May. The Russians, who were unsupported by naval force, recognized the hopelessness of their situation and agreed to withdraw on 16 May.

[2] Johan Christopher, Fieldmarshal Baron Toll (1743–1817), a former confidential adviser of Gustavus III, was governor-general of Scania.

Rear-Admiral Baron de Cederström, an event which affords me the highest satisfaction.

I beg your excellency to accept my best thanks for having caused my dispatches to be conveyed to Rear-Admiral Sir Samuel Hood, and I perfectly conform to your excellency's opinion respecting the islands of Bornholm and Eartholm. The acquisition of those islands would be of great importance and an object well worthy of consideration.

As soon as I have force that can possibly be spared from other services I shall lose no time to send it to the Baltic, and I hope to proceed myself in order to co-operate with the fleet of His Swedish Majesty. Sir Samuel Hood has my orders to cruise along the coast of Pomerania and to the southward of Gotland, and in the event of the Russian fleet coming from Cronstadt and Revel to join his force to the Swedish fleet. I have etc.

P.S. I have also cruisers off Rugen and the entrance of the Belts. I beg to assure your excellency of the high satisfaction it has afforded me in having the honour of your acquaintance and I shall be most grateful for any communication you will at any time be pleased to make to me that can tend to advance the important service we are employed upon.

19. *Thornton to Saumarez*

Stockholm,

28 May 1808.

Sir, I have had the honour of receiving your excellency's letter of the 18th inst. and learn with the greatest satisfaction the arrangement you have made with the Swedish Admiral de Rajalin relative to the distribution of the naval forces of the two countries, and which seems much more suited to the circumstances of them both than the one contained in that officer's *memoire*. The defence of their own coast, particularly where their own troops are engaged against the troops of Russia, seems the natural destination of the Swedish naval force, while the open sea, the coast occupied by France, the Belts and Sound are more properly confined to us, who have really a greater interest in these points than in common times the Swedes could have.

Your excellency will see from my late letters, that the force detached under Sir Samuel Hood will probably be more than enough for any fleet the Russians will venture to put out. The re-capture of Gotland is also a satisfactory circumstance. This event took place on the 16th. inst. by the capitulation of the Russian troops disembarked there, who have been allowed to return to a Russian port. I have etc.

20. *Rajalin to Saumarez*

Stockholm,

4 June 1808.

Sir, Your excellency's letter of the 27th. May have I received, and I can't enough declare the high obligation in which I rest for it and the pleasure it does me to correspond with your excellency.

Your excellency pleased to inform me in Gothenburg that you had mentioned to Rear-Admiral Sir Samuel Hood to take notice of Ertholmarna and Bornholm, how those islands should be conquered. If you has received answer, should I take as a particular favour if your excellency would let me know if you has made upp a plan for taking those places, and if you intend to do it.

A merchant whose name is N. Kemner has informed by a letter from Königsberg the 14th. May that he had freighted several vessels charged with rie or hemp, or others allowed articles for Stockholm on whose licences are marked the letters F.K.M.K.R. on one side and on the others *lämnad of N. Kemner* or delivered of N. Kemner. Without to mention the names of the vessels, wishes he, that those vessels should be taken; and for that purpose cruizers stationed by Memel or rather between Memel and Swalperort upon Oesel. It is necessary to explain your excellency why the vessels must be taken. The French consuls in Russia and Prussia has declared that the crew of vessels who at sea remark that the cargo is destined to Sweden may force the captain to return in the harbour and the crew has the half of the cargoes. Also is no truth in the crew; and the captain must be taken if the vessels shall come to Sweden. As all the Swedish armed vessells is employed, and your excellency has been good charged you with the coast from Libau, has I received order from His Swedish Majesty to let you know the merchands' demand, and that your excellency would be kind order a cruizer on the mentioned cruizing to take such a vessells and to escort they same to the entrance by Landsort, or Sandhamn, to Stockholm. And may your cruizer, since they pilots is coming on board they licenced vessels, return to his station. I beg your excellency would be assured that I have etc.

21. *Saumarez to Mulgrave*

Victory, off Gothenburg,

5 June 1808.

My dear Lord, In consequence of the various and important services incident to this station I beg to submit to your lordship the expediency of having another flag officer appointed to the squadron. Should the operations be carried on up the Baltic, I shall require the assistance of Sir Samuel Hood besides Admiral Keats who will be continued with the expedition. The service of the Sound and Belt, where four sail-of-the-line are stationed besides smaller vessels, requires the superintendance of a flag officer, and the extensive correspondence that frequently with H.M. envoy at Stockholm and the affairs of the Swedish government require the presence of a flag officer who should have the station off Helsinborg assigned to him.

I know not how far the appointment may be acceptable to Admiral Bertie,[1] but if it met with your lordship's approval I know no one to whom I could wish the proposal to be made in preference to him. I have etc.

22. *Moore to Saumarez*

Stockholm,

19 June 1808.

My dear Sir James, The plan the king of Sweden has proposed is that I should disembark the troops in the Russian territories in the bottom of the Gulf of Finland at Björkö, Viborg, Frederickshamn and Lovise in order to make diversions in favour of his troops whose head quarters are still at Brahestad opposed to the Russians at Gamle Carleby. This is so absurd that I of course must decline it. I must defer informing you with the detail of what has passed here until another opportunity, when less hurried, or until I have the pleasure of seeing you. It is difficult to give you an idea of the weakness and incapacity of this poor prince though a good man and meaning well. But he is absolute; he admits of no counsel or advice and expects to be implicitly obeyed. I am not without the hope that when I decline the operation he has proposed, that he will tell me officially, as he has already done in conversation, that he has no further service for the British troops. In this case I think it will be best to take advantage of it and to send them home; but I cannot bring myself, after what I know and have seen of him, to commit to his direction the force I command. I have written so to government at home and have said that nothing short of a positive order should now induce me to lead in Sweden or to undertake any operation, however solicited, which took from me the disposal of the troops or which I could not execute independent of the Swedes.

[1] Thomas Bertie (1758–1825) was born Thomas Hoare, assuming the name of Bertie on his marriage to Catherine Bertie in 1788. He was commissioned in 1780; promoted captain 1790; rear-admiral, 1808; vice-admiral 1813; admiral, 1825. Bertie, whose conduct at Copenhagen in 1801 was warmly commended by Nelson, did not serve after 1810 because of illness. He was created K.B. in 1813.

I hope to leave this on Tuesday, or at latest on Wednesday next. I beg to be kindly remembered to Captain Hope.[1] I have etc.

23. *Hood to Saumarez*

Centaur, off Moen [Møn],

22 June 1808.

My dear Sir James, Captain Lukin[2] brought me your very kind letters of the 13th and 14th. inst. the night before last, and I cannot do more than repeat my thanks to you for your very obliging attention. I should have sent the *Swan* cutter with my dispatches, but I deem the conveyance more certain by landing them at Ystad, and assuredly by far the most expeditious. Indeed the calms we have experienced would have been dangerous for the vessel to have passed the Sound, and she has been of most essential service here. Baron de Toll is very attentive to my wishes respecting them. I hope 'ere this you will be relieved from your unpleasant situation respecting the army and that all will be to your wishes. The *Mars* is a most essential reinforcement and I hope the *Salsette* will soon be back as she carried a fine wind up. The *Goliath* I shall detach to take charge of the coast between Danzig and the entrance of Riga and attach the *Magnet* with some other small vessel or a frigate, which will I think perfectly protect the trade. And one of the ships-of-the-line I must for the present place off Eartholm where the *Forward* now is. The gunbrigs would be of great use in the Baltic for the protection of the scattered trade, should the enemy fit out any small privateers. I tremble for our merchants; and if matters do not change I think they will find obstacles in Russia as they have, I fear, already in their speculations in Prussia. The French consuls are so very active and from the extent it cannot be long undetected where they are so many people of no principle concerned. We must collect the trade at Ystad guarding against any privateers from Eartholm of which lately I have not heard of any. I shall endeavour to arrange all for the best advantage, and I trust our accounts from the Gulf of Finland will be favourable and not require a larger force, which Admiral Baron Cederstrom seemed to wish for and, I thought, expected. This will go with my dispatches in a vessel Baron de Toll has sent out to me from Ystad. I therefore shall not add more than assuring you of my best wishes for your health and success.

[1] George Johnstone Hope (1767–1818) was captain-of-the-fleet to Saumarez; a post-captain of 1793; commander of the *Defence* (74) at Trafalgar; rear-admiral, 1811; K.C.B., 1815.
[2] William Lukin, the commander of the *Mars* (74), was a nephew of the Hon. William Windham. He was commissioned 1793; promoted captain 1795; rear-admiral, 1814. There is no record of any service after 1815.

24. *Mulgrave to Saumarez*

Admiralty,
26 June 1808.

My dear Sir James, I have received your private letters of the 5th. and 19th. of June and in compliance with your wishes expressed in the former I have appointed Rear-Admiral Bertie to serve under your orders, and he will proceed without delay to the Baltic to hoist his flag in such ship as you shall direct.

You certainly could not do otherwise than you have done respecting the application of Baron Jacobi.[1]

The capture of the gunbrigs[2] and a large proportion of the convoy off Dragø is a very unfortunate event as the north country merchants are very clamorous about the protection of their trade, and some resolutions come to at Hull, complaining in general terms, have been recently published in the newspapers. I cannot therefore press too much upon your attention the importance of guarding as much as possible against the efforts of the enemy's flotilla. The returns from the Baltic are at this moment of the utmost importance.

The resistance to the tyranny and presumptions of Bonaparte in Spain continues by all accounts to spread rapidly through the northern provinces. From the southern parts of Spain we have not yet any certain or detailed accounts. If the Spanish troops on the island of Funen [Fyn] or in any other part of the coasts of the Baltic accessible to you should manifest a disposition to withdraw from the enemy you will of course afford every facility of transports or other means to convey them to some part of Sweden till the means of transporting them from thence can be sent out from Great Britain. From general rumour there is every reason to suppose that such a disposition exists amongst the Spanish troops serving in the north of Europe. It must necessarily be left to your discretion to decide how far you may have it in your power to promote the object above stated. I am etc.

25. *Saumarez to Mulgrave*

Victory, Flemish Road, off Gothenburg,
27 June 1808.

My Lord, I have the honour to inclose for your lordship's information the copy of a letter I have this morning received from Mr. Thornton by an express

---

[1] Baron Jacobi-Kloest, the late Prussian ambassador in London, had requested a passage home for himself and suite from Marstrand near Gothenburg in a British man-of-war; which request was turned down by Saumarez.

[2] A convoy escorted by the *Turbulent* and *Thunder* gunbrigs was badly mauled by a force of Danish gunboats, when becalmed off Malmö on 10 June. The *Turbulent* was taken by the enemy.

relative to the unexpected detention of Sir John Moore on the evening prior
to his intended departure from Stockholm, it appearing by a letter from Sir
John Moore which General Hope[1] has communicated to me that late the
evening of the 24th. he was called upon by an adjutant general of the king of
Sweden with a message purporting that he was not to leave Stockholm without the king's pleasure. From the importance attached to the circumstance
by Mr. Thornton and Sir John Moore I have judged it proper in concert
with Lt.General Hope to make every preparation for withdrawing the troops
from Gothenburg and to hold the transports in readiness to proceed at the
shortest notice according as circumstances may require. I hope Sir John
Moore will have been permitted to proceed to join the forces under his order
pursuant to his intentions. But as a packet was sailing for England with a
Swedish messenger on board and, as far as I could learn, without conveying
dispatches from His Majesty's envoy or Sir John Moore, I felt it incumbent
upon myself to make your lordship acquainted with the foregoing particulars. I have etc.

26. *Pole to Saumarez*

27 June 1808.

Sir, I lost no time in laying before my Lords Commissioners of the Admiralty your letter under date of the 13th. instant stating 'that you have just
received intelligence from Mr. Smith, His Majesty's consul at Gothenburg,
that one of our convoys in passing through the Malmö Channel was inter-
cepted by the enemy's flotilla and that seventeen of them fell into their hands
and that a gunbrig, after defending herself a considerable time was obliged
to surrender on the following morning', also 'that you have reason to believe
this is the convoy which sailed with the *Thunder* and *Piercer* on the 22nd. ult.,
which had been detained at Malmö, and which consisted principally of
neutrals most of which were in ballast.'

I also laid before their lordships your letter under date the 16th. instant
enclosing a letter from Sir Archibald Dickson of the *Orion* with copies of
two letters transmitted to him by Captain Baker of the *Vanguard* relating
to the same unfortunate affair; and I am commanded to express the great
regret their lordships feel at the disaster which has happened and to call
upon you for a more detailed statement of the circumstances which led to this
untoward occurrence, which statement their lordships trust will show that

[1] John Hope (1765–1823) served as adjutant-general to Sir Ralph Abercromby in the
West Indies, Holland and Egypt. He was promoted lieutenant-general in 1808 and
appointed second-in-command to Moore, in which capacity he afterwards fought at
Corunna. After distinguished service in Spain he was created Baron Niddry in 1815; succeeded to the earldom of Hopetown in 1816.

the force under your command has been distributed in the most judicious manner as well for the protection of the Baltic trade as for affording assistance to the king's ally. And they hope that the disaster which has unhappily befallen the convoy arose from unavoidable accidents and not from any deficiency in the force allotted by you for its protection, or through any misconduct in the officers to whose care it was entrusted.

I am commanded by their lordships to signify their directions to you to use your utmost endeavours to prevent any such captures in future, informing yourself of the means the enemy may possess of annoying the convoys entrusted to your charge, and assembling in due time at the entrance of the Sound a sufficient force to guard against any attempt that may hereafter be made by the enemy's gunboats or any other naval force he may possess, their lordships considering the security of the trade from capture or annoyance as of the first importance.

The force at present under your orders is considered to be adequate to the duties of your command, but if you should find it necessary to employ more small vessels than can be spared to you from other services, you are to make such arrangements as you may deem to be necessary for augmenting your gun vessels, either by purchasing or hiring craft for that purpose to be manned and armed from such of the line-of-battle ships under your orders as may be employed in protecting the convoys passing through the Sound, where, it is to be presumed, they will not have to cope with ships of equal force and where consequently these aids may be afforded with advantage to the service. But if you think it desirable to have any heavy guns or ammunition, for any craft you may procure as gun vessels, sent to you from England you are to state the same to me in order that no time may be lost in preparing such articles as you may demand and forwarding them to you.

It has been deemed proper to enter into these details in order to point your attention to resources which it may be necessary to resort to if the enemy continues to increase his flotilla of gunboats and armed vessels for the purpose of intercepting our convoys. Their lordships are aware that your original instructions under date of the 16 April last and my subsequent letter to you are amply sufficient and clearly express the necessity of giving full protection to the trade within the limits of your station, but they have thought it requisite in consequence of the very unexpected disaster which has happened to be thus particular in calling your attention to this most important object.

The protection of the convoys through the Sound and clear of the island of Bornholm and the Eartholm is a matter of such high moment that it is their lordships' command that you detach Rear-Admiral Keats (who appears by your last disposition to be at Gothenburg) upon this particular duty, placing

under his orders a force adequate to the service on which he is to be employed
and giving him such instructions as you may deem necessary for his guidance; and their lordships suggest for your consideration the propriety of a
line-of-battle ship or two being anchored with springs on their cables between Dragø Point and Saltholms to awe and prevent the enemy's gunboats
from coming out during the passage of convoys into or out of the Baltic by
the passage of the Sound, which passage, under all circumstances, their
lordships are inclined to think to be least dangerous. I am etc.

27. Rajalin to Saumarez

Stockholm,
28 June 1808.

Sir, Your excellency allow me to let you know that His Majesty has
pleased to call Rear-Admiral Baron de Cederström to Stockholm, and that,
for the present, Rear-Admiral Sir Henry Nauckhoff[1] has the command of
the Swedish fleet. I beg your excellency would by a letter to Sir Samuel Hood
recommand that he would inform the Swedish admiral where your cruizers
of men-of-war are stationed, that in case the Russian fleet should come out
and be stronger than the Swedish, he might replye upon these ships.

Rear-Admiral Baron de Cederström has probably sent cruizers upp
against Cronstadt to know with surety the force of the enemy, and I shall
have the honour to inform your excellency thereof as soon as I receive the
report. However it is assured that the Russian fleet will not come out; and
when the Swedish fleet now is 11 man-of-war, and when your excellency in
the letter of 27th. May did me the honour to say in the event of the Russian
fleet coming from Cronstadt and Revel that Rear-Admiral Sir Samuel Hood
has to unite his force to the Swedish fleet, has I thought in order to beg your
excellency be good to let the Swedish admiral be informed where the English
man-of-war are stationed in the Baltic, for the reason I had the honour to
mention, and by these to assure the Swedish fleet in all events.

I have laid at the feet of the king, my master, the content of your excellency's letters with your personal wishes to co-operate for the sake of the
good and common cause, and His Majesty has been pleased to order me to
transmit to your excellency his royal satisfaction and most gracious approbation of these sentiments. I have etc.

[1] Henrik Johan, later Baron, Nauckhoff (1744–1818) was commissioned in 1769. He
served in the French navy, 1778–83, being wounded and made prisoner at the battle of the
Saints. He commanded a ship-of-the-line in the war of 1788–90, was promoted rear-
admiral, 1797; vice-admiral, 1809. He was naval aide-de-camp to the king, 1812–15;
admiral and appointed to the command at Karlskrona, 1817.

28. *Saumarez to Mulgrave*

30 June 1808.

My Lord, I have great satisfaction in acquainting your lordship that Sir John Moore came aboard this ship yesterday evening and as it is his intention to detach Colonel Murray to England by the packet your lordship will be made acquainted with the circumstances that have occurred subsequent to the statements transmitted by General Hope and myself for the information of government.

As the proposed return of the troops to England will necessarily occasion some alteration to the instructions I have received, I beg to inform your lordship that on their making from this port I shall proceed for the Sound and detach Admiral Keats to the Belt. I have etc.

29. *Saumarez to Mulgrave*

Victory, off Gothenburg,

5 July 1808.

My Lord, Mr. Oakley[1] secretary of legation at Stockholm came on board the *Victory* last evening with letters from Mr. Thornton acquainting me that the king of Sweden had left the residence on the 30th ult. and sailed on board one of the royal yachts without its being known what could be the object of His Swedish Majesty's intention in so sudden a resolution. Amongst the various conjectures that may be formed is the probability of His Swedish Majesty going on board his fleet off Hangö Udd. I have therefore dispatched an express to Sir Samuel Hood directing him to collect all the ships under his orders; and I shall proceed to join him without loss of time taking Rear-Admiral Keats with me on my way thro' the Great Belt; and I shall be in readiness to act according to circumstances and to such further information as I may receive from Mr. Thornton. I have etc.

30. *Thornton to Saumarez*

Stockholm,

12 July 1808.

Sir, You will see by the letter of Lord Castlereagh to Lieutenant-General Sir John Moore, of which I have the honour of transmitting a copy to your excellency, that His Majesty's government had it in contemplation to

---

[1] Charles Oakley was appointed secretary of legation, 18 Dec. 1807; was chargé d'affaires at Stockholm from late Oct. to 20 Nov. 1808.

endeavour to employ the troops under his command in an attempt on the island of Funen, for the purpose of disengaging the Spanish troops and of bringing them away. This plan, as far as it depends upon the co-operation of our land forces or upon the immediate furnishing of transport, must be regarded as impracticable; but His Majesty's government dwell with so much earnestness upon the importance of any attempt to attain the object of bringing away the Spanish troops, that I cannot forbear impressing it upon your excellency's attention.

The messenger Ross who brought my dispatches this morning delivered me a packet directed in the first instance to General Sir John Moore, in the next to yourself or either of the two admirals under your excellency's command, or lastly to me in case of the absence of the preceding. I opened it for the purpose of seeing whether it contained papers of which I could make use; and now I have the honour of transmitting it under this cover exactly as I found it.

Mr. Canning[1] urges me to make every possible effort to convey to their destination the letters in the packet, which are addressed by the authorities of Gallicia and by the deputies from that kingdom, and from the principality of the Asturias, to the commander and other officers of the Spanish army in the north, with the injunction that great care must be taken to prevent their interception and to avoid exposing to danger the persons to whom they are addressed.

At the distance from the coast at which I am placed, and with all the difficulties imposed by this government upon any communication with Denmark or the continent, I have found it utterly impossible to open any correspondence or obtain any information as to the position of the Spanish troops or of their commanders. The German papers (*Correspondent of Hamburg*) which I have to the 21st. of June mention Bernadotte's having returned to Hamburg; but it seems to me less difficult by means of the navy to learn with some accuracy the position of the Spanish troops in Funen and perhaps to release them. There are plenty of transport ships at Nyborg which might be used for their conveyance.

I think it very possible that Baron de Toll might aid greatly in furnishing a person who might be charged with a message to some of the Spanish officers, but I must leave it to your excellency's opinion upon the spot to make use of this hint or otherwise. I am etc.

[1] George Canning, the secretary of state for foreign affairs.

Enclosure:

30a. *Castlereagh to Moore*

Downing Street,

30 June 1808.

Sir, The progress of the insurrection in Spain which has extended itself not only to the provinces but to the army renders it an object of importance to extricate, if possible, the Spanish troops in the north of Germany. A confidential person has been sent to open a communication with that army, to ascertain their dispositions and to concert measures for their being brought away. That you may be in possession of the latest information, Lieutenant-Colonel Mackenzie who has been sent to Heligoland to superintend the execution of this service has been instructed to report to you the results of his proceedings.[1]

It is not judged adviseable to detain indefinitely your corps at Gothenburg for the chance of any aid it might be enabled to afford to such an object, but should you, upon the state of the information you may receive, be of opinion that you can favour the escape of the Spanish army from its present perilous position by a movement upon Funen or such other part of the coast as it may now occupy, His Majesty is pleased to direct that you do make an effort for this purpose, unless you should be of opinion that there is no reasonable prospect of its being attended with success.

I should hope with the assistance of the navy and your own transports that the means of removing the Spanish troops to Gothenburg might be found, where, I have no doubt, under the pressing circumstances of the case the king of Sweden would permit them to be landed till a proper provision of transports can be sent from hence to convey them to Spain. I have etc.

31. *Saumarez to Mulgrave*

Victory, off the island of Moen,

15 July 1808.

My dear Lord, I have the satisfaction to inform your lordship that I was joined this morning by the detachment under the orders of Sir Samuel Hood. Altho' I have not received any letters from Mr. Thornton of later date than

---

[1] The confidential person was James Robertson, a priest of the Benedictine community at Ratisbon, lately employed as tutor in the household of an English catholic peer, who had been recommended to Canning for services abroad by Sir Arthur Wellesley. The most accessible account of his adventures after being put ashore near the mouth of the Weser in a boat hired at Heligoland by Colin Mackenzie is C. Oman, *A History of the Peninsular War*, vol. i, 1807–1809; *From the Treaty of Fontainebleau to the Battle of Corunna* (1902), pp. 370 ff.

the 5th. instant which was prior to his having received any returns to the dispatches relative to the detention of Sir John Moore, I think it necessary in consequence of his strong recommendation to use every precaution that can tend to give effect to His Majesty's government in supporting their demand for reparation to hold the squadron in readiness to act as circumstances may require, and with that view I shall keep the line-of-battle ships collected until I hear from Mr. Thornton the result of any representations he may have been instructed to make to the government of Stockholm.

It rather appears that the journey of His Swedish Majesty from the residence was with the intention to visit his fleet off Hangö Udd, but whether it is accompanied with any other object appears to be very doubtful.

I profit of the return of a messenger which joined me this morning with dispatches from England for Sir John Moore to send my letters being likely to prove the most expeditious conveyance. I have etc.

32. *Drafts of Letters by Saumarez dated 18–21 July 1808*

Monday, 18th. July. On Thursday the 12th. I entered the Baltic and on the morning following was joined by Sir Samuel Hood in the *Centaur*, with the *Implacable*, *Mars* and *Dictator*. The *Africa* was off the Malmö Channel and *Goliath* on her way from off Danzig which with the *Victory* and *Superb* gave me eight sail-of-the-line. Dispatches reached me from England to the 27th. June and a messenger with dispatches for Sir John Moore, which I opened, to the 30th. By these last it appears that the troops were intended to have landed in Funen with the view to bring off the Spanish troops. The letters transmitted by General Hope and myself relative to Sir John Moore being detained at Stockholm had been received by government and appear to have excited a strong sensation with ministers. My latest letters from Mr. Thornton are to the 5th. July, four days later than those brought me by Mr. Oakley on my departure from Gothenburg. Altho' they tend to remove the doubts entertained of the king of Sweden having any further object in view but that of visiting his forces in Finland, other circumstances incline me to consider his journey in a suspicious light. A letter from Baron de Rajalin of the 29th., who accompanied the king from Stockholm, takes no notice of his intention. Another letter of the 8th. from the person at the head of the marine department in Rajalin's absence, is equally silent upon it. In the meantime I have detached the *Rose* with a letter to Nauckhoff, who has superseded Cederström in the command of the fleet off Hangö Udd, with the view of opening a communication and, if possible, for Captain Pipon[1] to find out the king's intentions.

Thursday, 21st. I received two days ago letters from England to the 9th. instant, and also from Mr. Thornton to the 12th. As the former were prior to the accounts transmitted by Lt. Colonel Murray having arrived in England, no determination could have taken place on the purport of the dispatches he conveyed. I feel, however, confident that no measures will be adopted that can lead to a rupture with Sweden; and I expect that my next dispatch from the envoy will authorise me to allow the instalment due the end of this month to be sent to Carlscrona. At half-past one yesterday morning a Swedish officer came on board the *Victory*, who commands a Swedish cutter employed to cruise off the coast of Pomerania for the purpose of obtaining intelligence, his family residing at Stralsund, and informed me that a body of ten thousand troops had actually embarked on board transports and were in readiness to sail from that port. I immediately detached Rear-Admiral Keats in three sail-of-the-line and four small vessels to endeavour to intercept them. And as this expedition might probably be concerted with others fitting out in different ports in the Baltic, the rear-admiral was directed to send part of his force to watch the enemy's ports higher up the coast of Pomerania. In the meantime I remain here with Sir Samuel Hood in order the more readily to receive the dispatches I have so much reason to expect from England and from Mr. Thornton to be of the highest importance, and which must in a joint measure direct me in my further proceedings. I have stationed Admiral Bertie, who arrived from England in the *Calypso*, to take command of the ships in the Sound hoisting his flag on board the *Orion*.

33. *Thornton to Saumarez*

Stockholm,
20 July 1808.

Sir, I am so perfectly persuaded of the great advantage which will arise at this juncture from an interview with His Swedish Majesty, as well to the common cause as to the particular interests of His Majesty in Finland, that on receiving your excellency's private letter of the 15th. (marked private and confidential) I immediately resolved to mention your wish to Baron

---

[1] Philip Pipon (1771–1829), the commander of the sloop *Rose*, was born at St. Brelade, Jersey; lieutenant, 1794; commander, 1802; captain, Oct. 1808; employed in the Baltic, 1808–12.

d'Ehrenheim[1] with a desire to him to propose it at once to His Swedish Majesty. Baron d'Ehrenheim seized the suggestion with an avidity founded on the same motives as those which actuated me (at least in part) and said that he would write this evening to the king, who is by this time in Åland, and who, he was sure, would immediately send the necessary orders to Hangö to await your excellency's arrival. I agreed therefore with him that I would endeavour to induce you to adopt the resolution of immediately repairing towards Hangö Udd, or at least towards the entrance of the Bothnian Gulf with such part of your squadron as could be spared without exposing the defences in the Sound and Belt.

In mentioning the ground of your excellency's desire to have an interview with His Swedish Majesty, I adverted only to the great delays and inconvenience of a written correspondence which is sufficiently indeed exemplified by the date of Baron de Rajalin's letter of the 28th. ult. I hinted indeed at the apparition of our joint naval forces in the Gulf of Finland and before Cronstadt, because this is a point of essential advantage to the affairs of Finland, and because it is calculated to flatter the sentiments of the king. But I carefully abstained from the principal idea, contained in your letter, of inducing the powers of the North to make peace and to unite once more against the common enemy; for with the king of Sweden this point must be touched upon at present with great delicacy.

Your excellency is aware that His Majesty has made it a point of great accusation against General Moore and myself that in the midst of projects for combined operations we talked peace, and has deduced a reason for the inactivity of the troops from our desire to spare an enemy with whom we are wishing to treat. For my own part, and under the circumstances in which I threw out these pacific suggestions (the first opening of the affairs in Spain) I cannot cease to take praise to myself for advising a measure, dictated as well by every principle of general policy as by the peculiar circumstances of this country. But His Majesty's disappointment would not allow him to see the affair in the same point of view, and he would hardly, I doubt, (at least in the first moments) be induced to go up the Gulf of Finland, if he thought the appearance there was connected with a project of offering terms of peace. This, however, must not be lost sight of, and I only take the liberty of putting you upon your guard in the first interview with His Majesty.

If this project of coming to the entrance of this gulf or to Hangö Udd should be carried into execution, it affords me the most favourable oppor-

---

[1] Fredrik Wilhelm, Baron von Ehrenheim (1753–1828) was appointed, after much experience in the diplomatic corps, president of the chancellery with special responsibility for foreign affairs in 1801; which post he held until the revolution. He acquiesced in the king's belligerent policy whilst fearing its consequences. After 1809 he retired into private life.

tunity I shall perhaps ever possess of having an interview with your excellency. A gunbrig or any other vessel which you could spare from your squadron (perhaps that which will bring the silver near Stockholm) might come to Dalarö, which is not thirty English miles from this place, and might convey me to any point which your excellency might be pleased to name, to Hangö for example, or any nearer point. Nothing indeed would gratify me so much as to be able to accompany your excellency up the Gulf of Finland, before Cronstadt, particularly if there were a hope of bringing on a pacific negotiation. And with this possible contingency in prospect, I observed to Baron d'Ehrenheim this evening how favourable an opportunity this presented to me of an interview with you, and desired him to mention it to the king, that His Majesty might not meet me on board the *Victory* by surprize. This was the more necessary as the late discussions have excited in the king's breast a certain prepossession against me, which I scarcely had share enough in them to deserve.

On this subject of peace, I would beg your excellency to lose no occasion of making Denmark feel that we do not willingly continue her enemy. This may perhaps lead her to make the first overture, to which all her real interest ought to lead her. I have etc.

34. *Nauckhoff to Saumarez*

Gustav IV Adolf, off Hangö,

27 July 1808.

Sir, I have the honour to acknowledge the receipt of your excellency's of the 15th. of this month.

May it please your excellency to receive my most sincere thanks for your obliging congratulations on my appointment to the command of the fleet of my sovereign, and at the same time permit me assure that nothing can afford more satisfaction to my ambition than the honour to co-operate against the common enemy with so gallant and celebrated admiral as your excellency.

The squadron under my command having made a cruise here for eight weeks are at present in want of water and fresh provisions. The sickness among the crews on board of several ships increase every day, which I fear will soon oblige me to return to Carlskrona with 4 or 5 ships-of-the-line in order to relieve the sick and take fresh water; but as it will be of greatest consequence to guard this station with a force sufficient to make head against the common enemy, I find myself obliged to solicit that your excellency will be pleased to send a reinforcement to this station of 4 British ships-of-the-line with two or three frigates as soon as possible. The king of Sweden are at present at Åland. I have etc.

35. *Saumarez to Mulgrave*

Victory, off Moen Island,

28 July 1808.

My Lord, A vessel from Wismar was this morning brought into the squadron on board of which was a person eight days from Hamburg who reports that the Spanish troops in Holstein had been desired to take the oaths of alligiance to the pretended king of Spain, which they had refused, and that Bernadotte had detached several French regiments to compel them to it. Their number amounted to about 16,000; and 15,000 are said to be in Zealand.

Mr. McKenzie, who had been instructed to communicate with Sir John Moore from Heligoland, came on board the *Victory* yesterday from Ystad and I had furnished him with a gunbrig to convey him to the Belt when the information was obtained. It has therefore decided him to return to Gothenburg.

The report of an expedition being ready to proceed from Stralsund does not appear to have been correct, although the Swede from whom the information is obtained is a person entrusted by Baron de Toll to procure information and is represented as an officer to be relied upon. I have etc.

36. *Keats to Saumarez*

Superb, off Langeland,

5 Aug. 1808.

Sir, The *Mosquito* has just joined me, and I delay her with reluctance one moment. Unfortunately the *Tigress*,[1] when taken, was bearing dispatches to you from Captain Campbell[2] of the *Dictator*, which I will endeavour to supply in the best measure I can as soon as the Spanish officer at present in the *Edgar*, now near, shall come on board.

Don Lobo,[3] who came from England in the *Mosquito*, is now on board the *Superb* and, conceiving his services can be more useful to his countrymen here than by going on in the *Mosquito*, will remain.

The accompanying statement of the number and situation of the Spanish troops is by him collected from Don Antonio Fabragues, lieutenant of the 1st. regiment of Catalogne on the island of Langeland, who went off to the *Dictator*. As he was not sent by the commander of the Spanish troops, and the

---

[1] The gunbrig *Tigress* was taken in the Great Belt on 2 Aug. by sixteen Danish gunboats.
[2] Donald Campbell was posted captain in 1795 and promoted rear-admiral in 1814.
[3] Rafael Lobo y Campo, a Spanish naval officer, came to London as secretary to the deputation from Seville in July 1808 and was forwarded to the Baltic to open a communication with the Spaniards in the Danish islands.

Spanish officers appearing to be in extreme ignorance of the late transactions in Spain, on that account, as well as to connect if possible the movements and plans of those in Zealand and Jutland with those in Funen and Langeland, further communication will be necessary. To this end I believe a flag of truce may be most adviseable this afternoon to Langeland; and I shall proceed in the *Brunswick* and *Edgar* towards Nyborg with a view to act as circumstances may make it necessary. It occurs to me that it might be adviseable to move the troops from Funen to Langeland, which is a productive island and where they could support themselves till transports are ready. Samsoe [Samsø] is too strongly fortified and has too respectable a garrison to be made use of for that purpose. But perhaps the islands of Thornoe [Tunø] and Andalev [Endelave] might serve for those in Jutland; and it should seem desirable to contrive if possible that those at Roskilde in Zealand should seize upon some small port, suppose Corsaer [Korsør], at the same time. Nothing can yet be determined on till we have further communication; and, as the men in the fishing boat which brought the officer from Langeland were suffered to return, there is some fear of a discovery or at least suspicion. The occasion will, I trust, justify the detention of the *Brunswick* and *Edgar*. Assure yourself, sir, that no zeal or exertion shall be wanting on my part in this important business. I have etc.

37. *Nauckhoff to Saumarez*

Gustaf 4th. Adolph, Road of Orö,

7 Aug. 1808.

Sir, The frigate *Jarramus* who should forward to your excellency my letter of the 6th. by which I had the honour to inform your excellency that the Russian fleet was discovered the 5th., by the 3 ships and two frigates who were left cruising off Hangö, consisting of 20 sails ranged in a line-of-battle, giving chase to the said ships obliging them to retreat and join me in this road, are stopped by contrary winds in the outer skerries where he is watched by the enemy's cruisers. And I am therefore obliged to try another expedient, sending a small brig along the skerries where I hope he will find the opportunity to escape the enemy's vigilance and be happy to forward your excellency this important information. And 20 sails of the enemy were yesterday seen from the top of this ship. One line-of-battle ship and a frigate cruised before the entrance off this road; the main force of the fleet are cruising off Hangö. I am in the greatest concern for the fate of vessels with stores and provisions for the fleet, which are daily expected from Carlscrona and are likely to fall into the hands of the enemy, if the British fleet under the command of your excellency will not soon appear and oblige the enemy to retire in his ports.

I wait with impatience for that happy moment; and if any of the British cruisers should appear before this road, making reconnoitring signals, I shall in the moment send a pilot out to meet them. The entrance to this road are to the west of a small rock named Bengtskjär in the charts, situated W.S.W. ¾ West 14 miles from Hangö Udd. I have etc.

38. *Saumarez to Rajalin*

Victory, off Carlscrona,

8 Aug. 1808.

Sir, I have had the honour to receive your excellency's letter dated 29th. July acquainting me that His Majesty the king of Sweden had been graciously pleased to order your excellency to communicate with me on the plans and intentions of His Majesty respecting the co-operations of the squadrons in the Gulf of Finland.

I have the honour to inform your excellency that the contrary winds have prevented these last five weeks the arrival of the victuallers I expected from England with the provisions for the squadron under my command. It was not until four days since that they have been enabled to join Rear-Admiral Sir Samuel Hood off Moen island, and I waited here for those supplies in order to proceed off Hangö Udd and join the squadron of His Swedish Majesty.

The information I have since received of the important events which have taken place in Fuen and the other islands in the Belts, in consequence of the Spanish troops having manifested a disposition to withdraw themselves from the service of the enemy and follow the example of their brave country-men in Spain and unite in the common cause against the detested *Tyrant Bonaparte*, I have been impelled to forego my intentions of going to the Gulf of Finland, and to proceed to the Great Belt with a view, if possible, to extricate the Spanish troops from being any longer in the service of the enemy. The letter I have had the honour to receive from your excellency makes me the more sensibly regret being prevented putting my first intentions into execution, from the happiness it would have afforded me to have co-operated with your excellency in fulfilling the views of His Swedish Majesty. I can only reconcile myself to so great a disappointment in being able to detach an officer of such high and distinguished merit upon this service as Rear-Admiral Sir Samuel Hood. He will take under his orders four line-of-battle ships and such smaller vessels as I can possibly spare; but your excellency must be very sensible of the necessity of having a great number of vessels stationed in the Belts and other parts of the station for the defence of Sweden and the protection of convoys, which even with the greatest vigilance can scarcely be secured from the attacks of the enemy's flotilla, which in the Great Belt alone consists of above sixty sail of large gunboats exclusive of smaller vessels.

I shall be happy to find that my proceedings are honoured with the approval of His Swedish Majesty, and I request your excellency will be pleased to honour me with your commands to be forwarded from Stockholm by way of Ystad. I have etc.

39. *Saumarez to Mulgrave*

Victory, off Bornholm,

9 August 1808.

My dear Lord, I have received your lordship's letter by Don Raphael Lobo who Admiral Keats very properly kept on board the *Superb* for the purpose of communicating with the Spanish officers that may join him from Fuen or the other islands when opportunity offered; and your lordship may be assured that I shall be most happy in showing him every possible attention as well as to any of the commanders of the Spanish army, who I may be so fortunate to meet with. I enclose with my official dispatch the last letter I have received from Admiral Keats, and I am hastening to the Belt as fast as the calms we experience here will permit; and I form the greatest expectation of being enabled to extricate the whole of the Spanish troops in the Danish islands and to provide for their subsistence until supplies of provisions are received from England.

I think myself fortunate in having so closely anticipated the purport of the instructions which I received the day after I sent off my dispatches with the account of the communication having been opened in the Belt. Your lordship will be assured that I shall devote every possible attention to this important object. I have etc.

40. *Saumarez to Keats*

Victory, off Dars Head [Darsser Ort],

15 Aug. 1808.

Sir, By the *Ariel*, which joined me last night, I received your letter of the 11th. instant acquainting me of the measures you had taken to carry into execution the duplicates of the secret instructions which had been transmitted to you by the secretary of the admiralty and which you had received

3

by the *Mosquito*; and informing me that the Marquis de la Romana,[1] with nearly six thousand of the Spanish troops under his command, had embarked that morning at Nyborg, which place he had taken possession of on the 9th., also that one thousand of the Spanish troops had joined you the same morning from Jutland and the same number had been thrown into Langeland to strengthen the post occupied by the Spanish troops in that island; also informing me that in consequence of the adverse winds and currents you had left the *Superb* on the 8th. and that on the 9th., two hours after your flag was hoisted on board the *Brunswick*, the Spanish general had taken possession of the town, and that the *Fama* brig of 18 guns and a cutter of 12 guns, having rejected every remonstrance, had been attacked by Captain Macnamara[2] of the *Edgar* with such small vessels and boats as could be collected and captured by them, with the loss of Lieutenant Harvey[3] of the *Superb* and two men wounded; and further informing of your having, for the greater expedition, hoisted your flag on board the *Hound* in the harbour, and that the artillery, baggage and stores had been embarked that night and the following day and removed to Slypsham [Slipshavn], four miles from Nyborg, at which place the army were embarked without opposition and, notwithstanding the state of the wind and weather, were placed under the protection of His Majesty's ships off the island of Sproe [Sprogø].

In the important service you have rendered to the country in extricating the Spanish troops from being any longer in the power of the enemy, I cannot too highly applaud the skill and judgement you have displayed, and the perseverance and zeal of the captains, officers and men under your command, as also Captain May of the Royal Artillery and the detachment under his orders; together with the great cheerfulness [with] which they appear to have supported the harassing fatigue in the performance of this important service, which I doubt not will be duly appreciated by the Lords Commissioners of the Admiralty when the various documents which I have transmitted to their secretary are laid before their lordships. I request you will be pleased to accept my thanks and convey the same to the captains, officers and men under your command. I have etc.

[1] Pedro Caro y Sureda, 3rd marquis de la Romana (1761–1811), was commander-in-chief of a corps of Spanish troops sent to northern Europe at Napoleon's request in 1807. He afterwards served in the peninsular campaign, dying near Badajoz of heart disease.
[2] James Macnamara (1768–1826), lieutenant, 1788; captain, 1795; was acquitted in 1803 of a charge of manslaughter arising out of a duel, several naval officers testifying to his aimiability of character; rear-admiral, 1814.
[3] Robert Harvey, whose commission was dated 2 April 1806.

41. *Draft of Letter by Saumarez*

Victory, off Baltic Port [Baltiski],

30 August 1808.

I wrote you by the *Rose* which I detached last Saturday off Stockholm as I had received information that the Russian fleet consisting of 13 sail, and as many frigates, were blocking up the Swedish fleet near the entrance of the Gulf of Finland. I was under some anxiety respecting Sir Samuel Hood and the *Implacable*, who I had detached to join the latter—and also for my being able to effect a junction with them without having the whole force of the enemy opposed to the few ships I had with me. It was not till this morning I was agreeably relieved from this state of suspense by falling in at daylight with a Swedish frigate whose commander informed me that last Friday the Swedish squadron with the *Centaur* and *Implacable* had chased the Russian fleet into this port, and that an 84-gun ship which was rather pressed by the *Implacable* had run on shore before she could reach the port, and had been set on fire by her people. This unexpected event has somewhat reconciled me to the state of anxiety and suspense I have been in since I left Admiral Keats with the Spanish army ten days ago, and I am not without hope that something may be effected against the enemy; but as I am only in sight of the place I must wait till I have communicated with our ships. Vessels I understand to have been detached to meet me, but they all missed the squadron. Indeed it is no way surprizing as we have had a very rapid voyage up the Baltic wishing to be in time to relieve our ally. This success will give a turn to affairs in this part of the world, and I hope set Sweden perfectly at ease with regard to the Russian fleet. But more of this by and by.

Thursday evening. We anchored about 2 and I had the satisfaction to see Sir Samuel Hood and Captain Martin[1] after their glorious exploits[2] which was still more brilliant than had been represented to me, the Russian ship having actually struck to the *Implacable* but was rescued for a time by their fleet. The Swedes' bad sailing not having allowed them to come up she was after attacked by the *Centaur*. Having got aground she was set on fire after the crew had been removed to our two ships. Nothing could excel the very gallant conduct of Captain Martin in his attack upon this ship, and also of the *Centaur* in afterwards boarding her.

Both he and Sir Samuel Hood are regarded with admiration by the Swedes

---

[1] Thomas Byam Martin (1773–1854) was the third son of Sir Henry Martin, bart., comptroller of the navy. He was made lieutenant in 1790 and promoted captain in 1793. He attained flag rank in 1811, became vice-admiral in 1819, admiral in 1849. Martin was comptroller of the navy, 1816–31; K.C.B., 1816; G.C.B., 1830.

[2] For an account of this engagement see Sir Richard Vesey Hamilton (ed.), *Letters and Papers of Admiral of the Fleet Sir Thomas Byam Martin*, vol. ii, pp. 31 ff. (Navy Records Society, vol. xii).

who beheld their heroic conduct with awe and amazement as the Swedish admiral expressed it to me. Their bad sailing prevented their coming up with the enemy and bringing on a general action which would have terminated in the capture of the whole Russian fleet.

August 31. I cannot too much lament not to have arrived a few days sooner, but it was impossible, and not a moment was lost in making the best of our way to join the Swedish fleet.

We remain at anchor about 5 miles from the Russian ships, who have had all the time since the action to fortify themselves in the best manner.

Flags of truce pass daily between them and the squadron relative to the exchange of prisoners, and everything appears to be conducted in the handsomest manner on their part, and very different to what it would be under French influence.

Pipon, who I had sent off to Stockholm, joined me last night, not having waited for the information I expected he would have brought me. I expect we shall continue in these seas till October, and I have directed my letters to be forwarded for me to the minister at Stockholm.

The ship destroyed was called the *Vsevolod* (74).

42. *Hood to Saumarez*

Centaur, off Rogervik,

30 August 1808.

My dear Sir James, I had the pleasure to write to you yesterday to congratulate you on the success of the endeavours of the *Implacable* and *Centaur*, and I have only to lament the enemy had a port at hand when we had the good fortune to arrive up with them, which in no other way would they have avoided a general action. Captain Martin's bravery and whole conduct has been delightful, and the *Implacable*'s superior sailing he made the greatest advantage of. Had not the enemy entered Rogervik at the time they did, in one hour a three-decker and a 74 must have been weathered by both ships, and it would have completed our wishes; but I think that you will feel that every exertion and energy was made, and that you will approve of all that has been done.

If there had been with us about two or three thousand troops the island might have been carried, and the whole fleet destroyed, for there were only the batteries on it for the defence of the port. Now the only chance would be by a *coup-de-main*, or the trial of fireships, as they lay very thick, with the bombs to throw them into confusion. I understand that Admiral Nauckhoff has written for some fireships. Indeed any old vessels would answer the purpose by taking a leading wind as they are all very close.

I hope you have been successful with the Spaniards in Zealand, and that the transports will soon arrive to relieve you from them. I am endeavouring to enter into an arrangement to get rid of the Russian prisoners. On my sending in the wounded of *Sewolod* I received a very civil letter from Admiral Hanickoff.[1] Today I send in a nephew of his. I hope we shall effect it on account of our provisions and water.

The Swedish fleet are moored in a line a little to the westward of the port, but for anything I may have omitted I must refer you to Captain White.[2]

I hope you have had good accounts from Lady Saumarez and the others of your family, and believe me etc.

43. *Saumarez to Gustavus IV Adolphus*

Victory, off Rogervik,

31 Aug. 1808.

Sir, It is with the highest satisfaction I do myself the honour to congratulate Your Majesty on the distinguished and brilliant success that has attended the late attack on the enemy's fleet by the capture and destruction of one of their line-of-battle ships and their precipitate flight into their port before the fleet of Your Majesty and two of His Britannic Majesty's ships under my orders.

I shall be most happy if this important success can be followed by any further advantage and I shall lose no time to concur with Admiral Nauckhoff in such measures as may be most adviseable for the annoyance of the enemy, and I propose to order a small detachment off Cronstadt which cannot fail having a good effect appearing at this juncture before the enemy's capital.

With the most ardent wishes I can form for a continuance of every success to attend the arms of Your Majesty.

44. *Saumarez to Pole*

Victory, off Rogervik,

2 Sept. 1808

Sir, You will please to inform the Lords Commissioners of the Admiralty that in consequence of all the different services required for all the line-of-battle ships here I have been prevented from sending the detachment, stated in my letter to you of the 30th. ultimo, towards Cronstadt under the orders

---

[1] The commander-in-chief of the worsted Russian squadron.

[2] Thomas White, commander of the *Ariel* (18); lieutenant, 1790; commander, 1798; captain, 1810. He saw much service in the Baltic during Saumarez's period of command; promoted rear-admiral in 1846, the year of his death.

of Captain Martin; and that I have appointed Captain Martin to act as first captain to the fleet under my orders, during the absence of Captain Hope, and appointed Captain Pipon of the *Rose* to the command of the *Implacable* and Lieutenant Mansell,[1] my flag lieutenant, to command the *Rose* until further orders; having also appointed Lieutenant John Ross[2] of His Majesty's ship *Victory* on board the ship bearing Rear-Admiral Nauckhoff's flag, in the room of Captain Pipon, for the purpose of explaining signals and assisting in the manoeuvres of the Swedish squadron.

Finding from Admiral Nauckhoff that most of the ships were in a very sickly state owing to the length of time they had been at sea and the want of refreshment, I recommended his detaching one of the ships-of-the-line under his orders to Carlscrona with the worst cases, amounting to four hundred; and having sent Mr. Duke,[3] surgeon of the *Victory*, to visit different ships in Admiral Nauckhoff's squadron, and he having represented to me that a supply of lime juice and sugar would be very beneficial, I have directed them to be supplied with those articles from the squadron. I am etc.

45. *Thornton to Saumarez*

Stockholm,
4 Sept. 1808.

Sir, I entertain the same apprehensions as your excellency that the inevitable delay which must intervene before the arrival of troops (if after all they can be spared) will render the attack of the port of Rogervik and the reduction of the Russian fleet a matter of great difficulty and even of doubtful success from the opportunity this delay will afford of augmenting and strengthening the defences of the port.

This, I think, is a circumstance to be lamented, and if the final abandonment of the hope of obtaining possession of this fleet should be the consequence of it, I am afraid that it will confirm Russia in her present system and encourage her to persevere in her war with England.

There appear to be among politicians (our own among the rest) two opinions as to the mode of conducting this war on our part against Russia. The one proceeding upon the ground that Russia has been driven into hostilities against us by the superior terror which France has inspired in her, rests upon

---

[1] Thomas Mansell (1777–1858), a native of Guernsey, first went to sea in 1793 on board the *Crescent*, Captain James Saumarez whom he followed into the *Orion* being present at the battle of Cape St. Vincent; lieutenant, 1798; served under Saumarez in the Channel and Baltic fleets; commander, 1808; captain, 1814; K.C.H., 1837; rear-admiral, 1849.
[2] John Ross (1777–1856) was commissioned in 1805 and served under Saumarez, of whom he was the biographer, continuously until 1812. He became commander in 1812; captain, 1818. He made a reputation after the war as an Arctic explorer; K.C.B., 1834.
[3] Valentine Duke, surgeon of H.M.S. *Victory*.

the principle that she is to be brought back to a better system by the operation of the same means, and that nothing but a greater or at least a more immediate dread, acting near at home and threatening the internal safety and tranquillity of the country, can make her change her line of conduct. The attack and bombardment of Cronstadt and of other fortified ports, and the menace of Petersburgh itself, are among the measures recommended by those who hold this opinion.

The other is that, as the war itself is an unnatural one and is condemned as such by the most thinking and the soundest part of the nation, nothing ought to be done by us which should offend this portion of the Russians, or which should appear to affect the dignity and honour of the country and give the war a national character. With persons of this way of thinking every forbearance of attack is a merit, and the absence of our ships from the Gulf of Finland and from the ports and coasts of Russia forms a topic of praise, and is thought to render a future pacification more easy and more cordial.

I do not know, sir, that I could add any weight to the one or the other of these opinions by mentioning to your excellency to which of the two my own is inclined; but I can safely affirm that the present position of the Russian fleet in Baltic Port and the fortification of that harbour offers a fairer occasion of trying the validity of these opinions, and with less risk of mischief than will easily occur again.

If the former idea is the most just, the attack and destruction of the Russian fleet in a harbour fortified to a certain degree are circumstances sufficiently calculated to give a salutary lesson of terror, if hereafter still more vigorous measures should be thought necessary. The affair of the *Implacable* and *Centaur* gives a specimen of the English mode of sea fighting which the Russians, I should think, would scarcely court the repetition of; and the invasion of Rogervik would be as useful, and a somewhat less offensive, measure than the attack of Cronstadt.

If on the other hand the system of forbearance is the most just, the favourers of that opinion can hardly be offended with the conduct of Great Britain in attacking an enemy who came out to seek the attack and to invite the king's fleets to a contest. It may be securely said, from our conduct hitherto at least, that we have not, and perhaps should not have, sought the Russians in their own ports; but it was hardly to be expected that a Russian squadron was to menace the fleet of the ally of Great Britain and not be resisted by an English squadron, who, if the former had not come out, might have still remained at the other end of the Baltic, quietly pursuing the views of its own government.

You can see, sir, very clearly, I believe, what are my opinions and what are my wishes as to the operations of the squadron under your excellency's command. On the possibility of carrying them into effect it would be most presumptuous in me to utter a sentiment; and if I have mentioned them at all, it is always with a view to the great object of all wars, a peace with the belligerent parties. I believe in no war was ever this object so much in view and so earnestly desired by His Majesty's government as in the present with Russia; and if the sparing of the Russian fleet could accelerate that event or its destruction remove it to a greater distance or render a pacification less easy and less cordial, I should be most earnest for the former, and perhaps this may be the idea of government itself. Possibly, however, and probably, a great blow in this way might accelerate it. I have etc.

46. *Duke to Saumarez*

Victory, off Port Baltic,

12 Sept. 1808.

Sir, Agreeable to your desire I have the honour to represent to you that from the 30th. August to the date hereof, I have visited the ships of His Swedish Majesty's fleet in order to ascertain and if possible to remedy the prevailing indisposition with which they have been for some time afflicted.

After a careful examination I am decidedly of opinion that *scurvy* of the most obstinate and dangerous nature, threatens the safety of the whole fleet. In order to account for the introduction of this unfortunate complaint it will be necessary to mention that in the months of January and February last their ships were fitted out and have since that period continued at sea without having received any regular supplies of fresh provisions; and the greater part consisting of country farmers, in general accustomed to live on vegetable diet, fully explain the origin and cause of their present state.[1]

The rapid progress which this disease is making cannot fail to excite the greatest alarm, as already twelve hundred men have been sent to the hospital (every hour is adding to the number of sick); and it is painful to remark that not less than four hundred have died on board one ship since yesterday. All those means which our service points out both for the cure and prevention of the formidable evil (consistent with the situation of both fleets) have been suggested and put into practice with the utmost alacrity by the physicians and surgeons. Many of the latter I am sorry to say are exhausted from fatigue.

[1] The Swedish manning system depended very much upon the recruitment of reservists who were maintained, when not required for service, upon smallholdings in coastal areas. The lack of seagoing experience explains the poor sailing of the Swedish warships in pursuit of the Russian squadron. The change of diet undoubtedly explains the outbreak of scurvy; but its unchecked progress reflects the inadequacy of the Swedish medical service.

As the present proportion of lime juice with which they are supplied is insufficient to effect a radical cure, and as much debility is manifested throughout the whole, should any exertion be required during the approaching season I am of opinion that every danger is to be apprehended from their sinking under the excess of harassing duty; and I felt more fully warranted in giving this statement in consequence of having examined on board each ship a certain number of those men considered most healthy whom, with four exceptions, I find labouring under the latent symptoms of scurvy.

It may not be improper to add that in this representation I do not stand alone: the surgeons of H.M.S. *Centaur* and *Implacable* perfectly coincide with me and the Swedish captains are satisfied of the inadequacy of their ships under the circumstances already mentioned, and of the urgent necessity of going into port. I have etc.

P.S. Having visited the fleet again this morning I find the progress which the disease is making even exceeds the opinion already formed; and if advantage is not taken during the present mild weather of getting immediately into harbour a few days longer must eventually incapacitate them.

47. *Saumarez to Pole*

Victory, off Rogervik,

14 Sept. 1808.

Sir, You will please to inform the Lords Commissioners of the Admiralty that from the uncertain state of the weather I have found it adviseable to move a greater distance from off the harbour of Rogervik and to anchor about six miles from Packerort lighthouse for the greater security of the united squadron. On Monday evening, the weather appearing favourable for the *Erebus* and the two fire-vessels to proceed upon service, they were got under weigh for that purpose, and at 8 o'clock bore up from the *Victory* for the entrance of the harbour under cover of the *Salsette*, *Magnet*, *Alaart*, and *Swan* cutter. But it having again cleared up, and Captain Autridge,[1] finding it too light to make the attempt, hauled out of the harbour and directed the two fire-vessels to do the same. The Russian prize brig which had been fitted up with combustibles and put under the command of Lieutenant Thomas Graham[2] of the *Victory*, who had very handsomely volunteered his services on that occasion, not being enabled to clear the harbour owing to the heavy swell, was taken in tow by the *Salsette*, but the tow-rope having given way close to the shore, Lieutenant Graham was obliged to set her on fire after taking the men out of her.

[1] William Autridge, lieutenant, 1802; commander, 1804; captain, 1812.
[2] Thomas Graham, lieutenant, 1799; commander, 1809; captain, 1811.

His Majesty's sloop *Rose*, which had been ordered to look out between the passage of east and west Raga, unfortunately got aground about 8 o'clock in the evening. I received information of it at midnight, when every possible assistance was sent to her. And after the greatest exertions on the part of Lieutenant Mansell (acting captain) and the officers and men of that sloop, assisted after daylight by the *Magnet* and *Alaart* and *Swan* cutter, she was got off yesterday afternoon, after putting some of his guns on board the *Alaart* and throwing the remainder overboard together with her iron ballast and shot, and being cleared of her provisions, without receiving greater damage than I hope may be repaired without being under the necessity to order her into port. Herewith I enclose for their lordships' further information Captain Mansell's statement of his proceedings relative to the *Rose* being grounded. I am etc.

48. *Saumarez to Gustavus IV Adolphus*

Victory, off Baltic Port,

17 Sept. 1808.

Sir, I have received the letter Your Majesty has had the condescension to honour me with dated the 13th. instant. Nothing can afford me higher gratification than to know that my services are honoured with Your Majesty's gracious approbation, and my utmost zeal and exertions will be devoted to prove deserving of it. The enemy's fleet in Baltic Port offers no opportunity of attacking them with any probability of success, and the operations of the united squadrons must be confined to keeping them strongly blockaded until a suitable opportunity offers of attempting to destroy them by means of fire vessels, after those which Your Majesty has been pleased to order to join Rear-Admiral Nauckhoff from Stockholm arrive. The day after my junction with Your Majesty's fleet, I hastened a line-of-battle ship to her station upon the coast of Scania with other vessels for the security of convoys, and I have left a sufficient force to frustrate and defeat any attempts of the enemy from the side of the Belts and the coast of Pomerania, that no apprehension need be entertained from those quarters.

It is ardently to be wished that the benevolence that dictated Your Majesty's appeal upon the humanity of the emperor of Russia could be attended with due effect, and that His Imperial Majesty would profit by the events which have recently taken place in the southern parts of Europe to unite his endeavours with the other powers in establishing a lasting and general peace, so much to be desired for the welfare of all nations.

I fervently pray the Supreme Being to bless and prosper Your Majesty's pious undertakings.

With a firm reliance on His Divine Blessing on Your Majesty's person and government and the prosperity and welfare of your august family, I have etc.

49. *Mulgrave to Saumarez*

Admiralty,
18 September 1808.

My dear Sir James, I have received your private letter of the 30th. of August. I am fully persuaded that if anything can be done to follow up the brilliant enterprize of Sir Samuel Hood, it will be effected by you. The importance of the object to the Swedes and the impression which you state their officers to have received from the speciman which they have witnessed of the vigour, skill and success of the British navy, gives every reason to hope that the king of Sweden will be eager to furnish the military means necessary for removing the obstacle which the island you mention opposes to the destruction of the Russian fleet.

It cannot fail to make a good impression in Russia when it is perceived that your force is sufficient to enable you to make a detachment off the port of Cronstadt.

You will perceive by my former letter that I have taken care of Capt. Pipon. The public will wait with impatience for news from you, but with no unreasonable expectations. The gazette will point out the difficulties and obstacles which exist; all that comes therefore will be clear gain. Your dispatches did not arrive in time from Windsor to appear in the gazette of last nights. They will be published on Tuesday. Believe me with the highest esteem and regard etc.

50. *Saumarez to Pole*

Victory, off Rogervik,
28 Sept. 1808.

Sir, You will please to inform the Lords Commissioners of the Admiralty that Captain Hope, first captain of the fleet under my command, having this day returned to [from] his leave of absence, Captain Martin proceeds to England and is the bearer of my dispatches; to whom I beg leave to refer their lordships for a more particular account of the proceedings of the squadron off Baltic Port.

The state of the weather having proved very unsettled for the last few days and the wind having set in this morning to the S.E., I thought it adviseable to get under sail. I propose to leave His Majesty's ships named in the margin [*Mars, Orion, Goliath, Ariel, Alaart*] between Dagerort and the coast of Sweden for the protection of trade and to intercept any detachment the enemy might send down the Baltic, altho' I have every reason to suppose they would take the first opportunity to repair to Cronstadt after they are refitted from their present dismantled state.

I propose to give directions to Rear-Admiral Sir Samuel Hood to proceed in the *Centaur* with the *Implacable* thro' the Great Belt; and I shall repair to the Sound in this ship or, according to circumstances, hoist my flag on board the *Salsette* and proceed thro' the Malmö channel for the greater expedition in order to comply with such orders as I may receive from their lordships for the further distribution of the force under my command.

His Majesty's envoy at Stockholm having strongly recommended that two line-of-battle ships should remain upon this station during the winter months to rendezvous at Marstrand or off Gothenburg, I request their lordships' directions upon that subject. I am etc.

51. *Saumarez to Gustavus IV Adolphus*

Victory, Carlscrona,
16 Oct. 1808.

Sire, I do myself the honour to inform Your Majesty that the weather having proved too unfavourable to have remained off Baltic Port without the greatest risk and danger to the united squadron, it was thought advise-able in concurrence with Rear-Admiral Nauckhoff to get under sail, leaving a detachment of two line-of-battle ships and some frigates to watch the enemy's movements. I have received information from Captain Lukin of His Majesty's Ship *Mars* who reconnoitred Baltic Port on the 4th. instant that the enemy had quitted Baltic Port and proceeded up the Gulf of Fin-land; and Your Majesty's ship *Camilla* which has arrived here this morning has brought the account that the detachment, having had a favourable opportunity of looking into the port, had observed one of the enemy's large frigates had driven on shore in the bad weather and was a complete wreck. As the advanced season of the year must prevent the possibility of further naval operations in these seas, I propose to avail myself of the first favour-able weather to proceed with the squadron under my command thro' the Belt to Gothenburg, happy if my exertions upon this station have been found to meet the honour of Your Majesty's royal approbation. I have etc.

52. *Saumarez to Pole*

Victory, in Hawke Road, Gothenburg,
29 Oct. 1808.

Sir, You will please to inform the Lords Commissioners of the Admiralty of my having received on my arrival at this anchorage yesterday their lordships' orders dated the 15th. instant, directing me to return with the ships therein mentioned to the Downs, if it should appear that the services of these ships could no longer be useful to His Majesty's ally and that it is not necessary to leave them in the Baltic for the protection of the trade; and further directing me to place the rest of the ships and vessels under my command under the orders of Rear-Admiral Sir Richard Keats, furnishing the rear-admiral with copies of my instructions etc. and directing him to carry the same into execution, and calling his particular attention to the instructions I have received relative to the trade of His Majesty's subjects and that of his ally.

I request you will inform their lordships that I shall in pursuance thereof proceed in this ship with the *Centaur* and *Implacable* to the Downs, leaving directions for Captain Lukin, on his arrival off this port, to proceed also in His Majesty's ship *Mars* to that anchorage. The *Goliath* and *Vanguard*, in consequence of their defects, had been directed to proceed to the Nore previous to their lordships' orders, where I shall also be obliged to order the *Africa* in consequence of the damage she sustained in an action with the enemy's gunboats, as stated in my letter of yesterday.

I shall leave the remainder of the ships as per margin [*Superb, Brunswick, Orion, Edgar, Dictator, Salsette, Tribune, Magnet, Ranger, Ariel, Prometheus, Lynx, Kite, Erebus, Gorgon, Proselyte, Fury, Tartar, Fama, Snipe, Minx, Hearty, Earnest, Wrangler, Charger*] under the orders of Rear-Admiral Sir Richard Keats, directing him, on the arrival of the *Orion* in the Belt with the convoy Sir Archibald Dickson is directed to take under his charge from Carlscrona, appointed to sail after the 15th. of November, to repair off Gothenburg for the purpose of completing his stores and provisions.

As the station in the Sound will require to be occupied for the defence of the coast of Sweden and the protection of the convoys passing thro' the Malmö channel, I propose to leave the *Edgar* and *Dictator* with the small vessels at present under the orders of Rear-Admiral Bertie to remain upon that service, directing the rear-admiral to put himself under the command of Sir Richard Keats until their lordships' further pleasure is known.

I shall also direct Rear-Admiral Sir Richard Keats to remain at Marstrand during the winter for the purpose of protecting the trade of His Majesty's subjects and of his ally the king of Sweden, holding himself and the ships and vessels under his orders in constant readiness to co-operate with the Swedish fleet at the early part of the ensuing season; causing him to be supplied with such stores of all species as can be spared from the ships ordered to England, leaving all the provisions ordered for the supply of the ships under my command at the disposal of the rear-admiral. And I herewith enclose for the information of their lordships a statement of the supply of provisions on board the victuallers in Flemish Road.

I also enclose a copy of the orders I left with Captain Sir Archibald C. Dickson, which I also request you will please to lay before their lordships, by which their lordships will observe that I have directed the *Ranger* and the *Magnet* to remain in the Baltic for such part of the trade as may arrive at Carlscrona subsequent to the sailing of the convoy appointed after the 15th. of November; and I shall leave directions to Sir Richard Keats to order the *Tribune* and some of the heaviest sloops under his command to collect any others that may be destined for England from the Baltic. I shall also give directions to the rear-admiral, should he think it adviseable to leave the station in the Belt previous to the arrival of the *Orion* with her convoy, to repair off Gothenburg, leaving the vessels upon that station under the command of Captain Graves[1] of His Majesty's ship *Brunswick*. I am etc.

53. *Saumarez to Pole*

London,
21 Nov. 1808.

Sir, In compliance with the directions of the Lords Commissioners of the Admiralty, signified to me in your letter of the 16th. instant, to transmit for their lordships' information the explanation to the several memorandums therein enclosed, I herewith transmit an explanation to the said memorandums, together with the accompanying documents, viz., a report of convoys appointed for the protection of the trade to and from the Baltic, copies of the different letters I have received from the king of Sweden from number 1 to number 6, and also copies of my letters to His Swedish Majesty; all which I request you will lay before their lordships.

I also request you will be pleased to inform their lordships that there is no part of my conduct from my first appointment to the command in the Baltic to the present time that I am not perfectly ready to have submitted to the strictest investigation, either as to what related to the protection of the trade of His Majesty's subjects and that of His Majesty's ally, as to the security and defence of the coast of Sweden, and more particularly when in the presence of the enemy's fleet in Baltic Port; fully convinced that throughout the whole period of my command the honour of my most gracious sovereign and of his ally, the king of Sweden, and the interest of both nations will be found to have been supported to the utmost possible extent.

The state of the war with respect to Russia and Prussia is maintained in a

---

[1] Thomas Graves who was posted captain on 19 March 1794.

manner heretofore unprecedented. An immense trade is carried on by British merchants under His Majesty's licence with the different ports of those countries. Both nations are known to be amicably disposed towards Great Britain and openly avowed their earnest desire to be on terms of peace and amity with England as well as their abhorrence of their alliance with France. In informing His Imperial Russian Majesty of the events that had occurred in Spain and Portugal, a favourable opportunity presented itself of also making known to that monarch the declared sentiments of His Majesty's government, of their readiness for peace when Russia was disposed to return to her feelings of friendship and amity with Great Britain. With this view the letter was written; and I trust His Majesty's ministers will ascribe it to my earnest zeal for His Majesty's service and the welfare and interest of my country.

I also hope that the Lords Commissioners of the Admiralty, after a mature consideration of the explanation I have given, will be satisfied that during the whole period of my command everything has been effected to fulfill their lordships' instructions for the defence and security of Sweden, the protection of the trade and the annoyance of the enemy; and that I shall be found to have merited their lordships' fullest approval. I have etc.

Enclosure:

53a. *Explanation by Saumarez*

In answer to the first question, 'For what cause convoys have been so long detained, it having been represented by the merchants that the trade was suffered to collect till the convoys became almost too large for protection and that this practice has prevailed throughout the season at Carlscrona and Gothenburg', the vice-admiral has to observe he is not aware of any delay having occurred in the sailing of convoys except what may have arisen from contrary winds or from unavoidable circumstances. On his departure from Gothenburg on the 5th. of July, the strictest orders were left with the senior officer in Flemish Road to use his utmost endeavours to accelerate the departure of convoys that arrived there to and from the Baltic. The cause of the convoys having sometimes collected until they became so numerous as to be almost too large for protection has arisen from the immense trade carried on by British and neutral vessels under His Majesty's licence to the different ports in the Baltic; and it has at different times occurred that convoys sailing from Gothenburg for the Baltic have been joined by other convoys from England off that port.

One circumstance which occasioned some delay of the trade from Stockholm was from His Majesty's envoy, at the time of the arrest of Sir John

Moore by the king of Sweden, having ordered the *Piercer* to receive his
official papers and those of the lieutenant-general and proceed with them to
Gothenburg without waiting for the trade, when another convoy was
appointed as speedily as possible.

   Another circumstance which occasioned some delay was after the Spanish
troops were extricated from the Danish islands and a convoy from the
ports in the Baltic, under the charge of the *Leveret*, *Hearty* and *Centinel*, had
sailed for the Belt, it was judged necessary, on their falling in with the *Tribune*
and *Falcon*, to order those ships to accompany them to the northern extre-
mity of the Belt, when it became too hazardous for any other convoy to sail
from Carlscrona until it was ascertained they were returned to their station
off Femeren for their further protection.

   On the vice-admiral's receiving information that the Russian fleet had
put to sea, he judged it expedient to take the *Africa* to the Gulf of Finland
having at the time only the *Mars* and *Goliath* with him; to which he was
more particularly induced from the great probability that existed of falling
in with the enemy's force before he could form a junction with the Swedish
squadron and the ships under the orders of Sir Samuel Hood. On his arrival
off Baltic Port eight days after, and finding from reports then made to him
that the enemy's situation would not admit an attack to be made on them
with any prospect of success, he detached the *Africa* on the 31st. of August to
Carlscrona to take charge of the trade then laying in that port. She accordingly went to Carlscrona and found that a convoy had sailed previous to her
arrival. She sailed from thence with another convoy and returned with the
trade from Malmö on the 2nd. of October; and accompanied the convoy
which sailed on the 16th. of the same month under the charge of the *Thunder*.

   The *Victory*, with the *Centaur* and *Implacable*, having sailed on the 21st.
for the Belt, it was not judged expedient to take the trade that had subsequently arrived under their protection, more particularly as a convoy was
appointed to sail on the 25th. four days after, and another daily expected to
arrive under the charge of the *Alaart* and *Rose* from Stockholm. It is further
proper to observe another circumstance: that it is by no means expedient to
appoint line-of-battle ships for the protection of convoys in the Baltic, whose
draft of water will not admit their going thro' the Malmö Channel.

   The vice-admiral herewith encloses for the information of the Lords Commissioners of the Admiralty an account of the different periods at which
convoys have been appointed; by which statement their lordships will judge
how unfounded have been the complaints made by the merchants of the
trade being neglected, and how unjust the representations they have made
upon that subject.

   In reply to the second query 'to state the causes that in the vice-admiral's judgement rendered it necessary to quit his station off Rogervik and proceed down the Baltic before any bad weather had actually set in and before any gale of wind had blown from the north-west Captain Martin having stated that a north-west gale would throw a great sea into Port Baltic, and the proximity of the enemy to the shore made it presumable they might strike (at least the Russian officers sent in with flags of truce did not conceal their apprehensions of danger), and Captain Lukin had declared that had the Russian squadron remained in Baltic Port during the gale of the 2nd. of October, he is confident that many of their line-of-battle ships must have been driven on shore; which opinion of Captain Lukin is founded upon observing a frigate in Baltic Port wrecked by the gale of the 2nd. of October', the advanced season of the year and the dangerous state of the united squadron, at anchor within four miles of the enemy's coast in from 48 to 52 fathoms water, rendered it indispensable to provide for their safety on the first setting in of blowing weather. And, although earnestly urged to leave the station for several days by persons of experience in those seas, and in whose judgement great reliance could be placed, it was not until the 28th. of September that the vice-admiral was prevailed upon to get under sail, it having then come on to blow strong and the weather very thick which rendered it too dangerous for the united squadron to remain at anchor or to continue in the Gulf of Finland.

This was the opinion of Rear-Admiral Nauckhoff as well as that of the different officers in His Majesty's squadron; and altho' it was presumable that a north-west gale, as stated in Captain Martin's narrative, would have driven some of the enemy's ships on shore, it would at the same time have exposed the united squadron to greater danger from their situation. And the vice-admiral is desirous that a reference may be made to Captain Martin whether such was not his opinion at the time upon that head, as well as to the expediency of the squadron quitting the station in the Gulf of Finland. Captain Lukin, who was left with a detachment to watch the enemy's motions, expressed the same opinion and has since signified in the strongest manner the satisfaction he derived at the squadron having left the station before the gale of the 2nd. of October set in, from the imminent danger to which they would have been exposed had they continued off Baltic Port.

The sickly condition of the remaining line-of-battle ships under Rear-Admiral Nauckhoff rendered their immediate return to Carlscrona indispensable. It is a lamentable fact that out of the eleven sail-of-the-line which composed the Swedish squadron above four thousand sick have been landed; and the average of deaths to the 4th. instant have not been fewer than from 25 to 30 daily: a melancholy proof of the inefficiency of those ships and their inability to have kept the sea.

On the junction of the *Aboukir*, *Majestic* and *Minotaur* from England on the 30th. of September it was the vice-admiral's intention to have returned off Baltic Port, and he signified the same to Captain Hope, first captain of the fleet; but the weather having continued unfavourable the strongest representations were made by him and Mr. Squire, the master of the fleet, against risking the squadron at so advanced a season of the year in the Gulf of Finland. And the gale that soon after ensued impelled the vice-admiral to order the above three ships to return to England and to proceed in the *Victory* with the other ships to Carlscrona.

In reply to the 4th. query, 'to explain by what instructions the vice-admiral felt himself authorized to write his letter[1] of the 17th. of September to the emperor of Russia and the reasons for his not having reported a measure of such serious importance for their lordships' information'. The vice-admiral, having understood it to be the declared sentiments of his Majesty's ministers that when an opportunity offered for peace between Great Britain and Russia it would be eagerly embraced and that the arrangements of such a negotiation would neither be difficult or complicated, His Majesty being satisfied if Russia should manifest a disposition to return to her ancient feelings of friendship towards Great Britain, to a just consideration of her own interests and to a sense of her own dignity as an independent nation, the vice-admiral has to observe that he had received translations of various papers relative to the transactions that had taken place in Spain and Portugal in order to be circulated on the continent. And knowing at the same time the pains taken by the emissaries of France to prevent those transactions being known in the northern parts of Europe, particularly at St. Petersburg, in transmitting some of the papers to the Russian Vice-Admiral Hanickhoff the vice-admiral considered it a favourable opportunity to inform His Imperial Majesty of the events relative to Spain and Portugal with a view, if possible, to detach Russia from her alliance with the French nation and to return to her former ties of friendship with Great Britain.

The letter was written with the knowledge and concurrence of Admiral Nauckhoff, who strongly recommended its being transmitted; and His Majesty's envoy Mr. Thornton, who was at that time on board the *Victory*, having also decided to write to the Russian minister on the same subject, was consulted as to the expediency of sending the letter and expressed his opinion that much good might result from it and that he was not aware of its doing any possible harm. The copy of the letter was delivered to Mr. Thornton to be sent by him to Mr. Canning, which was the reason of its not being

---

[1] Saumarez's private letter to the tsar informing him of events in Spain and expressing the hope that they would 'induce the powers of the continent to unite with Great Britain to restore that peace so highly to be desired for the welfare of mankind' is printed in Ross, ii, p. 118.

transmitted for the information of the Lords Commissioners of the Admiralty.

In answer to the 5th. query, 'for the vice-admiral to explain his reasons for having omitted to communicate for their lordships' information his having received a letter from the king of Sweden dated the 15th. of October. The letter from the king of Sweden, dated the 15th. of October, was received on the 21st., the morning of the vice-admiral's departure from Carlscrona; by which letter it appeared that His Swedish Majesty was unapprized of the enemy's fleet having sailed from Baltic Port, which circumstance was communicated to His Swedish Majesty in a letter from the vice-admiral, dated the 16th. of that month, the copy of which is herewith enclosed; and wherein he informed His Majesty of his intention to proceed to Gothenburg in consequence of the advanced season of the year not permitting any further naval operations in the Baltic.

In answer to the 7th. question, 'for the vice-admiral to explain upon what grounds he conceived the ships he brought home could be of no further use to the king's ally or to the trade in the Baltic, and his reasons for not providing by means of the ships returning to England convoys for the trade assembled at Carlscrona or any of the trade that were ready at Gothenburg when he arrived at that port', it is to be observed that the letter from their lordships' secretary, dated the 12th. of October, directing the vice-admiral to co-operate with His Swedish Majesty was not received until his arrival at Gothenburg on the 28th.; at which time he also received their lordships' orders of the 15th. for the final distribution of the squadron. And in compliance with these orders he directed Rear-Admiral Sir Richard Keats to take command of the squadron and proceeded to the Downs with the *Centaur* and *Implacable*, after having provided convoys for the protection of the trade to and from the Baltic and directed such vessels as could be spared to cruise in the Cattegat and Belt for the annoyance of the enemy, the protection of the trade and to prevent supplies getting to the coast of Norway; deeming the services of a greater number of line-of-battle ships than those pointed out by their lordships' orders to be no longer required upon the station, and having previously left His Majesty's ship *Orion* with the sloops and vessels named in the margin [*Magnet, Ranger, Alaart, Rose, Aetna, Hound, Starling, Fama, Urgent, Sacorman*] for the further protection of the trade and having made application to the Swedish admiral commanding at Carlscrona to order such reinforcements as might be required.

The very trivial loss sustained by the merchants in the Baltic trade is a strong proof of the unremitted care and attention bestowed on that important subject, particularly when the intricacy of the passages of the Belts and Sound are considered and the various obstacles thrown in the way by the

numerous flotillas of the enemy. The vice-admiral begs to refer their lordships to your letter to him respecting the attack made on the *Thunder*'s
convoy in the Malmö Channel, wherein their lordships were pleased to
signify their approval.

54. *Extract of a letter from Keats to Pole*

Superb, in the Great Belt,

27 Nov. 1808.

My practice and services in the Belt enable me to speak with more confidence of the means and measures, which I conceive requisite to escort convoys thro' that passage, than I can possibly pretend to do of the Sound.

Here, as the enemy possesses both sides and has in every variety of situation a safe harbour for his flotillas to resort to, and as neither of the two
objects (the islands of Sproe [Sprogø] and Romsoe [Romsø]) which offer
themselves to us, where gunboat establishments could be formed, would in
my opinion answer the end proposed, I consider, under a view of all the circumstances, we are likely to do better by trusting altogether to our ships than
by forming a gunboat establishment on either of those islands; the services
of which might be required so distant from them as often to render their
return impracticable and their situation perhaps unsafe, unless ships of force
are appointed purposely for them to resort to, whose operations otherwise
they would be found frequently to cramp and impede.

I acknowledge I see no great advantage either we or our ally derives by
keeping such a force as we have been accustomed to do this summer in the
Belt. Small vessels cannot be trusted from under the guns of the large ones
lest they should be calmed; and the large ones are twelve leagues asunder.
We cannot possibly prevent communication between Zealand and the other
parts of Denmark. It is true we turn it from some of its old channels, but after
all we may be said rather to inconvenience than delay it even.

Convoys passing thro' the Belt, besides the escort requisite for the Cattegat and Baltic Sea, should be strongly guarded; for if the wind fails them,
especially in the navigation between Sproe and the south end of Langeland
which may be considered the centre of their flotilla force, they must expect
to be attacked by a formidable number of gunboats. I am of opinion two
ships-of-the-line with two frigates and a couple of sloops should always meet
convoys coming from the eastward off the island of Femeren [Fehmarn]
and from the northward off Seyer [Sejerø] to conduct them both ways thro'
the Belt. If the periods of convoys' sailing were fixed so that *dependence*
could be placed on them, the Malmö squadron might occasionally be employed on that service and the officer commanding the division in the Belt

for the protection of convoys, knowing the periods of their sailing, could perhaps place himself at either end of the Belt as might be requisite to receive them.

It may be said if we employ so considerable a force to keep open the Malmö passage why not give up all idea of convoys ever passing the Belts; to which it may be replied that if you do not use that passage at all, the flotilla force in it will be removed and applied against you in the Sound. And on that consideration alone it might be advantageous occasionally to send convoys by the Belt; and indeed it may be prudent to vary the course of the convoys in those passages according as circumstances may render necessary.

It will, I think, be evident to their lordships that as so considerable a force will in all likelihood become necessary to escort fleets thro' these passages it will not be possible to attend to particular applications. Individuals must give way to the general interest; and merchants must be content to conform to whatever plans upon mature consideration may be thought right to adopt. . . .

I hope to be excused for again repeating that, as it has been necessary to have some data to go upon, I have formed my estimate upon a supposition that the enemy's force will next year be double what it has been this. But, if instead of 70 or 80 gun and mortar boats, he brings two, three hundred, as some reports say he intends doing; if he turns the principal attention and resources of the kingdom to dispute the passages of the Sound and Belt, our efforts must exceed any calculation I have made in this paper.

55. *Saumarez to Pole*

Cheltenham,
16 Dec. 1808.

Sir, I have received your letter of yesterday's date acquainting me that the Lords Commissioners of the Admiralty, having had under their consideration the replies to the several queries relative to my proceedings during my command in the Baltic as required by your letter of the 16th. ult., their lordships were satisfied with the different explanations, with the exception of that which relates to my letter to the emperor of Russia. I am etc.

56. *Keats to Saumarez*

Superb, Hawke Road, Gothenburg,
25 Jan. 1809.

Sir, It is with much real concern I inform you of the disastrous fate of the *Salsette* together with her convoy of 12 sail and the escort named in the margin [*Salsette, Magnet, Urgent, Fama, Sacorman, Camilla* Swedish armed ship, two Swedish men-of-war brigs] which sailed from Carlscrona on the 22nd. December.

The *Salsette* and the whole, with the exception of the *Fama* and *Sacorman*, arrived off and anchored under Falsterbo on the 24th. Dec. where fresh easterly winds obliged them to remain to the 6th. of January, when with a strong southerly wind the convoy, not being able to weigh, cut from their anchors and attempted the Malmö passage. But the passage was so choked with drift ice that no ship but the *Salsette* was enabled to gain an anchorage in Malmö Road. The *Camilla* Swedish armed ship and six of the convoy were driven by the ice on the shoal named the South Flint; the *Magnet* and three others on the Saltholm shoal. Four others, for the convoy had been joined on its passage by one merchant vessel, were driven with the two Swedish armed brigs towards the Sound.

On the 9th. it appears that the enemy, having succeeded in getting boats over the ice from Dragø, attacked the ships on the South Flint and, notwithstanding the efforts of the *Camilla* to protect them, succeeded in getting possession of three. The whole, it seems, were carried into deep water by the ice; and the *Camilla*, with the loss of her anchors, was last seen standing towards the Baltic, some accounts say with one, others with two, sail near her. The two Swedish armed brigs and four of the convoy were driven thro' the Sound. One of the latter was cut in pieces by it. Two were taken by Danish boats to the northwards of Elsinore. The fourth I cannot trace. One of the two armed brigs, after having been carried by the ice under Cronenburg [Kronborg] Castle and lost two men by its fire, got with much difficulty into Warberg, as did the others into a port near it.

The fate of the *Magnet* will be seen by Captain Morris's[1] narrative of the unfortunate loss of that ship. The three ships that were with her were named the *Jaschental*, *Recommencement* and *Nadagsda*. The first after struggling against difficulties till the 11th. was bulged on the North Flint and burnt by the enemy. The second drove ultimately on shore near Falsterbo where part of her cargo is expected to be saved; and the *Nadagsda* was last seen under sail near Falsterbo, but whether in possession of the enemy is uncertain.

Captain Bathurst,[2] one of whose boats with an officer employed in assisting ships in distress is at Malmö, and who from various accounts used every possible effort to afford protection and relief to his distressed convoy, was

[1] George Morris, born in 1778, lost a leg as a midshipman at the Glorious First of June, 1794. He became a lieutenant in 1796; fought at Camperdown, 1797; commander, 1802; captain, 1812; rear-admiral, 1846.
[2] Walter Bathurst (*c.* 1764–1827), lieutenant, 1790; captain, 1799. In 1824, after nine years without employment, he was given the command of the *Genoa* (74); in which ship he was killed at Navarino.

enabled to ride in Malmö Roads till the 11th. witnessing the mortifying scene of the distress or capture of many of his convoy, was on that night driven from his anchors, forced on shore and afterwards carried off it by the ice. And the *Salsette* was last seen on the 12th. under sail near Falsterbo surrounded by much drift ice; and I know by a message that she had no anchor left and that Captain Bathurst intended to use his endeavours to get into Carlshamn, which port, we have the misfortune to know, is frozen up. And from all accounts Ystad is the only place from which it is probable he may be able to procure relief on that coast.

I still have the misfortune to state that the *Sacorman* has been wrecked near Ystad, her crew saved, and that it is reported with an appearance of truth that the *Fama* has shared the same fate on the island of Bornholm. The *Urgent* was sent by Captain Bathurst to me in the Belt on the 28th.

For your further information I herewith transmit two letters from Captain Bathurst (that which he mentions to have written to Rear-Admiral Bertie on the 29th. not having been received) and also one from Captain Morris respecting the state of the unfortunate convoy. From these, and from the accounts received from the commander of the *Charger* and Mr. Consul Fenwick,[1] has the account I now send been formed. Hitherto I have not been able to procure a list of the ships that composed the convoy. I have etc.

P.S. The *Camilla* is lost in Kioge Bay. The *Salsette*, I hope, is in sight. 10 Feb. 1809.

[1] Charles Fenwick, formerly British consul at Elsinore, crossed to Hälsingborg after the outbreak of war with Denmark. He resided at or near this place during Saumarez's period of command, whence he forwarded commercial and political intelligence. When the war was over he returned to Elsinore as consul.

PART II

1809

PART II

INTRODUCTION

There were changes amongst the flag-officers. Keats was recalled to serve in the Walcheren expedition. Hood went home because of illness. They were succeeded by Rear-Admirals Dixon and Pickmore. Bertie again occupied the station in the Sound. The Swedish revolution of 1809 made uncertain the role of the British fleet. Keats, for example, envisaged its being employed to defend the king against the revolutionaries (doc. 58). The rapidity with which the deposition of Gustavus IV became an accomplished fact forced the British government to tolerate the revolutionary regime without formally recognizing it (docs. 63, 68). Britain fully appreciated that Swedish interests could be preserved only by an early peace between the northern powers. The evidence that convinced Saumarez and the government of Sweden's determination to avoid, insofar as she could, a break with Britain is documented. The volume of trade under cover of neutral flags and false papers increased enormously this year. The increase was accompanied by the introduction of improved methods of trade protection. The important documents here are those relating to the capture of the island of Anholt and the establishment of the convoy service through the Great Belt. Light is also shed on the nature and organization of the expanding trade, particularly by the correspondence between Saumarez and Heinrich Hahn and the letters of Isaac Solly. Channels of communication, other than commercial, with the continent were put on a firmer basis by the provision, under the wing of the fleet, of regular passages both ways between Ystad and Colberg; at which last place E. F. Schröder, who was introduced to Saumarez by Keats (doc. 72), assumed a key role in expediting the movement of mail and persons.

57. *Pole to Emes, Möller and Emes*[1]

Admiralty Office,

7 March 1809.

Gentlemen, I am commanded by my Lords Commissioners of the Admiralty to send you herewith for the information of the merchants concerned in the commerce of the Baltic a statement of the arrangements for the ensuing

---

[1] William and Philip Emes, partners in the firm of Emes, Möller and Emes, corresponded with the admiralty respecting convoy arrangements on behalf of the Baltic merchants, 1808–12.

season drawn up according to the plan agreed upon with Mr. Emes yesterday morning; and I am to request that you will inform me whether the said arrangement is satisfactory to the merchants.

Outward bound convoys:

1st. One convoy will sail from the Nore to Gothenburg on the 1st April.

2nd. The convoys for the Baltic will sail once a fortnight from the Nore, calling off Yarmouth as they did last season, and also once a fortnight from the Humber and Leith; and convoys will sail from Long Hope Sound[1] whenever a sufficient number of vessels are collected there as they did last year. They will proceed off Wingo [Vingå] and the commanding officer of His Majesty's ships at Gothenburg will have directions to be on the look out for all outward bound convoys and to order them to proceed without delay either through the Sound or Belt whichever at the moment he may think most desirable; and he will be ordered not to detain convoys off Gothenburg or to make them enter that port, unless he shall deem it to be absolutely necessary so to do to ensure their safety. The ships bound to Sweden will be seen in safety to the several ports of their destination, and those bound up the Baltic will be escorted fifty leagues to the eastward of Bornholm.

3rd. Cruisers will be kept constantly off Danzig to check the enemy's privateers and also off the island of Gotland and upon the southern coast of the Baltic.

4th. The first convoy for the Baltic will sail on the 15th. of April from the Nore and from the Humber and Leith at the same period.

5th. The last convoy will sail from the Nore and from the other ports of Great Britain on the 15th of October.

For the homeward bound trade the following arrangement is proposed:

1st. Convoys from Carlscrona will sail for England once a fortnight, and the Carlshamn ships[2] to rendezvous at Carlscrona, the first convoy to be appointed as early as the season will admit.

2nd. Upon the homeward bound convoys appearing off Gothenburg the commanding officer will forward the trade to England, if possible without taking it into the port of Gothenburg; and no delay will be permitted, unless it shall happen from unavoidable circumstance that the commanding officer may not have a vessel applicable to the protection of a convoy at the time it may appear off Gothenburg.

3rd. The last homeward bound convoy to leave Carlscrona for England on the 15th. November.

---

[1] Long Hope Sound, an anchorage in the Orkneys, was the rendezvous where ships bound for the Baltic from Ireland and the west coast of Britain joined convoy.

[2] These were merchantmen which, having missed the last convoy to Britain in Dec. 1808, had wintered at Karlshamn.

I am to request that you will lay the foregoing arrangement before the merchants concerned in the trade to the Baltic and that you will acquaint me for the information of my Lords Commissioners of the Admiralty whether the merchants concur with the opinion that was expressed yesterday 'that the arrangement which I have detailed would afford the most ample protection to the Baltic trade which the nature of the case will permit'.

I am at the same time to inform you that a stationary force adapted to the protection of convoys from the enemy's flotilla is appointed for the service of the Sound and Belt which, their lordships hope, will greatly contribute to the security of convoys passing into and out of the Baltic. I am etc.

58. *Keats to Merry*[1]

Superb, Hawke Road, Gothenburg

11 March 1809.

Sir, A letter, which I have just received from Mr. Consul Smith, informs me that a revolt against the existing government of Sweden has broke out at Carlstad [Karlstad] in the province of Warmeland [Värmland] and that the insurgents were marching in considerable force towards Stockholm.[2] But no intimation of any discontents in this neighbourhood has been received.

Admitting Mr. Smith's information should prove correct, I presume it were proper in such an unfortunate situation of affairs to manifest my readiness and that of the squadron under my command to support and defend His Majesty and government as well against rebels as his declared enemies;[3] and if your excellency coincides with me in this opinion, I conceive it might be proper to make a corresponding communication to His Majesty or his minister. Although such is the opinion I have formed, still being directed in certain events to consult your excellency's wishes, I consider this one in which I should act in unison with my instructions in abiding by your recommendations.

Intermediately, I shall lose no opportunity of acting, should there be occasion, in conformity with my own sentiments; and it is my intention to proceed to the Sound, as soon as I can ascertain the anchorage is safe, as

---

[1] Anthony Merry was envoy extraordinary and minister plenipotentiary to the court of Sweden, Nov. 1808–April 1809.

[2] This movement led by Lieutenant-Colonel Georg Adlersparre of the western army marked the beginning of the *coup d'état* against Gustavus Adolphus. It prompted a powerful group of discontented civilian officials and military officers in Stockholm to take direct action against the king who was deposed on 13 March.

[3] Ministers in London did not share the supposition that Britain had a responsibility for, or an interest in, the political survival of Gustavus.

well for the purpose of moving the merchantships from Landscrona [Landskrona] as to deter the enemy from taking advantage of any insurrection or revolts. I have etc.

59. Emes, Möller and Emes to Pole

London,
16 March 1809.

Sir, In compliance with the wish expressed in your letter of the 7th. instant that we should lay the arrangement therein proposed for the protection of the trade to and from the Baltic for the ensuing season before the merchants concerned, we beg leave to state we had a meeting for that purpose when the particular points were discussed which, generally speaking, appeared to meet with the approbation of the gentlemen present. Only one part of the arrangement was objected to which was the convoys calling off Wingo beacon, it was feared, would be productive of the evil complained so much of last year, viz., the detention of the convoys at Gothenburg. However, Mr. P. Emes explained most fully the conversation that passed on that subject, as well as the other points, at the interview he had with yourself and Sir James Saumarez, which satisfied the greater part of the gentlemen of the necessity of the measure. But we were again requested to urge the strictest orders being given that no delay occurs (except absolutely unavoidable) in forwarding the convoys and not to bring them off Gothenburg. With respect to the Carlshamn ships to rendezvous at Carlscrona, we were requested to beg their lordships would be pleased to order that the commanding officer take care that a cutter or other protection be given to bring the ships from Carlshamn to Carlscrona previous to the sailing of the convoys.

We have endeavoured to impress the minds of the gentlemen concerned with what we feel upon the arrangements proposed, conceiving them to afford the most ample protection the nature of the case will permit, and we believe the greater part agreed with us in opinion; and we have satisfied them of its being the wish of their lordships to give the greatest security possible to the trade. We are etc.

60. Barrow[1] to Saumarez

Admiralty Office,
4 April 1809.

Sir, Having laid before my Lords Commissioners of the Admiralty a letter

[1] John Barrow (1764–1848), a native of Ulverston, was one of the two secretaries to the admiralty from 1804 almost until his death. He was interested in the history of the navy. His writings include the biographies of Anson and Howe. He was made a baronet in 1835.

from Mr. B. A. Goldschmid requesting that protection may be afforded to the neutral ships named in the margin [*Three Gehroeders, St. Johannis, Elizabeth*] to Pillau, I have their lordships' commands to send you herewith a copy of the said letter and to signify their direction to you to order protection to be granted to the said ships on their arrival at Wingo to the port of Pillau, Mr. Goldschmid having been acquainted that convoys for the Baltic are appointed to sail from the Nore every fortnight and that you have been directed to afford protection to the ships above mentioned from Wingo to the place of their destination. I am etc.

Enclosure:

60a. *Goldschmid to Barrow*

13 Angel Court, Throgmorton Street,

3 April 1809.

Sir, I take the liberty of troubling you to lay the following request before my Lords Commissioners of the Admiralty.

I am on the point of shipping for Königsberg and Pillau, on board the following ships all neutrals, viz., *Three Gehroeders*, Gauke Henderlis, *St. Johannis*, Nicholas Lemtake, *Elizabeth*, Peter Paterson, to the amount of from 100 to £120,000 of British manufactured goods and West India colonial produce, for which I have special permission from His Prussian Majesty that the ships may enter the port of Pillau and there unload. Therefore the great danger is to reach the port of destination in safety, and if you would be kind enough to represent the above to their lordships with a humble request that they would grant me a sloop-of-war for their protection until their arrival in the port of Pillau, for the risk is not only in the Belts or Sound but in the road of Pillau where ships are obliged to lay to before they can enter the port. I made a similar shipment last year, and unfortunately the vessels were captured by a small French privateer coming out of Danzig even in the very roads of Pillau; and as I intend to ship so large an amount, *if I can get my request granted*, it will be absolutely necessary that their lordships will take it into their consideration and appoint a convoy for the three ships as stated. Otherwise it will prevent my undertaking this speculation, for I cannot possibly get the insurance effected without the above security. The ships will be ready to sail about the 20th. of this month, and are to return to this country laden with all kinds of naval stores. And under all these circumstances I have no doubt but that their lordships will grant my request. I am etc.

61. Solly[1] to Thompson[2]

London,
8 April 1809.

Sir, I take the liberty of informing you that the following ships are about proceeding to the Baltic on account of our engagement with your honourable board, and I request therefore that such attention may be paid to them as the importance of their employ seems to require. The ships carry goods from this country in order to facilitate foreign purchases and the united value of their cargoes is equal to one hundred and fifty thousand pounds. The masters have orders to proceed to Memel where they are to receive instructions as to their port of delivery and their port of loading. They have orders not to go into any Swedish port; and I might be allowed to point out what appears to me most advisable. I should recommend that they should be convoyed through the Sound [to] within sight of the port of Memel without stopping or calling off any port on their voyage, that a vessel-of-war of the smallest description, as being the least likely to attract attention, should during the shipping season be constantly cruising off the ports of Memel, Pillau and in the Bay of Danzig for the protection not only of ships proceeding from those places in ballast for ports in Russia but likewise for the protection of the trade of those places, off Domesnäss for the protection of the trade from Riga, and off Dagö for the protection of the trade from the Gulf of Finland. It may be calculated that the ships lay three weeks to a month at their loading ports, that a convoy in the neighbourhood of each of those ports would be desirable at the interval of three weeks on which subject an intercourse might be had by means of the look-out ship.

I beg leave further to submit whether it would not be advisable to order that the ships that are engaged by me on account of my contract should have a special convoy, at least that they should not on any account be kept waiting for the accumulation of a large fleet. I am induced to suggest this because I believe they will run less sea risk, have a better chance of increasing their number of voyages to and from, and in this way increase the supplies as well as be subject to a less degree of risk of being captured.

The following is the list of ships:

| The Uranus | Pucke, master, | brig. |

[1] Isaac Solly, the head of the firm of Isaac Solly and Sons, holders of a contract with the navy board for the supply of hemp.
[2] Sir Thomas Boulden Thompson, bart. (c. 1766–1828) was comptroller of the navy, 1806–16. He first went to sea with his uncle Captain Edward Thompson in 1778, was commissioned in 1782, posted captain in 1790, advanced to flag rank in 1809 and promoted vice-admiral in 1814. Thompson, who lost a leg in Nelson's battle at Copenhagen, was created a baronet in 1806; K.C.B., 1815; G.C.B., 1822.

The *Estafette*,	Ticks, master,	brig.
The *Conjunctor*,	Leidke, master,	brig.
The *Alexis*,	Rhoder, master,	ship.

The above proceed from this port and will be ready next week. The following are to proceed from Liverpool and are nearly ready:

The *Maria*,	Martin, master,	ship.
The *Hercules*,	Paterson, master,	ship.
The *Aufang*,	Klawitter, master,	ship.
The *Invariable*,	Kermer, master,	ship.

The *February*, Prauschriever, a ship, has proceeded under convoy for Gothenburg on her way to Memel. The *Satisfaction*, Paterson, the *January*, Reatall, the *Elbe*, Burch, were at Gothenburg bound for the Baltic when the last accounts arrived from thence.

By the last accounts from Petersburg the *Watzymannick*, Schultz, was there waiting for wind and weather; and the following at Riga:

The *Speculation*,	Domeke, master
The *Marineuke*,	Adams, master
The *Superb*,	Henry, master.

And I hope that you will think it right that, when met with at sea, that they should be proceeded with direct to this country. I hope you will excuse my adding to the above request that Mr. Edward Solly, my agent, now residing at Königsberg should be attended to by the commander of His Majesty's ships in the Baltic, as far as practicable, as it may be of essential service to the undertaking in which I am engaged.

62. *Saumarez to Hood*

London,
15 April 1809.

Sir, Herewith I enclose the copies of three letters I have received from the admiralty together with the copies of letters enclosed therewith from Mr. Isaac Solly and Mr. Joseph Beckett requesting protection for the vessels therein named to which I have to call your attention and particularly to the

4

stationing one or more armed vessels to watch the enemy's privateers in the Bay of Danzig. I have etc.

Enclosure 1:

62a. *Solly to Thompson*

London,
18 March 1809.

Sir, I take the liberty of communicating to you the information I have received from Königsberg in a letter of the 20th. February: 'It is of the utmost importance that measures be taken to blockade the port of Danzig, as it will otherwise be impossible to make any shipments from other ports, in consequence of the privateers that are fitting out there'. These privateers are most of them small boats, one or two guns, half decks, and run along the coasts watching the loaded ships as they come out of harbour. Several vessels were captured last year off Pillau in this way.

The passage through the Belt, avoiding Gothenburg, and small convoys are pointed out as most advisable.

In regard to the Belt, I believe it to be a fact, that none of the ships which have been captured, were captured in their passage through the Belt. In regard to the stopping at Gothenburg, a fair wind for the passage through the Cattegat is a foul wind to get to sea from Gothenburg: and, in a great many instances, ships were detained three weeks at Gothenburg, partly for want of convoy and partly for want of wind. The time that is lost in getting a great number of ships ready to sail with convoy, the check they are upon each other in a narrow sea, are arguments against a large convoy. In addition to the delay which is necessary in order to collect a large fleet, the time employed in getting a large fleet under weigh serves as a signal to the enemy. Merchant vessels should be allowed to place themselves under the protection of ships-of-war whenever they pass to or from the Cattegat or Baltic. As the weather in the neighbourhood of Pillau and Danzig was mild with a S.W. wind and rain during the month of February, it was expected that the shipping season would commence in the month of March; but this cannot be done without the protection of British ships-of-war cruising off the coast. And unless captures by the enemy are prevented from taking place early in the year, a great damp will be thrown on the mercantile spirit of enterprize that would prove very detrimental to the interests of the country. I am etc.

Enclosure 2:

62b. *Beckett to Milton*[1]

Barnsley,

8 April 1809.

My Lord, We, the Linen Trade here, are informed by the merchants of Königsberg, Bramsberg, etc in Prussia that they can load yarn, flax etc., and protect the ship in and out of their own ports till she gets to sea. Accordingly a Prussian ship with a valuable cargo is now loading with a view to run to Carlscrona and there put herself under the protection of the British ships.

It is suggested in the present state of Sweden that it would be desirable that the commander of the armed ships in the Baltic should have a direction to dispatch an armed vessel to look into Pillau and bring away under his protection all such ships there as are ready and willing to come away.

Now will you have the goodness to make the question to their lordships (of the admiralty) if such a direction would be given and advise me of their reply. I have etc.

63. *Merry to Hood*

Stockholm,

17 April, 1809.

Sir, The last messenger who arrived here from England in the night of the 13th. instant brought to me a communication of the sentiments of His Majesty's government upon the late events in the country, which sentiments not being as yet known here, I must for this reason, as well as for others, beg leave to apprize you of such part of them as may be interesting to you in the most private, secret and confidential manner.

I have had His Majesty's commands to express, in the strongest and most earnest manner, to the present administration in Sweden the lively and anxious interest which His Majesty takes in the personal safety of the king of Sweden.

His Majesty has declined to receive a letter which the Duke of Sudermania[2]

---

[1] Charles William Wentworth Fitzwilliam, Viscount Milton (1786–1857) represented Yorkshire continuously in the house of commons, 1807–1831. He was elevated to the peerage as 3rd Earl Fitzwilliam in 1833 on the death of his father the second earl, whose liberal opinions he shared.

[2] Charles, duke of Södermanland (1748–1818) was the younger brother of Gustavus III; regent of Sweden during the minority of Gustavus IV, 1792–96; re-appointed regent following the revolution of 1809; elected king by the estates of the realm in June with the title of Charles XIII.

had addressed to the king and caused to be sent to the Swedish minister in London to deliver to His Majesty, because it has been considered that the acceptance and acknowledgment of such a letter would have implied a recognition on His Majesty's part of the change which has taken place in the government of Sweden.

It has also been declared to the Swedish minister in London that no article of the treaty of subsidy, signed here by me on the 1st of March, can be understood to remain in force after the purpose of carrying on the war has been avowedly abandoned by Sweden.

And I have received at the same time His Majesty's leave of absence, to return to England leaving, however, his secretary of legation as chargé d'affaire here:[1] a mode which has been adopted to avoid the embarrassment which would have arisen with respect to the form of my letters of recall, as well as to show that His Majesty means to continue his political relations with this country.

I have understood, sir, that directions have been given for a frigate to be appointed for my conveyance to England, and I have had great satisfaction in learning by Captain Webley's[2] letter to me that you had been pleased to appoint the *Alexandria* for this service, because Captain Cochrane[3] had the goodness to bring me from England. Particular reasons render it expedient and important for me to conceal as long as possible from this government all the circumstances which I have now had the honour of stating to you, except that of the interest which His Majesty takes in the personal safety of the king of Sweden. It is therefore impossible for me to fix at this moment the time when I shall reach Gothenburg; but I conceive that my departure from hence will take place immediately after the arrival here of the next mail from England, when I shall expedite my journey as much as possible. I have etc.

P.S. What I have had the honour to state to you in my public letter herewith respecting the reciprocal formal assurances in writing given by both governments of the protection to be afforded, in every event, to the British and Swedish property in the two countries is perfectly authentic.

---

[1] Augustus John Foster arrived in Stockholm on 20 Nov. 1808 as secretary of legation. He remained there as chargé d'affaires after Merry's departure until June 1810 when he left at the request of the Swedish government.
[2] William Henry Webley, lieutenant, 1790; captain, 1802; commander of the *Centaur* (74), flagship of Sir Samuel Hood. Webley, first lieutenant of the *Zealous* (74) at the battle of the Nile, later served under Hood in the Mediterranean and East Indies; C.B., 1815, in which year he assumed the surname of Parry.
[3] Nathaniel Day Cochrane, lieutenant, 1800; commander, 1805; captain 1806.

64. *Hahn[1] to Keats*

Königsberg,
8 May 1809.

Sir, I had this morning the honour to receive your letter of the 30th. April, forwarded me by Captain Thomas Richard Toker[2] of H.M. sloop *Cruizer* who appeared off Pillau yesterday.

I am happy to notice your arrival in the Baltic with the squadron under your command and being ever animated with the greatest zeal and desire to be useful to H.M's government I shall very eagerly embrace every opportunity to transmit you whatever information I may consider useful or interesting.

I shall pay every attention to your directions for the benefit and protection of the trade from Memel, Pillau and Danzig, and follow the instructions sent to me to that intent by Captain Toker with whom I hope to be able to keep up a communication.

Several vessels are now ready or nearly so, whereof I shall probably be able to transmit a list herewith; but notwithstanding the protection held out there cannot be any security for the trade until the port of Danzig is blockaded or some force stationed there to prevent the privateers coming out, which have done so much injury to the trade already by the capture of several vessels with valuable cargoes, the loss of which falls upon His Majesty's subjects as they were insured in England. Permit me to request you will have the goodness to take this into consideration and, if possible, to station a frigate or some other force in the Bay of Danzig.

As several of the vessels now actually lading and destined for a British port, owing to the interruption of intercourse, are not provided with British licences, I request you to inform me whether you will afford protection to the like, the same as those who have licences. It appearing evident that it is intended to encourage and protect all trade from these ports to any British port, I conclude such vessels would be allowed to pass and, by your recommendation, might apply for or take up the licences already made out for them, tho' not yet received on account of the difficulty of communication.

Under you kind permission to communicate without reserve, I make free to mention that the rendezvous appointed at the Utclippers[3] or at Hanö is

---

[1] Heinrich Hahn was the alias of Louis Drusina, British consul at Memel since 1798, who remained in Prussia in the capacity of a secret agent until his death in 1810.
[2] Thomas Richard Toker, lieutenant, 1800; first lieutenant of the *Colossus* (74) at Trafalgar; commander, 1805; principally employed in the Baltic, 1808–12; captain, 1813.
[3] The Utklipporna rocks off Karlskrona, variously anglicized as the Utclippers, Utklippors or Outclippers.

considered rather disadvantageous from being in a corner and difficult to get out of. I, and several others, have very frequently recommended the capture of the Eartholms and of Bornholm, and should the Swedes declare against England the former would more particularly be a desirable and perhaps even necessary station for H.M's. ships as well as for the trade. Or, if the Swedes declare against us, the island of Gotland might be easily taken and would afford a good station or sheltering place.

We have not any agent or consul at Riga, but I shall make the confidential statement you desire to a very respectable British house there on whose discretion I can rely.

I beg leave to mention also for your government that the gentleman who has acted for me several years at Memel in the capacity of vice-consul is Mr. John Griffin, whom I have instructed that if anything is put on shore directed for me to his care to send it forward and for fear of accidents request only to direct for me as below—to the same care as before.

The privateers now at Danzig are the *Tilsit* of 8 guns, the *Voltigeur* a row boat with masts to let down and some small boats to lurk along the coast. These are all French and beside them there are two Danish cutter privateers commanded by Captains Brosch and Henrichsen.

The River Neva opened at St. Petersburg on the evening of the 27th. April, N.S. The Dvina at Riga opened about a fortnight ago.

And now permit me, sir, to request you will from time to time have the goodness to transmit all the English newspapers you can spare, as we are, and have been, this many months from the difficulty of communication totally in the dark as to the actual state of things in our dear native country, only getting what few accounts the French allow to be inserted in the German papers; and you may guess how unfair and distorted they must be. I have etc.

65. *Saumarez to Foster*

Victory, in Wingo Sound,

11 May 1809.

Sir, Having arrived at this anchorage on the 4th. instant and Rear-Admiral Hood being posted for England in consequence of the ill state of his health, I opened your letter addressed to the rear-admiral, dated 7th. instant, informing him of your being appointed His Majesty's chargé d'affaires in the absence of Mr. Merry.

I have the honour to inform you that I shall feel highly gratified by any communication you may be pleased to make to me relating to His Majesty's service and which may be interesting for my knowledge as commander-in-chief in these seas; and I shall be happy in conveying to you any information in my power which may be connected with His Majesty's service.

His Excellency Mr. Merry sailed yesterday for England on board His Majesty's ship *Alexandria*. From him I received such information as he possessed to the period of his leaving Stockholm. I propose to detach Rear-Admiral Dixon,[1] who joined me the 9th. instant in the *Temeraire*, to relieve Sir Richard G. Keats. And I propose to continue here for some time longer for the more speedy communication with England as well as to receive what you may do me the honour to write to me, giving you due notice previously to my proceeding for the Baltic.

The accounts rumoured of the pretended defeat of the Austrians I trust will not prove correct; and we must not be surprized at the circulation of exaggerated accounts of the success of Bonaparte in the present state of affairs on the continent and in the northern parts of Europe. I have etc.

66. *Nauckhoff to Saumarez*[2]

Stockholm,
16 May 1809.

Your Excellency, I have had news that your excellency has happily arrived in the Sound and that the object of your fleet is to enter the Baltic Sea. We are obliged, through the remarkable revolution in Sweden, to remain strictly on the defensive with regard to our neighbours until peace is made. Russia is unwilling to make peace unless we give up Finland and declare that our ports will always be closed to England; it is necessary therefore to continue the war. As I trust that harmony still prevails between your court and ours, the sovereign duke hopes that your excellency will be so good as to send small gunboats between Åland and the coast of Sweden in order to protect us against the Russians as long as they are resolved to make peace with us only on condition that we give up Finland and declare war against England. There is good reason to believe that as soon as your fleet draws near the coasts of Finland and Sweden, the Russians will not dare to venture out and as a result will never be able to inflict further damage upon us.

The sovereign duke has written to your government in order to procure the rank of captain for that worthy and meritorious officer, Mr. Ross. No more have I forgotten the distinguished services rendered to the Swedish fleet during the last campaign by Mr. Duke; and it is with pleasure that I

---

[1] Manley Dixon (1760–1837), lieutenant, 1777; captain, 1790; commanded the *Lion* (64) at the capture of the *Guillaume Tell* (80) at Malta, 1800; rear-admiral, 1808; commander-in-chief South American station, 1812–15; vice-admiral, 1813; K.C.B., 1819.
[2] Editor's translation.

have the honour to inform your excellency that the king has bestowed on Mr. Duke the title of Doctor of the Faculty of Medicine at Uppsala and, at the same time, the diploma of honorary membership of the Royal College of Medicine in Stockholm; in addition to which the king confers upon him as a mark of distinction a gold medal to be worn on the chest with a blue ribbon. The moment I receive these items, I will have the honour of forwarding them to your excellency for delivery to Mr. Duke.

I am most grateful for the many kindnesses and favours shown by your excellency to my nephew Mr. Nordenskjöld[1] who, I hope, has done all that is possible to be worthy of your goodness. I trust you will remember me to our friend Admiral Hood. My wife sends you her kindest regards. I have etc.

P.S. The estates of the kingdom of Sweden formally declared on the 12th instant that the former king, as also his son, has lost all right to the throne and crown of Sweden for ever. The wretched direction of government, whereby the whole kingdom has been reduced to distress, is the cause of the misfortunes of the king and his family. Duke Charles is in the meantime regent with all the powers of king; and he will be declared king of Sweden as soon as the estates have had time to establish another form of rule.

News has just been brought that the Austrians have totally defeated the army of Napoleon. If this be confirmed, I have no doubt that great changes will result among the northern powers.

67. *Saumarez to Foster*

Victory, Wingo Sound, Gothenburg,

18 May 1809.

Sir, I have just received the honour of your letter of the 15th. instant by the messenger Mears acquainting me with the particulars of a conference you had with Baron de Lagerbjelke[2] on the present critical state of Sweden, in consequence, as he was pleased to state to you, of her desire to remain in amity, and maintain her commercial relations, with Great Britain; and requesting you to explain to me the full extent of her danger, in the confidence

---

[1] Carl Reinhold, later Baron, Nordenskjöld (1791–1871) became a sub-lieutenant in the Swedish navy, 1808; carried out liaison duties on board the *Victory*, 1808–09; aide-de-camp to Puke in operations against Norway, 1814; retired with rank of rear-admiral, 1863.

[2] Gustaf, Baron, later Count, Lagerbjelke (1777-1837) was secretary for foreign affairs in the Swedish cabinet, 1801–05; appointed acting head of the department for foreign affairs by the revolutionary government. On 9 June he was ordered to Paris as plenipotentiary with Count von Essen (*q.v.*) for negotiations with France; Swedish ambassador to France, 1810–11; dismissed on account of his alleged indiscretions in Parisian society; resided in France until 1814.

that I should give all the assistance in my power which her perilous situation required, without waiting for instructions from his Majesty's government; also informing me of the formidable preparations making in Finland for the immediate invasion of Sweden.

The assurances made to you through Baron de Lagerbjelke, on the part of the duke of Sudermania, that every effort will be made to repel the meditated attack of Russia, and that his royal highness has determined not to yield to the conditions of peace proposed to him, as long as he has the means of defending himself, will decide me in employing the fleet under my command in the best manner in my power for the defence of Sweden; for which purpose an adequate force will be stationed in the Sound and on the coast of Denmark, to intimidate the Danes from making any attack on the southern provinces of Sweden; and a squadron of line-of-battle ships will be employed in the Baltic to watch the Russian fleet, and prevent any attempt on their part to carry an invading army against the coast of Sweden from the side of Finland.

As the attention of the Swedish marine will be principally confined to the defence of Stockholm, and the coast within the Gulf of Bothnia, it is to be presumed that, with proper exertion, they will be perfectly adequate to that service; and as three Swedish frigates have been ordered to cruise on that station, with other armed vessels, and one hundred and six gun-boats, no doubt can be entertained of their being for the present sufficient to repel the enemy; and I shall readily order such further part of the force under my command, as can be spared from other services, to co-operate in that quarter. The important transactions going on in the southern coast of the Baltic, in which the interest of Sweden is materially concerned, require a considerable part of the force under my orders for that particular service; but I have the honour to assure you, that every effort will be exerted for the protection and security of Sweden against any attack of the enemy.

You will be pleased to take the necessary measures that orders may be given for His Majesty's ships to be supplied with water, and such necessaries as they may stand in need of, at Carlscrona and other Swedish ports; and pilots when they require them. I have etc.

68. *Saumarez to Foster*

Victory, in Wingo Sound,
18 May 1809.

Sir, I have replied to your public letter as fully as I can consider myself warranted without having received any special instructions on the subject from His Majesty's government. But, considering it to be the intention to maintain the terms of amity with Sweden so long as it can be done consistently and prevent the country from falling a prey to the common enemy, I trust to be right in using my efforts for that purpose; and I hope to receive the sanction of ministers on the measures I am adopting. I shall proceed for the Baltic the moment it lies in my power, but the late prevailing calms and adverse winds have prevented the arrival of the ships on their way to join me; and no accounts later than the 5th. from London have reached this place. I sent three days since a small detachment of ships to take possession of Anholt, where supplies of water could be obtained, and which would also be a proper place for convoys to resort to in the event of exclusion from the Swedish ports.

Any information you can favour me with respecting the state of the Russian fleet at Cronstadt will be highly desirable, and also the probable time they may be enabled to put to sea from that port. I have etc.

69. *Saumarez to Keats*

Victory, in Wingo Sound,

19 May 1809.

Sir, I yesterday received a letter from Mr. Foster, His Majesty's chargé d'affaires at Stockholm, dated the 15th. instant communicating to me a conference he had on the same day with the Baron de Lagerbjelke, minister for foreign affairs to the Swedish government, the object of which was to expose the critical situation in which Sweden is placed from her desire to remain in amity and maintain her commercial intercourse with Great Britain; and requesting him to explain to me the full extent of her danger and the confidence that I would give all the assistance in my power which her perilous situation required, at the same time giving the assurances of the duke of Sudermania that every effort should be made on the part of Sweden to repel the meditated attacks of her enemies.

It being an object of great importance to defend Sweden in the present crisis from the attacks of Denmark and Russia, and as it is the intention of the Swedish government to employ all the means in her power in defending Stockholm and the coast in the Gulf of Bothnia from the meditated attack from the Russian general in Finland, three frigates and what other force can be spared from Carlscrona in gunboats and other vessels having been ordered to proceed to the Gulf of Bothnia, I have to desire you will use all the means in your power for the defence of Sweden and that you direct Rear-Admiral Bertie in the *Stately* and *Africa* to repair off Helsingborg without loss of time, giving him orders to use his utmost endeavours for the defence of Sweden and for the protection of convoys pursuant to his former orders.

The *Owen Glendower* has been ordered to Kioge [Køge] Bay with such small vessels as can be spared from other services; and I propose to order a ship in Malmö road for the greater security in that quarter.

As the season is fast approaching when the Russian fleet fitting at Cronstadt may be expected to put to sea, it becomes highly expedient that the line-of-battle ships within the Baltic should be kept collected and to rendezvous off the Utklippors. You will be pleased to give directions for that purpose to Rear-Admiral Dixon on his joining you with the ships placed under his orders; to whom you will also please to communicate the contents of this letter. I propose to proceed for the Belt the moment the wind will permit. You will therefore transmit to me any information you may obtain thro' that channel. I have etc.

P.S. I have to observe that measures have been taken for orders being sent to Carlscrona and other Swedish ports for supplies of water and such other necessaries as the squadron may be in want of to be furnished.

70. *Saumarez to Pole*

Victory, in Wingo Sound,

20 May 1809.

Sir, I have great satisfaction in acquainting you for the information of the Lords Commissioners of the Admiralty that the detachment of His Majesty's ships named in the margin [*Standard, Owen Glendower, Avenger, Ranger, Rose, Snipe*] under the orders of Captain Hollis[1] of the *Standard* have succeeded in taking possession of the island of Anholt, the garrison consisting of one hundred and thirty men besides the militia of the island having surrendered to His Majesty's arms on the 18th. instant. The acquisition of this island will prove of considerable importance in furnishing supplies of water to His Majesty's fleet and affording a good anchorage to the trade of the country in going or coming from the Baltic.

Captain Hollis, who has executed the service trusted to him highly to my satisfaction, mentions in the strongest terms the conduct of Captain Selby[2] of the *Owen Glendower* who conducted the landing, and of the zeal and exertions of the other officers and men employed upon this service, as also of Captain Edward Nicholls of the Royal Marines of the *Standard* who, with Captain Peter Jones with a detachment of fifty marines belonging to the

---

[1] Aiskew Paffard Hollis (1764–1844) entered the navy in 1774 and was present at the battle of Ushant. Commissioned in 1781, he was wounded in the action of 1 June 1794. He was posted captain in 1798 and was regularly employed until 1821; rear-admiral, 1825; vice-admiral, 1837.
[2] William Selby, lieutenant, 1793; commander, 1798; captain, 1800.

Victory, had been selected for this service; and by whose intrepidity in the attack of the enemy they obliged them to surrender at discretion.

Captain Acklom[1] of His Majesty's sloop *Ranger*, whose exertions upon this station have been highly meritorious, will have the honour of delivering you this letter; and I beg to refer their lordships to him for any information relative to the island of Anholt. Enclosed herewith I transmit Captain Hollis's letter to me, with the return of ordnance and stores captured in the island. I have etc.

71. *Saumarez to Foster*

Victory, Great Belt,

29 May 1809.

Sir, I had the honour yesterday morning to receive your letter of the 19th., enclosing one from Admiral Nauckhoff addressed to me, and also the copy of General Wrede's[2] report on the state of the north. I have been detained by adverse currents and calms since my departure from Gothenburg, but think myself fortunate in having been as early as Admiral Dixon, who sailed eight days before me and with whom I fell in yesterday evening off Langeland.

The Danish force of gunboats in the Belt has been considerably increased since last year. The *Melpomene* frigate was attacked by several in the night of the 23rd. and had four men killed, besides about twenty wounded. Captain Warren,[3] in having drawn their attention, succeeded in preserving a numerous convoy at anchor near Langeland which seemed to have been principal object for which they came out. The *Ardent* having very injudiciously landed a party of men on the island of Romsoe [Romsø] for the purpose of procuring a supply of wood and water, they suffered themselves to be surprized and about eighty men were made prisoner.

I am hastening with all despatch towards Carlscrona, and I hope to have the honour of hearing from you in my way off Ystad. I think it right to mention *in confidence* that I shall not have more than six sail of the line-of-battle ships with me until I can be joined by those that may be on their way from England. I have etc.

[1] George Acklom entered the navy, 1788; lieutenant, 1794; first lieutenant of the *Neptune* (98) at Trafalgar; commander, 24 Dec. 1805; continuously employed in the Baltic, 1808–12; created a knight of the order of St. Anne and St. Vladimir by Tsar Alexander I as reward for his services in 1812; captain 1812; unemployed after 1813; died, 1837.

[2] Fabian, Count Wrede (1760–1824) began his military career in 1775, and reached the rank of lieutenant-general in 1805. Unemployed by Gustavus IV after 1807, he was recalled to active service by the revolutionary government and was one of the leaders of the expedition to Västerbotten in 1809. In 1811 he retired partly for reasons of health, partly because of his dissatisfaction with the foreign policy of Bernadotte.

[3] Frederick Warren (1775–1848), lieutenant, 1794; captain, 1801; rear-admiral, 1830; commander-in-chief Cape of Good Hope, 1831–34; vice-admiral, 1841.

72. Keats to Saumarez

Superb, off the Utklippers,

2 June 1809.

Sir, I beg to state to you that the gentleman alluded to in my letter of the 10th. May, who has been eminently useful in the correspondence and communications we have had with Colberg, was recommended to my notice by a Mr. Johnson,[1] diplomatically, as he gave me to understand, employed by government on the continent. Mr. Johnson, who from Vienna embarked at Colberg and came to me a few days previous to the commencement of the French and Austrian war, was landed by me at Ystad and took the route of Gothenburg to England.

As this gentleman, who is a merchant and whose real name is Schröder[2] has assumed that of August Schaeffer, was very useful to the gentlemen who came up in the *Prometheus*, has since sent off Mr. Maimberg, who was the bearer of my letter of the 25th. to you, and at considerable risk has otherwise manifested a zeal and devotion to our interests, I have considered it right to assure him I should not fail to represent to you in a strong light the advantages we have received from his services. As I found by Mr. Maimberg that he much wished for a boat the better to enable him to carry on his communications I sent him one, taken by the *Urgent* from the enemy, in the *Rose* and asked his services to embark the persons (without discovering who they are) she is gone for.[3]

Amongst the numerous applications I have had from merchants for licences and passports (not one of which I have granted) is one from Mr. Schröder to permit a vessel to pass from a Russian port laden to Colberg; and I mention the circumstance particularly to you in order, as I assured him, he would meet with every disposition on your part to pay every attention to services like his, that you may notice in such terms as you please the impossibility of complying with it on any occasion you may write.

I subjoin the mode that he wishes to be adopted in communicating with

---

[1] John Mordaunt Johnson (c. 1776–1815), a native of Dublin, was employed by the British government as a confidential agent in the Habsburg territories during the suspension of normal diplomatic relations. He was rightly regarded by Metternich as the most able and discreet of the British agents operating in Germany. After the war he was made consul at Genoa. He died at Florence in Sept. 1815.

[2] E. F. Schröder, a merchant and shipowner of Colberg where he was Danish consul, aided the passage of persons and correspondence between Britain and the continent during the period of exclusion. For an appreciation of his services, see C. B. S. Buckland, *Metternich and the British Government from 1809 to 1813* (1932), pp. 139–40. His motives may, however, have been less altruistic than is suggested therein, since it is clear that he was in receipt of commercial favours from the British government. He was rewarded after the war with an appointment as Hanoverian consul.

[3] This may well be an allusion to the passage of the prince of Orange (*q.v.*) and his suite *via* Colberg and Ystad to Gothenburg, where he embarked for Britain on 8 June.

him. And as he does not understand English he much wishes he might be written to in French or German; and he is very desirous vessels sent would not stand near in nor remain longer in sight of the town than may be absolutely necessary. I have etc.

P.S. It is recommended to any ship appearing off to disguise and hoist Danish colours and fire three guns to leeward if they have anyone to land. Mr. Schröder will in such case order a fisherman on board who, on approaching the ship, will show a red cloth; and on such person coming on board and showing a card with E. F. Schröder on it, to such person letters may be given addressed to him.

37. Stedingk[1] to Saumarez

Stockholm,
4 June 1809.

Sir, Mr. Foster, the chargé d'affaires of His Britannic Majesty, has done me the honour of communicating to me the letter of your excellency dated 30 May, by which your excellency signifies your intention to repair off Carlscrona. In like manner Rear-Admiral Nauckhoff has delivered to me your excellency's letter dated the 29th. of the same month. I have had the honour of laying the latter before His Royal Highness the sovereign duke and of reporting the contents of the former to His Royal Highness.

It is by command of the sovereign duke that I enter into correspondence with your excellency, and I am delighted to have the opportunity of fulfilling his orders. His Royal Highness has accepted with the utmost gratification the offers made to him by your excellency to defend the southern coasts of Sweden by stationing your forces in the Sound and Belt so that the Danes will be held in check and be unable to attempt anything against our coasts, and to prevent the Russian fleet from emerging from the Gulf of Finland. That way we will be in a position, as you say to Mr. Nauckhoff, to concentrate our forces in the Gulf of Bothnia and on the coasts around Stockholm; and I hope that, when our oared-fleet is completely joined to our frigates and small vessels in these areas, we will with God's help be able to face the formidable Russian oared-fleet with which we are threatened, despite the fact that according to reports, they have between 200 and 300 sail. Unfortunately this will take up all our forces, and we are obliged in order to gather our strength here to withdraw all our gunboats from the Sound. The forces for the defence

---

[1] Victor Carl Ernst Berend Heinrich, Baron von Stedingk (1751–1823), a native of Swedish Pomerania, was commissioned in the navy in 1769 and served in both the sailing ship navy and the *skärgardsflottan*; rear-admiral, 1793; vice-admiral, 1802; commander-in-chief Gothenburg squadron, 1807–08; naval aide-de-camp to the king of Sweden, 1809–12; admiral, 1811; admiral-of-the-fleet, 1818.

of our trade will thus be reduced to a few frigates, brigs and armed vessels, but since your excellency has had the kindness to promise protection to our trade in the Sound as well as in the Belt, His Royal Highness is easy in his mind on that subject. The activity of the English navy and its pre-eminent ability make all things possible, especially when under the command of your excellency. It is with the highest consideration that I have etc.

74. *Krusenstjerna*[1] *to Saumarez*

Wladislaff, Carlskrona,

4 June 1809.

Sir, May your excellency be pleased to accept my humbel and truly assurance that nothing can afford me more heartfelt satisfaction that the pleasure I feel on account of my being honoured with the remembrance of a commander-in-chief whose very excellent qualities I had the best opportunity to admire during the short but honourable time I had the honour to serve in his concordance with his directions against the common ennemies to our respective nations.

The noble and disinterested disposition of your excellency to employ the forces committed to your orders for the defence of this country and maintenance of its independence excites in me the warmest sense of gratitude, and I beg your excellency will be assured that I shall find myself most happy if circumstances will admit of my being employed on joint service against the common ennemies.

There is in my opinion no reason to believe that the Russian fleet will leave Cronstadt, but they have a great quantity of gunboats and galleys assembled at Åland ready to invade the northern coasts of this kingdom.

Our forces of gunboats, formerly stationed at Malmö and in the Sound are gone to unite with those assembled at Stockholm and in the Bothnia Gulf in order to prevent and oppose the ennemies' intentions. The Swedish coast from Gothenburg to Stockholm are in consequence left without defence, open to invasions of the Danes if not protected by the English. Never was this country in a more deplorable situation.

May your excellency always enjoy health, success and happiness and permit me the honour etc.

P.S. I have to express to your excellency my most sincere thanks for procuring me the pleasure to review my good friend Mr. Ross whom I give myself

[1] Mauritz Peter Gramén Krusenstjerna (1766–1813) entered the Swedish navy in 1779; fought in the war of 1788–90. He was flag-captain of the Karlskrona squadron, 1808; promoted rear-admiral, 1809. As squadron commander in 1810–11 helped to preserve diplomatic relations with Britain through his correspondence with Saumarez.

the honour to recommend to the favour of your excellency if anything can be done for his promotion and welfare.

75. *Saumarez to Puke*[1]

Victory, off Carlscrona,

4 June 1809.

Sir, It is with the highest satisfaction that I have the honour to inform your excellency with my arrival off Carlscrona being in my way up the Baltic with part of the fleet under my command for the defence of Sweden against the attack of the Russian fleet, and to use every possible effort to preserve that good understanding that has for so many years subsisted between our respective nations.

I shall be thankful to your excellency for any information you will be pleased to honour me with that can tend to the advancement of the great and good cause in which we are engaged, and I am happy in profiting of the present opportunity to transmit an official bulletin which I received last Friday giving an account of a most important victory over the French army commanded by Bonaparte in person. This glorious event it is to be hoped will unite the powers in the northern parts of the continent totally to extirpate the atrocious tyrant who has been so long the scourge of the human race.[2] I have etc.

76. *Tawast*[3] *to Bertie*[4]

Helsinborg,

6 June 1809.

Mr. The Admiral, I have received the letter which you have today done me the honour to address to me and I hasten to reply thereto. The hostilities of Russia having obliged the government to assemble a naval force in the

[1] Johan, Baron, later Count af Puke (1751–1816) gained his first experience of war at sea in the French navy, 1778–82; fought with distinction against the Russians, 1788–90; commander-in-chief Karlskrona, 1803–09; admiral-of-the-fleet, 1809; led the naval forces in the expedition to Västerbotten; councillor of state, 1812–15; commanded the navy in the campaign against Norway, 1814.

[2] Exaggerated reports of Austrian successes in the war of 1809 were frequently circulated. The British assumption that a resounding Austrian victory would automatically lead to the anti-French alignment of the northern powers reflected a shallow appreciation of Swedish interests *vis-à-vis* those of Russia.

[3] Johan Henrik, later Count, Tawast (1763–1841), an experienced soldier who was promoted major-general after the 1809 revolution and became senior aide-de-camp to the army on the west coast; sent on a diplomatic mission to Constantinople, 1812; ambassador to Denmark, 1814–21.

[4] Charles Fenwick's translation.

Gulf of Bothnia, it has seen itself obliged to leave exposed for a time the coasts of Scania; and Rear-Admiral Hjelmstjerna[1] has received orders to use every possible exertion to proceed to his destination with the flotilla under his command. His Royal Highness the duke regent has received the most satisfactory assurances respecting the protection of the coasts of Scania and of the Swedish trade by the naval forces of His Britannic Majesty; and it is in virtue of the perfect confidence His Royal Highness places in these assurances that he has not hesitated to employ the flotilla intended for the defence of Scania to repulse the attacks of the Russians.

I hope that I shall soon have at my disposal some decked gunboats which it will be more easy to station in a manner to protect the convoys.[2] I write to Rear-Admiral Hjelmstjerna to enjoy to give every assistance to the convoy that may arrive before his departure. I have given orders that a pilot be sent to you from Malmö and beg of you Mr. the admiral to be assured of my sincere desire to contribute by every means in my power to everything that may be useful to the *interests* of the two *countries*. I have etc.

77. Puke to Saumarez

Carlskrona,

7 June 1809.

Sir, I felicitate myself on my being so happy as to have occasion of renewing with your excellency the acquaintance I was favoured with last year. Your excellency's flattering letter of the 4th. instant gave me a very agreeable remembrance of it, and I may give you my hearty acknowledgements therefore, as also for the news your excellency was pleased to annex. The post arrived for a short time from Stockholm did not contain anything of importance, but that the matters stood well. The German mail was not come in; and in general the news are of so different a content that nobody knows which of them is to rely on. All our forces on the southern coasts being in necessity to be drawn up to the northern parts of the country for repulsing the attack of the Russians, the coasts on this side will be without sufficient defence. It is only in your excellency I may fix my confiance, convinced as I am that, by the good intelligence that subsists between the both nations and His Britannic Majesty's benevolence towards Sweden, your excellency will not omit to protect, as far as possible, the trade from Gothenburg and trough the Belts upwards, and retain all hostile enterprises. I would wish to

---

[1] Rear-Admiral Claes Leonard Hjelmstjerna (1742–1810) was commander-in-chief of the division of the *skärgardsflottan* stationed in the Sound.

[2] After the departure of the Swedish gunboats from Landskrona the British abandoned the practice of sending convoys through the Sound and concentrated upon providing an efficient convoy service through the passage of the Belt.

have as some such gunbrigs as your excellency's and other small vessels to send up to the Finnish gulf where they would be of no little service. I include myself in your excellency's friendship which I will be very proud to possess, and wish no better than that your excellency with all your brave officers and men may with their usual success defeat and frustrate the enemy's projects against us. It is with these sincere sentiments that I have etc.

78. *Extract of a letter from Hahn to Saumarez, dated 9 June 1809*

In my last letter to Captain Martin, No. 6, and in my former letters to Rear-Admiral Sir R. G. Keats, I represented the great difficulties merchants laboured under in not being able to procure licences owing to the difficulty of communication with England. And whereas it is evident that His Majesty's government intends affording every facility and encouragement towards a direct trade with the United Kingdoms, I suggested the idea that probably when my letter was laid before you, sir, as commander-in-chief of His Majesty's fleet in the Baltic, you might deem it for the good of the trade to issue substitute licences.

At this season of the year the produce of Russia and Poland usually comes down in floats; already many barks are arrived with hemp, flax, etc. which the merchants would readily buy up and ship for England, could they speedily be provided with licences. But before they can hope to procure such from England under the existing difficulties, the short season for shipping would elapse. Permit me, therefore, with all due submission, to recommend to your consideration whether it would not be furthering the aims of government if you could furnish me with some kind of substitute licences, which might serve as protections for ships bound to British ports under convoy. I should think there would be the less difficulty in granting such, were it inserted in such substitutes that the skippers or receivers of the cargo are bound to take out a proper licence on their arrival at the port of destination.

Enclosure 1:

78a. *Substitute for Licence*

Whereas it has been represented to me by a person officially connected with His Majesty's government that the trade is obstructed by reason of the want of regular licences and that the [name of ship] of . . . lasts burthen, whereof [name] is master, is laden with [list of cargo] and bound to a port in Great Britain, I do therefore consent to her sailing from the port of [name] and recommend it to the captains and commanders of His Majesty's ships to permit the said vessel to pass unmolested, unless she be found deviating from her course without apparent necessity. The description of the vessel, to which this pass is granted, will be on the back hereof endorsed by Mr. Heinrich Hahn.

The shippers or receivers of the above cargo are bound to take out a proper licence on the arrival of the vessel at the port of destination.

Given under my hand and seal on board His Majesty's ship [name] off [place] the [date] day of [month] 1809.

Enclosure 2:

78b. *Endorsement*

I do hereby certify that the [name of vessel], whereof [name] is master, is of the burden of . . . lasts, rigged as a [description of vessel], was built at [place].

Granted under my signature and seal at Königsberg, this [date] day of [month] 1809.

79. *Nauckhoff to Saumarez*

Stockholm,

16 June 1809.

Your Excellency, I have had the pleasure of receiving the obliging letter dated the 29th. ultimo which you had the goodness to address to me, and I return you my heartfelt thanks for the ardent interest you take with regard to the defence of Sweden against our mutual enemy. The great insincerity of the Russian ministry is apparent, for in the first instant Russia refused to make peace because we did not have a king, and now that we have one, Russia, instead of showing a willingness to negotiate and put an end to hostilities, makes warlike preparations on a big scale with gunboats at Åland and in the Gulf of Bothnia poised to attack the Swedish coasts. If your excellency can arrange for some warships to put in an appearance off the Åland coast, it would, I am sure, deter the Russians from undertaking any attack with their flotillas against the frontiers of Sweden.

I have the honour to send your excellency herewith the diplomas and the medal which the king has bestowed on Mr. Duke for delivery to him. The king's letter is written in Swedish and can be translated by Mr. Ross or Mr. Nordenskjöld. It would afford me a true satisfaction if Mr. Duke is gratified by this mark of distinction and by my appreciation of his meritorious zeal and the tireless service rendered by him to me and to the Swedish squadron.

I cannot thank your excellency enough for the kindness and benevolence always shown by you to my nephew Mr. Nordenskjöld when I once more recommend to you.

My wife is just now in the country. She will be most appreciative of your remembrances. I have etc.

80. *Saumarez to Keats*

Victory, off Carlscrona,

17 June 1809.

My dear Sir Richard, I learnt with the utmost satisfaction, on being joined by the *Phoebe* last Tuesday, that you passed the Belt with your valuable charge without accident or molestation from the Danish flotillas; and yesterday both your obliging letters of the 10th. and 12th. reached me, the latter mentioning that they were all safely housed in Wingo Sound. I hope the winds will have enabled you to sail before this time and that I shall soon have the pleasure to hear of your arrival in England.

I find from Bertie that the convoy under the *Cerebus* and *Alexandria* passed the Sound on the 14th. and that he had ordered the *Africa* to escort them clear of the Malmö Channel. Provided they have the patience to wait for a settled wind, I have no apprehension for their safety. The *Dictator* will have resumed her station in time to add her protection.

Admiral Pickmore[1] joined me yesterday with the *Saturn*. The station in the Belts is become of so great importance that I have decided on Admiral Dixon taking the ships employed there under his command, for which purpose he shifts his flag to the *Ruby*, and will take the convoy the moment the wind will admit their coming out of Carlscrona.

I have received no late communications from the opposite coast, but expect them hourly, the *Rose* being off Pillau and the *Cruizer* with the *Tilsit* off Colberg, the latter to be left for the purpose of carrying messengers etc. that arrive on their way to England.

The Swedes continue most friendly disposed towards us, and I am happy to find they have sent a strong force to the Gulf of Bothnia, equal I trust to keep the Russians in check in that quarter. I shall proceed with the squadron for the Gulf of Finland, and I hope the Russians will afford us an opportunity to attack them. Allow me to assure you of the sincere and unalterable sentiments with which I am etc.

P.S. The *Tartar* returned yesterday from off Rugen but could obtain nothing certain relative to the fate of Col. Schill,[2] but as he had not been found there is reason to believe that he may yet live.

[1] Francis Pickmore, lieutenant, 1777; captain, 1790; rear-admiral, 1808; vice-admiral, 1812; governor and commander-in-chief Newfoundland, 1816–18, the year of his death.
[2] Ferdinand Baptista Schill (1776–1809) was a colonel of hussars in the Prussian army who attempted to launch a military insurrection against French domination in Germany. He was surrounded with his small force at Stralsund and killed in the fighting on 31 May.

81. *Saumarez to Mulgrave*

Victory, Gulf of Finland,

23 June 1809.

My Lord, Baron de Platen,[1] councillor of state, having been directed by the king of Sweden to deliver to me the decoration of Commander Grand Croix of the Order of the Sword, accompanied with a letter from His Swedish Majesty the copy of which I have the honour to enclose, I request your lordship will be pleased to lay the same before the king my gracious sovereign, should His Majesty be most graciously pleased to permit me to avail myself of this mark of distinction. I have etc.

82. *Saumarez to Pole*

Victory, off Landsort,

24 June 1809.

Sir, You will be pleased to inform the Lords Commissioners of the Admiralty that on the 22nd. instant I made sail from off Carlscrona with the squadron as per margin [*St. George, Temeraire, Implacable, Saturn, Rose, Wrangler*], leaving Rear-Admiral Dixon off that port to collect the trade and proceed with them as soon as the wind would permit; and after seeing them in safety thro' the Great Belt to take the command of His Majesty's ships and vessels and remain there for the protection of the trade of His Majesty's subjects, and to prevent any intercourse between Zealand and the Danish islands in the Belt and the coasts contiguous thereto.

I arrived off Landsort this evening, and have sent the *Rose* in with this letter and to bring out any dispatches that Mr. Foster, His Majesty's chargé d'affaires in Stockholm, may have received for me.

You will also please to inform their lordships that I shall proceed without delay to the Gulf of Finland, after being joined by the *Minotaur* and *Bellerophon* with the *Owen Glendower* and *Phoebe* who I had detached to cruise off Dagerort. The only account that has reached me relative to the Russian fleet at Cronstadt has been from an American vessel spoken with by the *Minotaur* on the 16th. instant, stating that four sail-of-the-line with several large frigates were outside of the harbour at Cronstadt, and the rest in a forward state of preparation for sea. I have etc.

[1] Baltzar Bogislaus, Baron, later Count, von Platen (1766–1829) began his career in the navy and was wounded at the battle of Hogland, 1788; retired from the service in 1800 having incurred the displeasure of Gustavus IV. After the revolution he was promoted rear-admiral and appointed a councillor of state. An ardent advocate of union with Norway, he was one of the makers of Swedish policy in 1812.

83. *Extract of a letter from Hahn to Saumarez, dated 27 June 1809*

I am indebted for the lists of convoys you have favoured me with, as also for your goodness in forwarding my packets and letters.

I notice your having taken my representations respecting the want of licences into consideration, and in compliance with my application have transmitted me ten licences to fill up with the names and descriptions of such ships or vessels and masters' names etc. as I may deliver them to, copies whereof to be transmitted you without delay in order to be forwarded to His Majesty's government. To which and all your further instructions relative thereto, beg you will be assured I will pay most particular attention in every respect. Meantime permit me to return most sincere thanks for the facility and encouragement you have thus the goodness to afford for carrying on a direct trade with Great Britain, enabling the merchants to draw a pretty considerable supply of hemp, flax, timber, etc. from these ports. At present there is, unluckily, a great scarcity of ships in these ports, but [I] hope for fresh arrivals by the next convoy.

I observe you were proceeding with the squadron up the Baltic, and that Capt. White of H.M. sloop *Ariel* has directions to transmit my letters to you off Dalarö, and that you recommend sending my letters for England addressed to Mr. Foster, His Majesty's chargé d'affaires at Stockholm.

In respect to the latter, permit me to recommend it to your consideration whether my dispatches to Mr. Secretary Canning could not be more expeditiously forwarded *via* Carlscrona and Gothenburg, particularly should they be of such a nature as to require the most speedy conveyance. By my last respects of the 21st. I took the liberty to enquire if there was not a confidential person at Carlscrona to whom I could transmit my letters to forward to England. I had no good opinion of Mr. Lindegren,[1] he being a Swede, and been so very neglectful that I certainly cannot apply to him. Last autumn Lieutenant Ross, R.N. was left at Carlscrona, from whose zeal and attention I had the most pleasant assurance of my dispatches being punctually forwarded; and he had the goodness to embrace every favourable opportunity to transmit me useful intelligence. I understand the said gentleman has left that station. Probably you may have left some other person there. Permit me to entreat you to have the goodness to attend to my wishes in affording me the means of forwarding my dispatches to His Majesty's government by the shortest route.

---

[1] Hahn's criticism of John Lindegren, a merchant of Ystad who acted as British vice-consul there, was less than fair. He played a part in the maintenance of communications with the continent and also in the profitable business of provisioning the fleet with fresh supplies of beef.

84. *Dixon to Saumarez*

Ruby, Great Belt,

5 July 1809.

Sir, In consequence of the increased strength of the enemy's force in the Belt I consider it a duty incumbent upon me to represent to you for your consideration whether it would not be eligible to strengthen the squadron under my orders with one ship-of-the-line.

Although I may be of opinion that the enemy will not venture an attack upon two ships-of-the-line when anchored for the mutual support of each other, I am desirous of pointing out the necessity I think there is of having two ships-of-the-line which I can occasionally station at anchor to the northward of Sproe Island, about two miles, for the protection of the convoys from England, and two ships-of-the-line at the same distance to the southward of it for the protection of the trade from the Baltic.

As the trade cannot approach from the southward with safety the vicinity of Langeland with one ship-of-the-line only, unless the commander of the convoy can ascertain to a certainty that the ships with me are to the southward of Sproe, and the same respecting the trade from England unless I am to the northward of it; and as it may be very probable that my services may be required to give strength to both convoys at the same time, which has occurred on my entering the Belt, I beg to observe that the same is not likely to be effected with any prospect of security to the trade during the calm months of July and August, unless two ships-of-the-line from me are certain of joining it.

My wish therefore is that I may have four line-of-battle ships placed under my immediate orders, in addition to the two stationed to the northward and southward for the purpose of meeting convoys, being of opinion that the respectable strength in armed boats from four ships-of-the-line, in opposition to the enemy's flotilla force, will be more likely to keep the enemy in check than the line-of-battle ships themselves, as the calms and currents at this season of the year frequently baffle every effort to change their position to advantage. It is impossible to ascertain to any degree of correctness the immediate force of the enemy between Norskow [Naskov] and Nyborg, but on the evening of the 1st. of July 37 gunboats, besides several sloops and other boats, were formed from the N.E. end of Langeland in line. The day before, 14 were counted at Norskow, and at Corsoer 12. I believe the Langeland and Nyborg divisions had united. Whether they intended any joint attack or not, it is impossible to say. However, that evening at 8 o'clock, when they appeared in readiness to make some movement, a breeze sprang up from the S.E. which would have prevented it.

I beg leave to observe to you, which I forgot in my former letter to mention, that Captain Barker[1] of the *Alonzo*, to whose charge and direction I had appointed the armed boats of the squadron in opposition to the enemy's flotilla, conducted the force with much zeal and judgement; and the activity of the officers and men under him was very conspicuous. I have etc.

85. *Saumarez to Foster*

Victory, off Nargen Island,

11 July 1809.

Sir, By the *Mary* cutter which arrived yesterday I received your letters of the 2nd. and 4th. inst. marked *private* and *confidential*; and I return you thanks for the important communication you have been pleased to make to me of the rejection by Russia of the proposed armistice with Sweden, and of the intended plan of the latter to transport a force to Wasa to co-operate with General Wrede, and endeavour to force the Russian troops in West Bothnia [Västerbotten] to capitulate, which I sincerely hope will be attended with the desired success.

I have not seen Baron Platen yet; but, should he put in execution his intention of running to the squadron, I shall readily attend to any proposal he makes to me respecting a small part of the force under my orders being stationed off the Åland Haf, although the services in the Gulf of Finland occupy all the forces I can muster.

I remember to have had the honour of making the Baron's acquaintance, who appeared to me to be a clever and well-informed man. Be pleased to convey to him the information that, should he honour me with a visit, Captain Mansell has my directions to receive him on board, and that I shall be happy to concert with him any measures he may suggest for the defence of Sweden.

You will be happy to hear of the success that has attended a detachment of this fleet under the command of Captain Martin, of the *Implacable*, in an attack on the Russian flotilla, by the boats of that ship, the *Bellerophon*, *Melpomene*, and *Prometheus*, under the orders of Lieutenant Hawkey, who succeeded in boarding and carrying off six gun-boats, besides one sunk, and a convoy of vessels, fourteen in number, which were also captured, laden with stores and provisions for the Russian troops. It is with concern I have now to state the loss of Lieutenant Hawkey,[2] who conducted that attack and

---

[1] Edward C. Barker, lieutenant, 1798; commander, 1805.

[2] Joseph Hawkey was commissioned on 24 March 1807. At the time of his death he was first lieutenant of the *Implacable*.

Lieutenant Stirling[1] of the *Prometheus*, Mr. Mountenay, a midshipman, besides ten men killed and thirty-seven wounded.

The *Implacable* and *Melpomene* had, previously to this, nearly captured a large Russian frigate off Hogland; but she escaped to Aspö, and with four other ships of war, proceeded between the rocks to Frederickshamn. On the following day they captured nine vessels laden with naval stores belonging to the emperor, which they fell in with in Narva Bay.

I anchored here last Sunday in expectation of procuring a supply of wood and water; of the former I found an abundance, which had been ready prepared for the emperor's troops at Revel, but was disappointed in being able to obtain but a small supply of water.

I am in anxious expectation of receiving favourable accounts from the armies. If Napoleon can but be defeated, the cause of Sweden will be materially benefited, and the emperor of Russia kept within proper bounds. I am etc.

86. *Extract of a letter from Hahn to Saumarez, dated 11 July 1809*

My last respects were of the 4th. instant. Yesterday evening I had the honour of receiving your obliging favours of the 30th. ultimo and 6th. instant, for the contents whereof, as also for the newspapers, I am very thankful: particularly for the several copies of the *Courier d'Angleterre* which I send forward different ways.

I am infinitely obliged by the kind care you take in forwarding my dispatches and letters, and that in case of anything important occurring which I wish to communicate to Mr. Canning by the shortest route, you have had the goodness to instruct Capt. White to land them at Carlscrona.

I am curious to know the intent of Baron Stedingk's[2] mission and whether the Swedes will eventually shut their ports against the British. I have no good opinion of them.

It was ever my decided opinion that the Russian ports should have been strictly blockaded last year.[3] The dissatisfaction in the country was very great upon the prospect of not having any trade; and if they had not been allowed any, I am convinced the government must have changed their system, and then there would have been a free trade this year. It was,

[1] James Stirling.
[2] Curt Bogislaus Ludvig Christoffer, Count von Stedingk (1746–1837) brother of Victor von Stedingk, was a native of Swedish Pomerania. He was Swedish ambassador to the court of St. Petersburg 1790–1808 and plenipotentiary at the negotiations leading to the peace of Frederikshamn in September 1809, which is the mission alluded to by Hahn.
[3] The policy of strict blockade as the most efficacious means of forcing the Russians to change their system was constantly urged by discontented merchants and shipowners in Britain, whose arguments were in part akin to those of Hahn.

however, certainly expected the ports would have been blockaded and other vigorous measures recurred to this year. People said that last year it was the intention of the British government to show the Russians they might have trade [in] spite of the French decrees and their government; but, as this leniency had not produced the good effect expected from it, this year it was supposed most vigorous measures would be pursued against their ports, and particularly when we heard of the great armament preparing for the Baltic.

The Russians are not the only nation undeserving the generosity shown them. Instead of being thankful for the protection afforded their ships, they consider it as due to them and that the English cannot do without them. I had lately occasion to speak very boldly and warmly on this subject, on complaints being made to me in rather a rude way that the English cruisers had taken a vessel bound from Stettin to Pillau, on board of which were some private effects belonging to people in office.

I opened the letter directed to Messrs. Schröder & Co. in Colberg, expecting, as it proved, to be only a cover to one for Her Highness the princess of Orange, which I sent forward by messenger going off this morning; and shall apologize to Messrs. S. & Co. for what I have done on sending them the cover. The other letter shall also be forwarded by a safe conveyance. I shall also write to the princess of Orange at the imperial headquarters to advise her son's[1] safe arrival in England.

87. *Puke to Saumarez*

Adolf Frederick, off Tjorkö,

2 Aug. 1809.

Sir, I do myself the honour to inform your excellency that His Swedish Majesty has most graciously been pleased to entrust me the command of his sea and land forces who are to act in the coasts and in the Gulf of Bothnia against the common enemy to our respective nations; and I beg to assure your excellency that nothing can afford me more pleasure than receiving your commands if ever I can be of the smallest use to your excellency.

I submit to your excellency's own judgement if it should not be useful to the common service to have respective officers who are acquainted with the language placed a side of the commanders-in-chief. For my part I should find it very agreeable if Lieut. John Ross, who served last year on board the Swedish admiral's ship, would be permitted to resume the same employment

---

[1] William Frederick, prince of Orange (1772–1843), the son of William V last stadtholder of the Dutch republic, commanded the Dutch army in the campaigns of 1793–95; served later against France in the Prussian and Austrian armies; went to Britain after the French entry into Vienna, 1809; first ruler of the kingdom of the Netherlands established in 1815 with the title of William I.

on board of this. He is so well acquainted with the Swedish language and customs that I flatter myself he would have no objection to this proposition.

If winds permit I intend to depart tomorrow with 2 ships-of-the line, one frigate, 6 galleys, 50 gunboats and some transports carrying 7,000 troops and proceeding in the gulf in order to debarque the troops on a proper place so that they might fall in the back and destroy the enemy's troops who at present occupy the province of Wester Bothnia. Vice-Admiral Baron Cederström will remain with 100 gunboats and some galleys to protect the Swedish coasts opposite Åland. The *Camilla* frigate are left cruising in the Ålands Haf to act in conjunction with the British force stationed there by the orders of your excellency.

I should think it very useful for the service we are upon if a British frigate and some sloops of war could be stationed at Kökas in order to prevent the enemy from sending any reinforcement to Åland and also if your excellency should proceed farther up the Gulf of Finland with the British squadron and make such demonstrations as would contribute to keep the enemy in uncertainty of an attack on either of the coast in the gulf, he would thereby be obliged to disperse his forces which in the present case would be of greatest utility for the service. I submit all this to your excellency's invaluable judgement and have etc.

88. *Mulgrave to Saumarez*

Admiralty,

3 Aug. 1809.

My dear Sir, By this opportunity you will receive the expression of the high admiration with which the board of admiralty is impressed by the heroic attack in Porkala Sound. When the action was reported to the king, His Majesty expressed in the strongest terms his gracious approbation and applause, adding at the same time that 'His Majesty laments the loss of so distinguished an officer as Lieutenant Hawkey and of the other valuable men who fell with him upon this occasion'. The feelings of the whole nation must accord with those of His Majesty.

A commission of commander has been made out for Lieutenant Charles Allen[1] and Lieutenants Sheridan,[2] Skekel[3] and Rennie[4] who have served

---

[1] Charles Allen, the son of William Allen commissioner of Greenwich Hospital, lieutenant, 1799; commander, 1809; retired captain, 1840.

[2] John Sheridan, lieutenant, 1801; commander, 1810; captain 1815; retired, 1846.

[3] John Skekel, lieutenant, 1804; commander, 1811; captain, 1825; retired, 1846.

[4] George Rennie, was said to be a nephew of the famous engineer John Rennie. He was appointed lieutenant in 1807; commander, 1811; captain, 1814. He was dismissed the service in 1821 having been found guilty of inflicting irregular punishments on the crew of H.M.S. *Tees*, but was reinstated in his former rank in 1822.

the regular period. I shall give recommendations for promotion to the stations on which they will be most likely to obtain early advancement; and, in the interim, I request you to be so good as to add them to the list of those who are to be placed in vacancies that may arise in the Baltic. The merits of Lieutenants Houghton[1] and Vernon[2] are noted, and will not (as indeed they cannot) be forgotten. I am etc.

89. *Platen to Saumarez*

Stockholm,
4 Aug. 1809.

Sir, It is with great pleasure that I have the honour to return my best thanks to your excellence for all the numberless civilitys bestowed on me under my last visite.

It would be vanity to relate it to me personely, I can only account for it by serving the king and country your excellence so powerfull protects for wich His Majesty has ordered me to express his highest gratitude wich he wishes to have the pleasure personaly to express to your excellence.

As for the operations in the common cause as well as for some other small business I have written to Capten Hope to whom I send several charts and draughts. I hope he will make out what I mean tho' I cannot express my ideas as I wished in an foreign language.

Part of the expeditions to the north is already under way and the rest will tomorrow sett of under the command of Admiral Puke. May the Almighty crown the undertaking with success and soon send them back again. Perhaps something might be effected before bad weather puts a stop to operations with the small fleet. Till now every event seems favourable to the expedition, and the knowledge of the chiefs makes me confident that what is possible will be done. How much shall Sweden be indebted to your excellence for having so powerfully promoted the business by combined measures.

Ever I shall be glad for the opportunity it gives me to assure your excellence of the high estime where with I am etc.

P.S. It is by the order of His Majesty that I have the honour to announce your excellence Lieut. Ross being created a knight of the Order of the Sword on the particular request of the Admiral Puke.

---

[1] William Houghton was a lieutenant of 20 Nov. 1807. He received no further promotion.

[2] Frederick Edward Venables Vernon, a son of the Hon. Edward Venables Vernon, archbishop of York, entered the navy in 1803 and was commissioned in 1809, being appointed a lieutenant of the *Implacable* on 29 April. He was promoted commander in 1811; captain in 1814.

90. *Saumarez to Platen*

Victory, Gulf of Finland,

12 Aug. 1809.

Sir, With the greatest pleasure I have received the letter your excellency has done me the honour to write, and I have to express my sincerest regret at not having been able to enjoy for a longer time your valuable company on board the *Victory*; but when I considered how precious every hour must be to your excellency at this important epoch, I could not prevail upon myself to offer the least delay to your departure, however happy it would have made me to postpone it for some days longer.

I hope soon to have the satisfaction to be informed that the expedition has been crowned with the most complete success; and should the proposed enterprize against Åland be adopted, I trust to be able to reinforce the detachment under the orders of Captain Reynolds[1] and contribute, as far as my means will admit, to an expedition that has the security of Sweden for its object.

I return you my sincere thanks for the charts you have been pleased to send to Captain Hope, and for the attention your excellency has bestowed on the welfare of the squadron in directing that the ships may be supplied with fresh provisions from the island of Gotland should they require it.

The unremitted marks of friendship and regard shown to the fleet under my command in the different ports of Sweden have excited my highest gratitude, and I have not failed to express the same to my government.

I shall take the earliest opportunity to signify to Mr. Ross, who is at this time absent from the squadron on a particular service, the distinguished mark of favour His Majesty the king of Sweden has been pleased to confer upon him for his services. I have etc.

91. *Mulgrave to Saumarez*

Admiralty,

22 Aug. 1809.

Sir, I have the honour to acknowledge the receipt of your letter of the 23rd of June communicating to me the offer which had been made to you of the Swedish Order of the Sword. It has not yet been possible for me to take His Majesty's pleasure upon the desire which you have expressed to receive His Majesty's gracious permission to wear the insignia of the Swedish order. I have etc.

[1] George Reynolds, commander of the *Tribune* (36); lieutenant, 1790; captain, 1802.

92. *Mulgrave to Saumarez*

Admiralty,

22 Aug. 1809.

My dear Sir, I have sent you an official answer to your application for His Majesty's permission to wear the Sw. dish Order of the Sword, and I will write this private and secret letter to inform you of the grounds on which it has been necessary to send you that letter. Various and important reasons of state have rendered it necessary to delay acknowledging formally the Duke of Sudermania in the character of king of Sweden. It has on the other hand been, very naturally, the policy of the existing government in Sweden to obtain as immediately as possible the direct or virtual recognition of the present order of things in that country. The act of conferring an order of knighthood is a distinct and pure act of sovereignty unmixed with any consideration of public necessity or political expediency. Consequently the sanction of His Majesty to the exercise of such an act of sovereignty on the person of one of his subjects would be on the part of His Majesty a virtual admission of the competence of the authority in the name of which this distribution of honours should be made. It is most probable that from this view of the subject in Sweden, the offer to you of the Swedish ribband has originated. The Swedish chargé d'affaires in this country[1] is aware of the very delicate situation into which this measure has brought the Swedish government. He is therefore very desirous that the question should not be stirred; and it will be desirable that you should not enter into any explanation on the subject, nor indeed open the question at all, unless you should be addressed upon it by the Swedish government in which case my public letter to you would furnish a sufficient answer on your part. I am etc.

93. *Platen to Saumarez*

Stockholm,

23 Aug. 1809.

Sir, It was with great pleasure I received your excellence's kind letter of the 12 Aug. wherein I find new marks of the benevolence your excellency always has shown to this country, as well as the friendship against me who in various occasions has been so active, a particular instance whereof certainly was the commodious and pleasant manner in which I was brought over and back again by so polite a man as Captain Mansell, in the same time that his abilities and the skillful management of his vessel made the voyage so interest-

[1] Carl Gustaf von Brinkman, late Swedish ambassador to Britain.

ing to me. Only absolute necessity could bring me to the privation I feelt by
so soon leaving your excellency; but this is too often the case at sea, and is
realy to be reckoned one of the hardships of seamans.

Our expedition up the Gulf of Botnia arrived the 13 Aug. at Härnosänd
and set of in the best ordre and high spirits the 14 and 15 with a fair wind,
without till then having sustained a single loose or accident, and no more
than seven sick on the whole armament. The days before the Russians had
declared the armistice to be ended and an attack was to be expected the 13
but took not place. The admiral was willing to debarque at Ratan to the
north of Umeå where, with a good wind, he hoped to be at there back in 30
or 40 hours, if they have not already been retreating, which may have
obliged him to go as far as up at Piteå. These are the last news we have had
from that quarter, and we expect now to hear something every moment.
May it please the Almighty to give success to the enterprise, and it would
certainly highly contribute to the welfare of this country. An other point of
the highest consequence is certainly Åland, the island being in all points of
view of the greatest weight to Sweden and particularly if, we are obliged, as
may be the case, to renounce the possession of Finlandia by a peace. Therefore, whatever steeps, who can bring us to the possession of this spot, are
capital to us in the present moment when we are negociating for peace. This
is the reason why by the autorisation of His Majesty I have the honour once
more to request your excellency to by all possible means co-operate for the
purpose in the way an plan I had the honour to communicate in my last to
Captain Hope. The entrance of Kökar is certainly deep and safe for the
largest ships, and a squadron of consequence and strength at that place, with
some smaller vessels threatening to advance further to the common inward
way, on the line I have marked out, would highly distract the Russians from
other quarters of the island where our attacks would be performed.

As the English government almost in every dispatch requests Sweden to
come to an accomodation with our enemies, and as a very capital tar and
wood trade is carried on upon both shores of the Gulf of Botnia, I should
think it of an high interest to England not to enable Russia by the possession
of Åland to shut up this gulf. An officer, who knows very well the entrance
of Kökar and who at the place will find out pilots, will be sent to your excellence as soon as I hear the northern expedition succeed, as I am confident that
the only appearance of an English squadron in those quarters, who are a
principal point of contest, would give more weight to the negociation than
any other blockade in the Gulf of Finlandia. Could the retirement of the
English fleet from the inner part of the gulf induce the Russian fleet to come
out I should be very glad of it.

Your excellence will excuse if there is anything incorrect or not well expressed in my letter. My making use of a foreign language, I hope, will induce your usual kindness to make amendments for it.

Just at this moment a report from the Admiral Puke is arrived and in a particular letter he marks that having set of on the 15 he passed along the coast of Finland having twelve gunboats in tow of each line of battle ship and a frigate; and, without being observed every object being covered by a dreadful fog, under which he the sixteenth stod into the shore at Ratan, without having a man on bord who had ever been there, and came to an anchor so close to the shore that his last gunboat was between the breakers while at anchor; all without being detected. At 4 in the morning the 17 the coast was perceived and instantly the troops were landed without opposition, a guard of about 100 men instantly leaving the field. Against all what I dared expect he has effected the whole landing without the lose, as he tells me, of an single oar and without the enemys knowing the least of the matter, tho' absolutely acting, except a very small corps who is to the north, for which reason he was sending a division of gunboats to Piteå. Every instant I wait anxiously for decisif news from those quarters an the admiral tells me that if heaven protects his enterprise he will make another attempt at Wasa before coming down again. I hope that under so brave commanders the Swedish name will once more be vindicated from what it has suffered in the eyes of the world under the direction of a fool!!

In particularly once more recommending the plan for Åland to the consideration of your excellency I have etc.

94. *Saumarez to Mulgrave*

Victory, Gulf of Finland,

28 Aug. 1809.

My dear Lord, I had the honour to receive your lordship's letter yesterday and I am exceedingly happy at the favourable manner His Majesty has been graciously pleased to consider the attack of the Russian flotilla in Porkala Sound. I have communicated to Lieutenant Allen and to the other officers employed upon that service the distinguished manner in which their gallantry has been appreciated by your lordship and of your intention to recommend Lieutenants Sheridan, Skekel and Rennie for promotion to the stations on which they will be most likely to obtain early advancement. In the meantime I shall comply with your lordship's desire to add them to the list of officers who are to be placed in vacancies that may arise in the Baltic.

Within the last few days the troops that were encamped in the vicinity of Revel have been removed, and, it is reported, are on their way to Poland where it is understood a large body of Russian troops has been ordered in consequence of the proceedings of Bonaparte in that country.

The embargo on all Russian vessels still continues, but I am happy to find the trade under neutral colours is permitted to proceed as usual. I have etc.

95. *Foster to Saumarez*

Stockholm,
7 Sept. 1809.

Sir, Your private letter of the 5th. inst. has reached me with extraordinary dispatch. By this time you will, I trust, have had mine of the 2nd.; and I have nothing to add to the statement I then made to you of the appearance of affairs in Sweden, except that an armistice has been offered by General Kamenski,[1] which will probably be accepted. Platen is in great despondency, and says he never will be sanguine about anything again. The generals have certainly not done as they might. As far as the council and the navy were concerned, all was well combined, but the army was ill-posted, and Wachtmeister[2] has shown that he has but a very poor head. Unless the Russians are disposed to change sides, the negotiation at Frederickshamn is not likely to be benefited by these events. You must calculate on this country yielding, if the ministers are pressed strongly, to the terms demanded. I see no means they have of resisting. It is a mutilated land, and the resources that remain are ill-managed, while the debt is rapidly increasing.

Baron de Platen desires me to say he will send you the plan you demanded of St. Petersburg by the next opportunity; it is copying, and not quite ready. I have the honour to send to you a couple of the last French papers. Lieut. Allen delivered to me your letter, and I shall endeavour to get him a seat in the messengers' carriage to-morrow night.

I should be glad to know when you think of quitting the gulf with the fleet, and how soon the navigation becomes dangerous. If an armistice between the hostile armies in West Bothnia takes place, in all probability the squadron in Åland's Haf will be no longer necessary there. I have etc.

---

[1] Lieutenant-General Nicolas Mikhailovitch Kamenski, whose professional abilities were highly rated by his opponents, was given command on 13 July of the Russian army corps which had since the spring advanced from Uleåborg into Västerbotten. He arrived at Umeå at the end of the month with orders to drive southwards and force the Swedes to an early peace. The Swedish expedition to Västerbotten was designed to halt his progress by establishing a threat to the rear of the Russian army.

[2] Gustaf, Count Wachtmeister (1757–1826) entered the army, 1770; lieutenant, 1776; major, 1780; major-general, 1790; general, 1809 when he assumed command of the army on the Västerbotten expedition; for the failure of which his indecisiveness was in part responsible; retired, 1813.

96. *Saumarez to Foster*

Victory, Gulf of Finland,

8 Sept. 1809.

Sir, I had the honour to receive yesterday your letter of the 2nd. inst., and I am truly concerned to find the success of the Swedish expedition has been so very inadequate to what was reasonably to have been expected, and that the delay in endeavouring to cut off the retreat of the Russian troops will render it too late to make the intended attack upon Åland. The terms persisted in by Russia appear to be very severe; but I apprehend Sweden will be obliged to make the most of them from the slender means she has of defending herself during the winter months, when the country will be exposed to danger of an invasion. It is a fortunate circumstance that the navigation has been so long protracted as to enable the trade to proceed hitherto out of the Baltic, and as considerable delay must still take place before the peace can be ratified, it will afford sufficient time for the ships that are loading in the Russian ports to assemble at Carlscrona before the exclusion can be enforced. The period agreed upon for the last convoy to sail from Carlscrona was fixed to the 15th Nov., till which time, at least, we must hope the ports will be open both to ships of war and the trade. Should you think it advisable, it might be mentioned to the Swedish minister that if the stipulation of exclusion is absolutely insisted upon, that it is hoped that it will not be put in force till the winter is too far advanced to admit any ships sailing from the ports of Russia.

It will be proper to know from Baron Engeström[1] if the notice that was signified in the spring, of not allowing more than five or six pendants at a time at Carlscrona or other ports in Sweden, is insisted upon at present, in order that I may regulate myself accordingly. At the same time, as tempestuous weather in going down the Baltic, or other circumstances, may render it advisable for the whole squadron to enter Carlscrona, I would wish orders to be given for that purpose, and that the pilots may be directed to go out to ships making the signal. I shall be obliged to you to let me know by the return of this vessel the determination of the Swedish government upon this point.

It is my wish to remain in the Gulf of Finland as long as is possible, consistent with the safety of his Majesty's ships; but as the equinoctial gales may soon be expected, and as it will become indispensable to withdraw the ships, particularly those stationed in Makelato Bay, I could wish to be informed

---

[1] Lars, Baron, later Count, von Engeström (1751–1826) held posts in the Swedish diplomatic service in Vienna, Warsaw, London and Berlin, 1782–1803. In 1809, after six years of unemployment because of his pro-French sympathies, he succeeded Ehrenheim as president of the chancellery with responsibility for foreign affairs. His influence waned following the election of Bernadotte, but he remained in public life until 1824.

whether it becomes of importance to Sweden for the squadron to remain in this sea any longer, and which I also request you will let me know, by the return of the vessel that conveys this, with as little delay as possible. I forward some papers I yesterday received from Pillau; you will find the armistice[1] has been prolonged for a fortnight with fourteen days' warning, but it was expected hostilities would re-commence the middle of the present month.

I sincerely congratulate you upon the surrender of Flushing. I hope we shall soon hear that the other objects of the expedition[2] have been accomplished, particularly as far as regards the capture or destruction of the enemy's ships in the Scheldt. I delivered to Captain Ross the Cross of the Order of the Sword, which was enclosed to me by Count de Mörner.[3] He will be happy to avail himself of this signal mark of distinction, on receiving His Majesty's gracious permission. Permit me to request your having the goodness to forward the enclosed to Count Mörner. I have etc.

97. *Extract of a letter from Hahn to Saumarez, dated 14 Sept. 1809*

Late last night I had the honour to receive your much esteemed favour of the 8th. instant and beg leave to return sincerest thanks for your obliging communications and for the newspapers.

The information given by the masters of vessels from St. Petersburg and Revel, I am sorry to say is not confirmed by the accounts received here, they, on the contrary, not giving any hopes of a change of system in Russia.

I am sorry that the Swedish expedition has not answered the expectation formed of it. It is generally supposed here likewise that the Swedes will make peace with Russia. It is not probable that Sweden will regain Finland by force of arms or that Russia will restore it voluntarily. Perhaps if the possession was secured to Russia and Sweden received an equivalent elsewhere, matters might be arranged to the satisfaction of both; and Russia might then listen to what it will probably not now attend to, if the restoration of Finland is to be a condition. Should a change in the politics of Sweden occasion any alteration in respect to the convoys, I request you will have the goodness to give me timely notice thereof.

I am particularly grateful for your obliging care in forwarding my dispatches and private letters. Permit me again to recur to your goodness in forwarding the enclosed.

---

[1] A reference to the Franco-Austrian armistice agreed upon after the battle of Wagram fought on 5 July. Austria acknowledged defeat by the treaty of Schönbrunn, 5 Oct. 1809.
[2] The results of the Walcheren expedition disappointed the hopes entertained by Saumarez.
[3] Gustaf, Count Mörner was privy chamberlain to the king of Sweden.

According to letters from Danzig General Bertrand[1] has not yet arrived there, but was still expected. And it is said the fortifications of that place are to be demolished, which causes many surmises as the French have laid out so much money upon them. Perhaps they have not sufficient spare troops to garrison it and fear it falling into other hands.

We hope soon to hear of the success of the expedition you advised having detached against the Eartholms,[2] as the possession of these is considered of moment. For should P[russia] join against the French and again be unfortunate, where could the r[oyal] f[amily] fly to? They would be greatly averse to take refuge in R[ussia].

98. *Platen to Saumarez*

Stockholm,
22 Sept. 1809.

Sir, At the conclusion of the peace, hard as it is, we cannot yet deny that in an high degree we are indebted to you for our existing as a state.[3] I therefore anew congratulate myself on our personal acquaintance as it enables me to express to you my thankfulness, confident as I am that these are the feelings of the whole nation. Hard is the separation from Finland, but it was of course a necessity. For the rest, the king and the election of the prince of Augustenburg is recognized.[4] Denmark is no way included in the peace except well wishes, the common fate of small allies and a slender consolation to be not absolutely the meanest.

As for the continental system, it is easily to be seen by the treaty that the Russian interest is not alike with the French and that it is mentioned only because it ought to be so. For the first moment I am authorized to say that no

[1] Henri Gratien Bertrand (1773–1844) accompanied Napoleon to Egypt; promoted general, 1800; after serving with distinction in the campaigns of 1806–07 was created a count of the empire; governor of the Illyrian provinces, 1811; followed Napoleon to St. Helena; returned to France, 1821.
[2] Intelligence of a mutiny amongst the garrison of the Eartholms prompted Saumarez to order a bombardment by two ships-of-the-line and three bomb vessels, the results of which confirmed the general opinion of naval officers that the place could not be reduced without the aid of an army.
[3] The treaty of Frederikshamn, signed on 17 Sept., registered the cession to Russia of Finland, the Åland Islands and a strip of territory in the far north and made formal provision for the adherence of Sweden to the continental system with certain reservations concerning the import of salt and colonial produce, the confirmation of which was made conditional upon the agreement thereto of France and Denmark.
[4] Christian August, duke of Augustenborg (1768–1810) was Danish commander-in-chief and governor of Norway, 1807–09. His defensive policy, the product of pan-Scandinavian sentiments, recommended him to those Swedes, including Adlersparre and his followers, who sought a union between Sweden and Norway. He was elected crown prince of Sweden and made an adopted son of the childless Charles XIII, entering upon his duties immediately after the signing of the peace of Jonköping between Sweden and Denmark, Dec. 1809; died suddenly at a military review in Scania, 28 May 1810.

alteration will take place in what was before mentioned to Mr. Foster, and he probably will have advertised of. Our ports are open to so brave an ally, to so successful a protector, for so many sails as your excellency judges fit to send in into them for the remaining of the harvest, confident that a man as Sir James is incapable to make other than proper and amical use of it; and the treaty, as far as I now conceive, is no hinderness for it for this whole year. Should in time it prove different proper communication will be made in very convenient manner at a due period.

If your excellence should wish for any refreshments at Gotland, such as may be had there of sheeps and greens, proper steps are taken by the governor. The best way might be to send a small vessel with an advertisement, and then a little after let the fleet proceed to Östergam and Katthammars vicken. I am confident the governor Baron Rajalin will make his outmost for to by all possible means assist.

Your excellence will pardon my incorrect letter for the sake of the hurry I am under for not to lose the opportunity with the sending of a vessel this night affords me for to repeat the feelings of constant gratitude and high estime wherewith I always shall have etc.

99. *Pole to Emes, Möller and Emes*

Admiralty Office,

29 Sept. 1809.

Gentlemen, I am commanded by my Lords Commissioners of the Admiralty to request that you will call the attention of the merchants trading to the Baltic to the arrangement made at the commencement of the season with their concurrence respecting convoys and that you will remind all those concerned in the trade that the latest period fixed for the sailing of the outward bound convoys to the Baltic from the ports of Great Britain is the 15th. October.

Referring to the many losses and inconveniences which occurred last season in consequence of ships sailing contrary to the advice of the admiralty at a very late period by which not only the trade suffered severely, but several of His Majesty's ships were wrecked and many exposed to the most imminent peril, my lords have commanded me thus early to desire you will apprize the merchants that the engagements made for the protection of the Baltic trade (approved of on the part of the merchants by your letter to me of the 16th. March last) will be adhered to with the utmost exactness, and that no outward bound convoys will under any circumstances be granted after the 15th. of October.

I am further directed by their lordships to remind you that, by the arrangements already alluded to, the last homeward bound Baltic convoy is to leave
Carlscrona for England on the 15th. November, and I am to request that
you will inform the merchants that it is their lordships' intention to adhere
strictly to this regulation, and that they have given orders to Sir James
Saumarez, commanding His Majesty's ships in the Baltic, to make his
arrangements accordingly, and on no account to suffer the last convoy to be
detained longer at Carlscrona than the 15th. November.

In making the present communication to you for the information of those
concerned in the Baltic trade, my Lords Commissioners of the Admiralty
have commanded me to explain that it is not from any apprehension that
you are not already aware of the necessity of adhering to the arrangements
made after due deliberation for the protection of the Baltic trade, that they
have thought it proper thus to call your attention to the subject, but in order
that the very extensive body who are concerned in the ships employed in this
important branch of our commerce should be apprized in time of the great
danger to which they must be exposed if they do not rigidly adhere to the
plan agreed upon for their protection. I am etc.

100. *Saumarez to Hahn*

Victory, Carlscrona,

9 Oct. 1809.

Sir, By the *Ariel* which joined me here two days since I had the honour to
receive your letters of the 21st and 26th. ult. the former enclosing one from
Baron Wessenberg[1] and also a translation of the general orders issued out by
the Emperor Francis on opening the negotiations at Altenberg. I am as yet
uninformed whether hostilities have been renewed, but the intelligence
brought here from Colberg states that they were expected to recommence on
the 5th. instant. We must hope therefore that every possible success should
attend the Austrian army in the grand and great cause, and in which they are
so nobly supported by the brave Tyroleans.

With respect to the enquiry you make whether any quantity of arms and
ammunition could be supplied by the fleet under my command, particularly
gunpowder, I beg to acquaint you that a considerable supply of the latter
could be spared from the different ships, but I should not consider myself at
liberty to order such a supply without receiving instructions from govern-

---

[1] Johann Philipp, Baron von Wessenberg-Ampringen (1773–1858) was a distinguished
Austrian diplomat, strongly attached to the anti-French cause. During his residence at the
court of Berlin from Feb. 1809 to Nov. 1810 he was in continuous contact with British
agents and served as an intermediary between the Austrian and British governments.

ment for that purpose, except in case of Prussia being engaged in actual hostility against France. I request you will be pleased to inform me whether you think such application will be made in order that I may leave instructions upon that subject with the senior officer at Carlscrona on my quitting the port. It is much to be desired that the trade should be hastened as much as possible that they may arrive at Carlscrona the beginning of November. The time limited for the admission of ships-of-war in the Swedish ports, Mr. Foster informs me, is fixed to the 12 of next month.

I have great satisfaction in informing you that the convoy, which had been detained here by contrary winds, sailed on the morning of the 6th. (last Tuesday), consisting of 240 sail and was joined by 40 others off the port from Stockholm. They are escorted by two line-of-battle ships and four smaller vessels to England.

Convoys will be provided as fast as the trade assemble here till after the 15th. of next month and as the wind is so favourable I hope it will bring all the ships from Riga and the other ports. The transports that conveyed the Russian seamen to Riga are now off this port on their return to England.

I omitted to mention in my last letter that I have had cruisers on the coast of Pomerania in consequence of the information that the enemy had fitted out privateers at Stralsund.

101. *Extract of a letter from Hahn to Saumarez, dated 30 Oct. 1809*

Last Saturday I had the honour to receive your very obliging favours of the 23rd. and 25th. instant by the *Tartarus,* for which, as also for the accompanying papers, permit me to return sincerest thanks, feeling much obliged by your kind attention and favour.

I duly notice the contents of your letters particularly what relates to the sailing of the convoys, and that the last still remains fixed for the 15th. November. It has, however, been represented to me that it will be impossible for a number of ships, now in these ports, to be ready laden in time to join the last convoy so appointed and fixed; and I have been requested to apply to you on this subject. Permit me therefore to recommend this to your consideration and to request that, if possible, you will have the goodness to extend the period of the departure of the last convoy either to the 30th. November or 1st. December.

There are now about 50 vessels at Memel. The greater part may be able to sail thence next week. 10 or 15 of them may be ready by the 15th. only, but several cannot be ready till a week later as they are now loading new flax seed for sowing, destined for Ireland where it is much wanted, and can only be drawn hence late in the autumn and should arrive at its place of destination this year. Now, unless you have the goodness to leave a ship-of-war or two to protect these vessels, they run the risk of wintering in Sweden, and in all probability could not afterwards arrive early enough next spring in Ireland for sowing the seed, which would not only occasion great loss to the merchants, but also be a very great disappointment to the growers of flax in that country.

At Pillau there are also several vessels now loading, and about to load, valuable cargoes for the British markets with which they cannot be ready in time for the convoy of the 15th. Nov. At Libau there are also several in the same situation. From Riga I have not yet got the returns, but from what I can learn, I presume there are about 100 sail of vessels that could not be ready in time to join the last convoy of 15th. Nov. At St. Petersburg (Cronstadt) several large vessels are loading valuable cargoes. By what Mr. Foster writes me, I conclude there were several ships in the Swedish ports which would not be ready by the 15th. Nov., and therefore he has probably also solicited a later convoy.

I flatter myself on considering the immense property invested in [the] said ships and cargoes which will want protection, you will have the goodness to appoint another convoy as late as possible, and acquaint me with the period you are pleased to fix. As the convoys of this year proceed by the passage of the Belt, those disasters and losses which befell His Majesty's ships last year by going thro' the Sound cannot recur.

102. *Extract of a letter from Hahn to Saumarez, dated 6 Nov. 1809*

Just after I had sent off my last respects of the 2nd. instant, I had the honour to receive your obliging favour of the 30th. ult. by the *Alban* cutter to which [I] pay due attention, and am particularly glad to notice that you will have the goodness to extend the period of the sailing of the last convoy from Carlscrona to the first of December. This information has given the greatest satisfaction to those concerned here and at all the ports. At Riga it will be particularly pleasant as so many vessels are still detained there. My correspondent informs me under date of 28 Oct. that there were at that time 143 vessels which had not yet got permission to discharge and load again. All of these cannot possibly be at the place of rendezvous even by the 1st. Dec., and they will be at a loss, if they arrive after the appointed time, where to take shelter for the winter. Perhaps you would have the goodness to point out the place either for that, or where to go if they arrived off Carlscrona a day or two only after the convoy was gone.

103. *Saumarez to Hahn*

Victory, Hawke Road, off Gothenburg,

14. Nov. 1809.

Sir, I have had the honour to receive this morning your letters from the 30th. October to the 6th. inst. which have been forwarded to me from Carlscrona by Rear-Admiral Pickmore who has also enclosed under cover to Mr. Consul Smith the two letters addressed to Lord Bathurst.[1]

It affords me the greatest satisfaction to find that the measure I adopted for protecting the sailing of the last convoy from the Baltic is likely to be attended with such beneficial effect to the commercial interest of the country. Permit me to assure you that was it in my power to fix even a later period than the first of December I would most readily avail myself of it; but the great delays that must be expected at so late a season for convoys passing thro' the Belt, where a strong protecting force of line-of-battle ships must remain stationed for the latest convoys, the different winds required through the different passages and the inevitable necessity of coming to anchor during the long nights, added to other serious impediments, may make it six weeks or even a longer time before a convoy can get through so intricate a channel unless particularly favoured by wind and weather. The convoy that sailed from Carlscrona three weeks since under the charge of the *Bellerophon* was only enabled to clear the Belt yesterday, and has been obliged to take shelter in Hawke and Flemish roads from contrary winds. Another numerous convoy that sailed on the 4th. under the protection of the *Edgar* remains in some part of the Belt and most probably very insecure from tempestuous weather. All these circumstances makes me most seriously apprehensive for the safety of the remaining convoys should they be retarded in their sailing by any continuance of adverse and contrary winds.

With regard to the information you require, of what would be the most proper place for ships to take shelter in during the winter that may arrive too late for the last convoy, I can point out no other than Carlscrona; but under the existing circumstances, and also taking in view the late treaty of peace concluded between Russia and Sweden, it is very uncertain how far it may be secure for the trade to resort to that port after the squadron have left the Baltic, unless they can depend upon the papers and other documents that have enabled them to clear from the ports in Russia or the other ports in the Baltic.

You will observe, sir, that the security of the trade will chiefly depend upon their own exertions in order to be in time to take benefit of the last convoy

[1] Henry Bathurst, 3rd Earl Bathurst, was secretary of state for foreign affairs, 11 Oct.–6 Dec. 1809.

appointed for their protection; but the safety of His Majesty's ships, as well as that of such ships and vessels as may be in time to sail with the convoy must not be hazarded by waiting for those that have been delayed beyond the time appointed.

I beg you to accept my thanks for the communication of the events that have taken place in consequence of the late lamented treaty that has been concluded. Happy will it be for Prussia if the tyrant will permit her to rest tranquil without taking his vengeance for any supposed aggression he may impute to her; but it is scarcely to be expected from his insatiable disposition.

I take the opportunity of sending to you my latest papers. You will view with exultation the patriotic loyalty and zeal displayed by all ranks of people in the commemoration of the fiftieth year of our gracious and revered sovereign's accession to the throne.

I shall desire the communication to be kept up as long as possible, but Colberg, as you have very properly pointed out, will be better adapted, and thro' means of Mr. E. F. Schröder at that place the intercourse may be kept up till the squadron sails from the Baltic.

I shall use my best endeavours respecting the two detained vessels, but I am concerned to say that it is without any great hopes of success, the *Erebus* being at this time absent, and no expectation of her joining before my return to England.

With my sincere and fervent wishes for your health and every happiness.

104. *Foster to Saumarez*

Stockholm,
14 Nov. 1809.

Sir, I have had the honour to receive this day your excellency's letter dated Wingo Sound on the 7th. instant. My letters subsequent to the 27th. ult. will have informed you of the disposition of this court towards Great Britain.

In answer to that part of your letter in which your excellency expresses that you are induced to hope that the trade would be admitted into any of the ports of Sweden until the latest part of the season, I beg to refer you to my letter of the 1st. October in which, in consequence of the communication of the Swedish government to me, I had the honour to inform you that the 12th. instant was fixed upon for putting into execution the stipulation imposed by Russia upon Sweden regarding British ships. It has since been removed, as you know, to the 15th. inst.; but I am assured that there will be indirectly every kind of facility afforded to the trade and that the mere hoisting a Swedish or neutral flag will be sufficient to ensure the merchantships the entry of the ports; and ships-of-war will be received singly if they declare themselves in distress.

As to the departure of His Majesty's ships I have already had the honour to communicate to you that the proclamation does not interfere; and Admiral Pickmore is at liberty to remain in Carlscrona until the end of the month, or longer if necessary, as I have written to him. There seems to be every disposition in this government to avoid taking any measure which shall unecessarily commit them in their relations with England; and I hope to hear from you that you find no difficulty in your communications with Gothenburg. As you entered the harbour before the 15th. I imagine you do not come within the scope of the proclamation. I have etc.

P.S. I am informed officially that even prize vessels that have been brought in before the 15th. inst. may be sold at Gothenburg.

105. *Saumarez to Croker*[1]

London,

7 Dec. 1809.

Sir, I have received your letter of yesterday's date, enclosing the copies of two letters from Mr. Isaac Solly to the commissioners of His Majesty's navy requesting protection to be afforded to several hemp ships now in the Baltic; and signifying the directions of the Lords Commissioners of the Admiralty to let you know for their information whether under the present circumstances of the season I am of opinion His Majesty's ships may with safety be sent upon this service.

I request you will be pleased to inform their lordships that having taken upon myself to extend the time originally determined upon with the chairman of the committee of merchants concerned in the Baltic trade to the 1st. of December, which was a fortnight later than the period at first fixed upon with their concurrence, I was impelled to it in consequence of the number of ships that, I was informed, were delayed in the ports of St. Petersburg and Riga and that were at that time shipping their cargoes for England. But I do not consider it to be consistent with the safety of His Majesty's ships appointed for the protection of the trade and those stationed in the Belt to defend them against the attack of the Danish gunboats that they should be ordered to remain in the Baltic to a later period, particularly after the disastrous events that occurred last season when so many of His Majesty's ships

---

[1] John Wilson Croker (1780–1857) succeeded Pole as secretary to the admiralty in 1809, which appointment he held until 1830. He was a regular contributor to the *Quarterly Review* and author of various editions of essays and papers; M.P. for different constituencies in England and Ireland, 1807–32.

were lost and others exposed to imminent danger, besides the number of valuable vessels which were wrecked and fell into the hands of the enemy.

I am not without very serious apprehensions that if the present westerly winds should prevail any time in the Baltic and a sudden change of easterly wind set in that similar occurrences may again take place this year. A convoy of near one hundred sail, that left Carlscrona under the protection of the *Edgar* on the 4th. of November, has been detained in the Belt till the 26th. and arrived at Gothenburg, most of them with the loss of anchors and cables; and two of the convoy lost. Another numerous convoy of one hundred and forty sail, that sailed from Carlscrona under Rear-Admiral Pickmore on the 17th., I have reason to believe are still detained in the Belt. In all probability the convoy appointed to leave Carlscrona on the 1st. instant are still detained there and, should westerly winds prevail, may be even later than the time when the *Salsette* left that port last year, which was on the 22nd. of December; and they were anchored off Falsterbo on the 24th. instead of the beginning of January as stated in Mr. Solly's letter.

I further beg to observe that Danzig Bay, as pointed out in Mr. Solly's letter of yesterday's date, is in my opinion very unfit for the rendezvous of the trade, and for the very reasons mentioned in that letter, as it is on the southern side of the Baltic. On the setting in of an easterly wind it is possible that the northern side may be frozen up, as well as the Sound and Belt, when the ice may not have extended to that part of the Baltic; to which I have to add that a northerly wind, which is favourable for a convoy to sail from Carlscrona to the Belt, would be unfavourable from Danzig Bay. Under these circumstances I cannot take it upon myself to recommend any of His Majesty's ships being sent upon the service pointed out in your letter. I am etc.

106. *Barrett*[1] *to Saumarez*

Minotaur, Carlscrona,

7 Dec. 1809.

Sir, Since I had the honour of addressing you last scarcely anything worthy of remark has occurred except the arrival of a few vessels from Riga, Memel etc., a list of which I herewith enclose.

On the 30th. ult. I acquainted you with my intention of putting to sea the next day, the wind being then at N.E. During the ensuing night it came round to south, and has continued nearly in that quarter since.

A few days ago I received a letter from Mr. Hewletz, agent to the house of

[1] John Barrett, lieutenant, 1793; captain, 1795; died in the wreck of the *Minotaur* (74) off the Texel, 22 Dec. 1810.

Solly, and another from Mr. Amburgh of the house of Schröder requesting me to defer the sailing of the convoy until the 12th. or 15th. in expectation of the arrival of several sail from Riga, which, they say, will positively be here by that period. On the other hand, I am informed by old masters of vessels in the Baltic trade, lately arrived from different ports in the gulfs, chiefly Riga, that the ice is so very strong as to prevent those which now remain from attempting to get out this season. The latter of course I am most inclined to give credit to, as they certainly must be the better judges of the weather in this part and at this season of the year. I have not yet given any answer to the request of the beforementioned agents; [n]or do I think it at all necessary, for were I to pay attention to all their frivolous pretexts, it would not only be delaying the present valuable convoy collected here, but would in my opinion be attended with great inconvenience and risk to them as well as to His Majesty's ships, the season is so rapidly advancing.

The *Tartar* and *Lynx*, which were appointed to remain for the vessels which may arrive here after the departure of the convoy under my charge, are not in a condition to remain on the station any longer, both being reported to me to have made much water in the late gales.

I have lately received a letter from Mr. Hahn dated 22nd. ult., wherein he says I may not expect any more vessels from Colberg or its adjacent ports this winter, the harbours on that coast being entirely frozen up without the least appearance of the ice breaking. I also this day received one from Mr. E. Solly of Memel who likewise mentions the severe weather they have experienced in that part, but says that several vessels will be able to get out about the end of the first week in December at the soonest. I conclude therefore it will be the middle or latter part of the month before they arrive here.

Under all these circumstances I think my best mode of proceeding will be to take the first favourable opportunity of wind and weather and, with the very valuable convoy under my protection, make the best of my way to England agreeable to my orders, as I understand from Mr. Consul Smith that Rear-Admiral Dixon has appointed the 15th. inst. for the sailing of the last convoy from Gothenburg.

From the additional convoy list you will see what the vessels are which have arrived within these few days, and will of course be the most competent judge of my proceedings, which I trust will meet your approbation.

I herewith transmit the state and condition, and return of sick and wounded, of His Majesty's ships and vessels under my orders, and have etc.

PART III

1810

PART III

1810

PART III

INTRODUCTION

Dixon resumed his station in the Great Belt. Pickmore was succeeded by Rear-Admiral Reynolds. Though excluded from the ports of Sweden as a result of that country's having made peace with Britain's enemies, the fleet was able to resort to undefended anchorages off the Swedish coast. It obtained supplies from, and preserved a correspondence with, the land. In these circumstances the expansion of the Baltic trade continued in the first half of the campaigning season. The good will felt toward Britain by many Swedes, their sense of dependence upon Britain and their desire to avoid a severance of relations are amply documented. The documentation of Anglo-Swedish relations is incomplete, since Saumarez's correspondents did not include those Swedes who believed that Swedish interests would benefit from a French alliance. The existence of good will towards Britain was, therefore, no guarantee that the *status quo* would be preserved. The sudden death of Christian August, the former Danish governor of Norway, who had been elected crown prince of Sweden in 1809 as successor to the childless Charles XIII, was a critical event. The revival of the succession problem opened the way for the election of a candidate, who had necessarily to be approved by Napoleon. And, as things turned out, the candidate who was at once acceptable to a majority of Swedes and to Napoleon was Marshal Bernadotte, prince of Ponte Corvo (doc. 135). The result of the election and the vulnerability of Sweden at the close of the year, when the British fleet was about to withdraw, to pressure from Paris threw a dark shadow over the future course of Anglo-Swedish relations. It was lightened only by the receipt of unofficial assurances that the declaration of war issued from Stockholm was not intended as a prelude to belligerent action. Another serious cause of disquiet was the sudden imposition by Napoleon of rigid control over the German ports which disturbed the flow of trade, lowered confidence and threatened the extinction of British intercourse with the Baltic. The difficulties are illustrated in the documents. John Barrett of the *Minotaur* (74) perished with his crew in a shipwreck off the Texel on the journey home.

107. *W. and P. Emes to Croker*

London,

9 March 1810.

Sir, In consequence of the desire expressed to our P.E., when last he had the pleasure of waiting upon you, that we should call a meeting of the merchants trading to and from the Baltic in order to collect their sentiments as to the arrangements most desirable for the protection of the trade this year, we beg leave to state for the information of their lordships that we have convened a meeting of the gentlemen concerned to take the subject into their consideration. But the political situation in which we stand with respect to Sweden precludes them from pointing out any decided plan for the homeward bound trade. However, from what we could collect, the general sentiment appears to be in substance as follows: that a strong force should be stationed in the Belt and that convoys do sail from the Nore once a fortnight direct to the Baltic and the ships to be protected as near to the ports of destination as possible in the way they were last year, and that vessels should be kept cruising near the different ports not alone to prevent any privateers getting out, but likewise to protect the ships downward bound.

That for the protection of the Gothenburg trade a separate convoy should be appointed at the same periods to see the ships off that port; and, as it may be deemed adviseable by many merchants that vessels bound up the Baltic should first go into Gothenburg to change their clearances[1] in order with more security to enter the ports in the Baltic, it becomes necessary for the protection of that part of the trade, and which will be considerable, that we should have several ships on that station to receive the ships coming out of Gothenburg and to take them into the Belt, in order that they may be conducted through by the force there.

With respect to the homeward bound trade from the Baltic they felt a greater delicacy in pointing out to their lordships any fixed place, as so much depends upon the political relations that exist with the continental powers, as to the place of rendezvous for the ships, and which their lordships are more competent to act upon than they are to offer an opinion. At the same time they beg most particularly to impress upon their lordships' minds the absolute necessity of having a place of rendezvous for the vessels without which the trade cannot possibly be protected; and that such place of rendezvous as their lordships may deem most adviseable should be secured to the ships and the merchants acquainted with it as early as possible, in order to make the necessary arrangements for the ships now laying at the different ports loaded and ready to get away. At the same time they beg leave to suggest that in looking to a place of rendezvous a material point is to be considered, that of being as centrical as possible for the lower as well as the upper ports in order that the advantages may be general, and that when such rendezvous is fixed, the convoys be appointed to sail from thence for England once a fortnight, and oftener provided more than thirty vessels should be collected in the intermediate time, as the losses which have occurred the two last years

---

[1] This meant having the ship's papers endorsed to certify that the vessel's port of departure was Gothenburg, not a port in Britain or the British colonies.

have been chiefly occasioned by the convoys being too numerous to be properly protected.

They also beg leave to call the attention of their lordships to the number of vessels now laying at Carlshamn and Carlscrona bound to Great Britain which were left there in the autumn, and as it is of the greatest consequence that they should reach this country as early as possible, it is hoped that so soon as our force reaches the Baltic, a protection for those vessels may be immediately sent to conduct them through the Belt.

With respect to the period of sailing of the first convoys from this country, it is hoped by the merchants that their lordships will be pleased to appoint a convoy for Gothenburg not later than the first day of April, and for the Baltic not later than the fifteenth day of April to sail from the Nore.

Indeed should the force destined for the protection of the trade be collected and ready to sail earlier, it would be still more satisfying to the merchants. We are etc.

108. *Saumarez to Croker*

London,

17 April 1810.

Sir, You will be pleased to inform the Lords Commissioners of the Admiralty that I have directed Rear-Admiral Dixon to take under his command His Majesty's ships and vessels named in the margin [*Hero, Plantegenet, Vanguard, Ganges, Dictator, Prometheus, Snipe, Earnest*] and to proceed with them to the Great Belt, and to station them in the different parts of the Belt in the best manner for the protection of the trade to and from the Baltic and for intercepting and cutting off any communication between the island of Zealand and the coasts upon the continent adjacent. I also propose to detach Captain Pater[1] of His Majesty's ship *Princess Carolina* to Hawke Road, Gothenburg; and I have to request their lordships will be pleased to place under my command such further force of frigates and smaller vessels as they may deem necessary for the various services incident to the station in the Cattegat and Baltic. I have etc.

109. *Saumarez to Foster*

Victory, Hawke Road,

21 May 1810.

Sir, I have the honour to acquaint your excellency of my arrival here with part of the squadron under my command and of my intention to proceed

[1] Charles Dudley Pater, lieutenant, 1779; captain, 1795; rear-admiral, 1814.

into the Baltic as soon as the wind will permit. It will afford me the highest satisfaction to renew a correspondence from whence I derived such great benefit during the time I was employed upon this station last year; and, although the unfortunate exclusion of British ships from the ports of Sweden will render it more difficult at this time, I hope it will not be the means of entirely depriving me of the honour of hearing from your excellency. As I propose calling off Ystad on my getting into the Baltic, I shall detach a vessel to that place for any letters you may have done me the honour to write. I have etc.

110. *Croker to Saumarez*

Admiralty,

24 May 1810.

My dear Sir, You will with this receive a public order for strictly blockading Elsinore which, as it in some degree seems to contravene what was settled when we parted, I wish privately to explain to you.

It arises out of the following circumstances; that (by the Danish regulations) all the ships must touch and pay certain rates of duties at Elsinore[1] under penalty of confiscation if they can be taken. This places the trade in an embarrassing situation. If they go to Elsinore they may be confiscated for fake papers and on any of the thousand pretences that we know would be set up against them. If they do not go, and that they happen to fall in with Danish cruisers, they are liable to confiscation for not having been there. It is therefore with a view to furnish them with an *excuse* for not going to Elsinore that you are to place it in blockade, and, as this is the case, you will see that vessels bound for any of the Swedish ports in the Sound may be permitted to pass, the single port of Elsinore being the object of blockade and that with a view not so much to prevent ships that *choose* to go there from doing so (tho' that also is an object as it will cripple the Danish revenues), as to take away a ground of confiscation from those who never intended to enter that port.

I hope you have found everything to your satisfaction hitherto and that before you return you may have an opportunity of trying what stuff the Russians are made of. Ever, my dear sir etc.

---

[1] The Sound dues paid at Elsinore since the fourteenth century by all ships sailing to and from the Baltic.

111. *Foster to Saumarez*

Stockholm,

25 May 1810.

Sir, I hasten to reply to the letter which you have done me the honour to write from Gothenburg and to return you my best thanks for the communication of your arrival off the Swedish coast. It is with great pleasure that I renew a correspondence which, as you are kind enough to say, was of benefit to you last year, and from which I certainly derived most important assistance and the highest satisfaction.

I am afraid, however, that the opportunities of writing to you will be few. Ystad, from its neighbourhood to Denmark, seems to be too exposed to observation for this government to wink at the correspondence passing that way. It has been hinted to me, however, that it might proceed without difficulty through the small town of Sölvitzborg [Sölvesborg] on the frontiers of Blekingen [Blekinge] and Scania; and I write to Mr. Fenwick by this day's post to recommend his making arrangements for the purpose.

Mr. Consul Smith has transmitted to me a copy of an article in your printed instructions which, he says, you allowed him to make known at Gothenburg and which, if acted upon, will strike at the coasting trade of this country in a manner that I scarcely think was contemplated by government. Indeed it appears to me, particularly when I consider the previous notice that has regularly been given in Sweden, where measures have been taken against His Majesty's interests, that it will be liable to the imputation of unfairness if acted upon immediately, vast quantities of Swedish shipping, which was sent to sea in the confidence of security from capture, being exposed to its operation. I was in hopes that I should have heard from you on the subject, and I cannot but flatter myself that His Majesty's government will have forwarded to me explanations respecting it.

The Danes have annoyed the Swedish trade so considerably that I understand strong representations will be made on the subject at Copenhagen, and possibly some retaliation may take place from this side of the water if they do not cease their proceedings.

I trust you will have the goodness to let me know if it is your intention to order the capture of Swedish ships of all kinds which shall be proceeding from one port of Sweden to another. I am etc.

112. *Nauckhoff to Saumarez*

Stockholm,

30 May 1810.

Excellency, Although we are much disturbed here by the declaration which your excellency has made about blockading the ports of Sweden, I cannot believe that this will lead to acts of hostility against the Swedish flag, and accordingly you will allow our merchantmen to proceed to England and pass between the ports of Sweden and Germany.[1] Without such immunity Sweden will be completely lost; and I cannot imagine such to be the intention of your government.

Relying upon the friendship and benevolence which your excellency has always shown, I trust you will not take it amiss if I beg you to inform me whether it is permissible for a gallias named *Anna Louisa*, Captain J. Kullberg, of 50 lasts which some time ago left here for Riga to load corn for conveyance to my iron-works estate can pass to this place freely without licence.

A business house here, by name Bernt, Beskow and Co., have entrusted me with the task of representing to your excellency that last autumn they dispatched a vessel to Riga which was [there] laden with hemp, oil, etc. for England. But after quitting Riga this ship had the misfortune to be cast by a gale upon the coast of Finland, and went aground among the rocks off Åbo and Lorssö, but as it is hoped to save part of this cargo and to send a ship there to carry out the work it is desirable to have your excellency's assurance that this reshipment can be done without prevention by your cruisers. I venture also to ask your excellency if ships belonging to Finland and Åland, laden with firewood and other products of the country which Swedes in residence there need to send here, can pass without being molested.

Once again I beg your excellency to be so kind as to enlighten me with regard to all that I have had the honour to point out to you; and I pray your excellency will be convinced of the most high consideration with which I have etc.

113. *Saumarez to Croker*

Victory, off Ystad,

6 June 1810.

Sir, You will please to inform the Lords Commissioners of the Admiralty that I arrived off Ystad this afternoon, having seen the convoy that left

---

[1] The ports of Swedish Pomerania which was restored to Sweden by the treaty of peace with France signed at Paris on 6 Jan. 1810.

Gothenburg last Saturday, consisting of 36 sail, in safety thro' the Great Belt, and am now proceeding up the Baltic. The *Princess Carolina* with the convoy under her charge, consisting of 366, were clear of the Belt on Monday last, and are by this time far on their way to their respective ports of destination.

His Majesty's ship *Edgar*, with the *Orion*, *Saturn*, *Alexandria* and *Sheldrake*, were at anchor off Romsoe Island with the homeward bound trade, about 150 sail; and another convoy of 73 sail, which had been directed to assemble in Hanö Bay, are now in sight on their way towards Dars Head under the charge of the *Martial* gunbrig.

I found off Moen Island Rear-Admiral Reynolds[1] with His Majesty's ships named in the margin [*St. George, Formidable, Resolution, Standard, Swan*], and I shall, after having had communication with Ystad, proceed to Hanö Bay in the further execution of my orders. I am etc.

114. *Saumarez to Croker*

Victory, off Ystad,
6 June 1810.

Sir, Herewith I enclose two letters which I have received from Captain Mason[2] of His Majesty's ship *Fisgard* stating his having taken and destroyed three of the enemy's privateers off Wismar and the Trindelen lighthouse, also another letter I have this day received from him, giving an account of the capture of a privateer under French colours by the boats of that ship, together with a galliot she had taken, in the harbour of Warneyminde [Warnemünde], in which Captain Mason details the piratical conduct of the privateers upon that coast. And you will please to lay the same before the Lords Commissioners of the Admiralty. I am etc.

Enclosure 1:

114a. *Mason to Saumarez*

Fisgard, off Wismar,
30 April 1810.

Sir, I have the honour to inform you that having yesterday chased an armed schooner close in shore off Wismar and it falling little wind, I sent in

---

[1] Robert Carthew Reynolds (c. 1748–1811) entered the navy, 1759; lieutenant, 1777; captain, 1790; commanded the *Amazon* (36) in the action with the *Droits de l'homme* (74), 1797; rear-admiral, 1808; died in the wreck of the *St. George* (98) off the Jutland coast, 24 Dec. 1811.

[2] Francis Mason, lieutenant, 1799; captain, 1806; employed in the North Sea and Baltic, 1808–12; C.B., 1815; rear-admiral, 1838; K.C.B., 1841; second-in-command Mediterranean fleet, 1841–43.

the boats of this ship under the command of Lieutenants Barclay[1] and
Hessleden.[2] Upon their approach, the crew of the vessel took to their boat
and escaped on shore. She was brought out and proved to be the *Juliana*,
Danish privateer of Kiel, carrying two long four-pounders, four smaller
ones, besides musquetoons. By her *role d'équipage* her crew consisted of the
commander and 22 men. By the log it appears she has made two captures.
One part of the captain's instructions, of which I enclose you a translated
copy, directs him to capture every vessel having an English licence and give
him the names of some; which information, I understand, the owners of the
privateers gain by their agents in the Swedish ports, and most probably in all
other ports of the Baltic. I have etc.

Enclosure 2:

114b. *Instructions to the commander of a Danish privateer*

In the cruise which you commence to-day you must principally be careful
that you send no ships into the harbour of which you are not persuaded
firstly that they come from England, or have a licence on board, or have been
examined by an English vessel, or are laden with English or colonial commodities whether *Danish*, *Russian*, *Swedish*, *Mecklenburg*, *Prussian or
neutral vessels*.

Secondly, the ships which come from Russian harbours are generally
bound for England, whether laden with goods or in ballast, and are cleared
for *Norwegian* or other *allied ports*. The lading of these ships must be signed
and accompanied with a certificate from the French consul in Petersberg. All
these vessels have English licences on board which you must find, or else you
cannot take them as prizes. You can obtain them by promising the ship or
money to the captain. You must promise the men the same; and everything
you promise in order to get these licences I will keep quite faithfully.

Thirdly, you must look out particularly for such vessels as are going to
Russia or Prussia. They have generally colonial wares on board, and are of
great value. As soon as you have taken a prize send it to Danzig, if out at sea,
directed with your account of the transaction to Mr. Peter Andriel Meicht.

Fourthly, your log must be as exact as possible. You must observe (a) the
longitude where you saw a ship, (b) the longitude where you boarded her,
(c) under what colours she sailed, and if she refused to heave to or defended
herself.

---

[1] John Barclay, acting lieutenant of the *Britannia* (100) at Trafalgar; lieutenant, 20 Nov.
1805; retired commander, 1838.
[2] James Hessleden (or Hesledon), lieutenant, 1807.

Fifthly, as soon as you come on board you must take possession of all papers, and examine the whole company, and see if they have nothing concealed about the body. The clothes also you must examine. After you have done this, take each man separate and examine him strictly. Show him the decree of the Emperor Napoleon of January 11th. 1808 in which a third part of the prize money is promised to anyone who will declare that the vessel has been examined by the English, or that she sailed from England, or has an English licence. Tell the men that everything will be kept silent and that they have not a better opportunity of making their fortunes. The decree I have sent enclosed.

You must cruise from Colberg to Pillau and Memel and send your prizes to Danzig. If you cannot go thither endeavour to sail to Warnemünde and Rostock where you must apply to Mr. Leynis in Warnemünde or Mr. Sekleider in Rostock. You must give him an accurate account of everything. He will take you to the French consul who will take care of the rest. All the papers you find in the prizes you must put into a sack or packet, and seal it with your seal; and afterwards make the captain of the prize seal it. You must make the captain sign a declaration of all th circumstances you found against him. The examination must be made before the captain and two sailors and signed by each of them. If you are obliged to go into any harbour with the *Juliana*, keep her in the roads that none of the men may have any communication with the land, which you must observe very strictly.

Should you chance to meet a vessel with French licence, endeavour to find an English licence on board, *which you cannot fail to do*. Her you must take as a prize. All the ships which have certificates from French consuls you must examine and all their papers. These vessels are generally cleared from two places, and are to be condemned as prizes even if they had a licence. The captains hide their papers under the hearths or about the body. As soon as you have detained a ship, you must treat the men with the greatest kindness and politeness; and endeavour to make them afraid of the punishment inflicted on anyone who does not declare the truth.

You will find many Swedish vessels which you must examine, very accurately. If they come from Calmar [Kalmar] or that part, they are generally laden with tar, deals, lime etc. All Swedish vessels coming from Gothenburg, Carlshamn, Stockholm have colonial produce only under another name. But as we are at peace with Sweden you must be very careful not to occasion me any expenses. You must scrutinize everything closely, both men and goods. Every vessel you fall in with at sea is subject to examination; only you must take care not to bring them up as prizes if the papers are right. I leave everything to your own sense and thought, and recommend you to observe my observations very accurately. Remember, if you fulfill everything, you will make your own, and my, fortune off Colberg, Pillau, Memel and Libau.

You are to sail from here today and steer for Warnemünde. In Warnemünde there lies a vessel of 26 German lasts, called the *Hungarian Wolf*, a schooner, Capt. Lange. This Lange lives in Warnemünde where he keeps a public house. He is bound for Colberg. You must wait for him at Grønsund. Sunday at 3 o'clock he is to sail. Perhaps he may not sail then. If you do not meet with him there, you can wait for him at the Goels[1] by Dast not far from Stralsund. The Goels lie north of Stralsund.

This morning a great number of ships sailed from Neustadt, viz., *Thol. Harder*, *Kocker*, *Woll*, *Werde*; and many more, whose names I have not heard, all from Lubeck cleared for Stralsund. Some are probably laden with colonial wares and, if not, they have English licences, which you will find concealed behind the captain's desk or about the body. You must accuse the captain boldly as if you knew of the whole affair. Three vessels will lie at anchor under Gasmund or Feird. There are two vessels coming, one from Elsinore, the other from Copenhagen, laden with colonial wares bound for Rostock or Wismar. Three vessels lie at Wismar icebound; but their lading is unknown. These, however, you need not examine.

115. *Saumarez to Foster*

Victory, off Ystad,

7 June 1810.

Sir, I had the honour to receive both your letters, dated 25th. ult., on my arrival at this place yesterday evening, and I request you will accept my best thanks for them. I was much surprized before I sailed from Hawke Road to find from Mr. Consul Smith that you had not received from government any communication relative to the restrictions upon the trade of Sweden, having taken it for granted at the time I received instructions upon the subject that intimation of it would have been made to you by the same conveyance. I trust that you have before this received explanations respecting it, and that they will prove as satisfactory to the government of Sweden as the circumstances will admit.

I have hitherto acted on that part of my instructions with the utmost moderation; but, in conformity to these instructions, it will not be in my power to desist in future from allowing the cruisers to make captures of such Swedish vessels as they fall in with who are not provided with licences from

---

[1] The shallows off the Dars peninsula.

England. The depradations of the Danish armed vessels have determined me
to give orders to His Majesty's ships stationed off Kioge Bay not to admit
any vessels to enter the Sound, which I have signified to our government.

The place you have been pleased to point out for the correspondence in
future is perfectly well adapted, more particularly from its vicinity to Hanö
Bay, the rendezvous which I have appointed for the trade, and where I propose to proceed on receiving dispatches which I daily expect from Gothenburg. I shall therefore hope to have the honour of hearing from you next by
way of Sölvitzborg.

The information I have received from Mr. Fenwick of the lamented death
of the crown prince[1] must have thrown the government under very considerable embarrassment and possibly may lead to some change in the politics of
the country.

I request you will favour me with any information you receive relative to
the Russian fleet, as it will in a great degree decide the time when I may proceed towards the Gulf of Finland. It is with great satisfaction I have the
honour to inform you that the numerous convoys that have sailed from
Gothenburg have all cleared the Belt without loss; and the two homeward-
bound convoys are, I hope, by this time far on their way. The one under the
protection of the *Edgar* and *Saturn* was off Romsoe last Sunday, and one
which sailed more recently was yesterday off Dars Head.

I hope the time is yet very distant, but I trust you will be pleased to signify
to me the proposed period of your leaving Sweden. I will give directions for
one of the ships under my orders to convey you and suite to Yarmouth or
any other port you prefer. I have etc.

116. *Yorke[2] to Saumarez*

Admiralty,

7 June 1810.

Dear Sir, Since the supplementary instructions of this day are sent off on
the subject of your not interfering with the *coasting trade* of Sweden or
capturing vessels within the ports or harbours of that kingdom, except in the
cases specified in your former instructions, the Marquis Wellesley[3] has communicated to me that he has received information that some of the ships

---

[1] Suddenly on 28 May 1810, confronting the Swedes with the necessity of electing a new
heir to the throne.
[2] Charles Philip Yorke (1764–1834), the half brother of Philip Yorke, 3rd earl of
Hardwicke; first lord of the admiralty, May 1810–March 1812.
[3] Richard Colley Wellesley, 1st Marquis Wellesley; 2nd earl of Mornington (1760–
1842) was secretary of state for foreign affairs, 6 Dec. 1809–4 March 1812.

under your orders have detained or captured some ships sailing from a Swedish port and destined for the port of London.

Tho' I am persuaded that there is some mistake or exaggeration contained in the statements that have been made by the merchants concerned in the Swedish trade, or by others, on this subject (the admiralty hitherto having received no information whatever of a detailed or specific nature relating to it) yet it appears to me necessary to trouble you with this letter for the purpose of apprizing you that no Swedish ship can require a licence to sail to England or to any place from whence the English flag is not excluded; nor from England or any such port back again to Sweden. I am persuaded that should any seizures of the kind alluded to have taken place through the misconception of any [of] your officers, you will lose no time in giving the most precise orders for preventing any such mistakes in future; in directing the ship or ships so detained to be set at liberty, it being the anxious wish and intention of H.M's government (as you are already informed by your former instructions) to avoid as much as possible, and consistently with the honour of the nation, any cause of misunderstanding with the Swedes. I have etc.

117. *Saumarez to Nauckhoff*

Victory, off Ystad,
9 June 1810.

Sir, I have received the honour of your letter of the 30th. ult., and it is with inexpressible concern I find it out of my power to comply with your wishes to allow the vessel you mention to proceed from Riga to a port in Sweden without being furnished with a licence from England, it being absolutely contrary to the tenor of my orders. I therefore can only hope she will arrive in safety and without being interrupted by any of my cruisers. I am very happy in complying with the other part of your letter respecting the ship belonging to Messrs. Bernt, Beskow & Co. stranded last winter upon the rocks in the vicinity of Åbo; and I have sent to these gentlemen a certificate under my hand to prevent their being molested in their attempts to save any part of the cargo.

Knowing the dependence of Stockholm upon receiving supplies of fire-wood from the coast of Finland, I shall give orders for open boats loaded with that article to be allowed to pass unmolested.

I most sincerely hope that the accustomed harmony will be preserved and maintained between our respective countries, and that a lasting peace will speedily be restored to all nations.

I beg my respectful compliments to Madame Nauckhoff and to your aimiable daughter I had the pleasure to see on board this ship; and with sentiments of the highest regard and perfect esteem, I have etc.

118. *Questions proposed by Rear-Admiral Krusenstjerna*

Off Ystad,
9 June 1810.

His Swedish Majesty having received the unexpected information of the intention of the British government to adopt against the Swedish trade His Britannic Majesty's orders in council of the 1st. and 25th. November 1807, and that these orders are immediately to be put into execution by the naval forces acting in the Baltic Sea under the command of His Excellency Vice-Admiral Sir James Saumarez has graciously charged the underwritten to submit the following remarks to his excellency's consideration, and also humbly to solicit his excellency will be pleased to communicate his opinion on the subject in consequence.

1st. His Britannic Majesty's orders in council of the surmentioned dates establish a distinction between blockaded ports and those *under restriction incident to a state of blockade*. They prescribe that vessels and cargoes belonging to nations not in war against England may in certain cases sail and be transported from and to ports of the latter qualification.

His Majesty concludes and expects in consequence that Swedish or neutral vessels who sail from such Swedish ports, which are not actively blockaded by the English forces, and are bound to England or the English dominions in Europe may be permitted to pursue their voyage with-

Vessels and cargoes from Swedish ports destined to ports in England, altho' unprovided with licences from the English government, or from ports in England bound to Sweden will not be molested in their voyage.

out being liable to capture even in the case she should not be provided with licences, and that the same freedom might be accorded to vessels who have been loaded in England with salt, either of English production or there lawfully imported, being bound to Swedish ports under the said qualification.

2nd. His Majesty wishes to be informed how far Swedish vessels or open boats, loaded or in ballast trading from one Swedish port to another, will be liable to capture, and also if it is the intention of his excellency to station any ships-of-war in the Ålands Haf, Gulf of Botnia or in general within the Swedish skerries.

Open boats or small vessels carrying seeds, bricks, lime, grain, fuel or other small articles from one Swedish port to another along the coast will not be interrupted, or from Finland across the Gulf of Bothnia.

3rd. However, it is not to be presumed that unarmed vessels, acting under His Swedish Majesty's flag and commission, carrying provisions or stores of any kind belonging to His Majesty from any foreign or Swedish ports to any port of His Majesty's dominions, also the packet who carries the mail between Sweden and the Swedish Pomerania, and the boat who conveys the Swedish post through the Belt to and from Germany could be liable to capture, yet I think it proper to submit this matter as a question to his excellency.

The packets with the mails from Ystad to Stralsund will be continued to pass unmolested, so long as the packets with the mails from England are admitted at Gothenburg.

4th. It is a flattering hope to His Majesty that the justice and equity unseparated from the well known respectable and noble character of his excellency will induce his excellency to spare from capture those Swedish vessels who, not being informed of the latest decree from the British government for an ignorance which ought not to be imputed to them.

119. *Saumarez to Croker*

Victory, in Hanö Bay,

13 June 1810.

Sir, You will please to inform the Lords Commissioners of the Admiralty with my arrival here on the 10th., where I found Rear-Admiral Reynolds with His Majesty's ships under his orders and about thirty sail of the trade which had assembled at this anchorage since the departure of the last convoy; since which they have been coming in daily from the different ports of the Baltic. And on the arrival of others that are daily expected from Petersburg, I shall appoint a convoy to see them to the Belt.

Hanö Bay is remarkably well adapted for collecting the trade during the summer months, where a supply of excellent water is easily obtained. By different ships arrived here which sailed from Cronstadt the 1st. instant, it does not appear that the Russian fleet are ready for sea or in a state of equipment at that period, with the exception of a few frigates and smaller vessels. The ice was but just broke up in the Gulf of Finland; and as the seamen composing the Russian fleet are confined in barracks during the winter season in the vicinity of St. Petersburg, they may be fitted for sea within a short time. They are stated to consist of twelve sail-of-the-line with a great number of frigates.

Seven Swedish line-of-battle ships under jury masts are moored across the entrance of the harbour of Carlscrona, with a strong boom outside of them extending across the channel within the batteries. Six frigates are stated to be getting ready for sea.

I have this morning received information from Mr. Consul Smith that sixteen Norwegian gunboats had passed to the Swedish territory under pretext of escorting their trade detained in the Swedish harbours by the cruisers. I have directed Captain Honeyman[1] of His Majesty's ship *Ardent* stationed in Hawke Road to be upon his guard should they advance as far as that anchorage; and I recommend that another ship carrying heavy metal should be sent from England and placed under the orders of Captain Honeyman. I am etc.

120. *Foster to Saumarez*

Gothenburg,

14 June 1810.

Sir, I should have written from Stockholm to inform you of my being obliged to quit that capital, but the Swedish minister's letters to me, con-

---

[1] Robert Honeyman, lieutenant, 1790; captain, 1798.

veying the wish of the government that I should depart, gave me but forty hours to prepare myself, and I had scarcely time for any other occupation than that of getting ready during so short a period. I left Stockholm on the morning of the 8th. inst. and arrived at Gothenburg this evening. I am anxiously waiting to receive orders from home in order to take my departure.

The Swedish government has not notified in London its orders to shut the ports of Sweden to His Majesty's packet boats. Therefore I expect from day to day that an order will arrive for their exclusion. Captain Honeyman of His Majesty's ship *Ardent* has been kind enough to offer me a passage on the *Chanticleer* if she can be detained a few days, and I shall very willingly and thankfully accept the offer.

Baron d'Engeström considered my departure and the cessation of correspondence between England and Sweden as a necessary consequence of the treaties of peace[1] lately concluded by this country and therefore as not likely to produce any change in the present relations with Great Britain. Indeed they have both long been announced as being to take place. The communication, therefore, will still be winked at, as I have reason to believe, by the Swedish government; but it must be done privately. I have etc.

121. *Puke to Saumarez*

Carlskrona,
19 June 1810.

Sir, I have had the honour to receive your excellency's benign letter of the 17th. instant and accepted with the greatest satisfaction the good information that was contained in it of the permitted and unhindered passage of the Swedish coasting trade; and I hasten to make notice of it to the king my sovereign.

I experience in this happy event an indubitable testimony of your excellency's benignity and benevolent sentiments towards this country, arisen and founded during former relations between Great Britain and Sweden.

May your excellency allow me to profit by this occasion to assure of that most unfeigned consideration and high regard, independent from all political relations, with which I have etc.

---

[1] The clauses in the treaty of Paris regulating Sweden's commercial relations with Britain were much more stringent than those of the treaty of Frederikshamn. The only concession granted by Napoleon concerned the import of foreign salt.

122. *Saumarez to Yorke*

Victory, Hanö Bay,

20 June 1810.

Dear Sir, I have this morning received the honour of your letter on the subject of the trade of Sweden in which you are pleased to observe that the Marquis Wellesley had communicated to you that he had received information that some of the ships under my orders have detained or captured some ships from a Swedish port and destined to the port of London, to which I beg leave to state that the information must have been incorrect, the detention or capture of any vessels of that description being contrary to the orders I have given to the cruisers upon this station, and no report having been made to me of any being detained.

I beg further to observe that to every application made to me by any of the merchants I gave my decided opinion that Swedish ships trading to England or to those countries where British produce was admitted were not liable to detention and that they would not be molested by the cruisers under my orders.

Knowing the extreme distress that Sweden must suffer from the interruption of her coasting trade, I acted upon the instructions I received with the utmost possible moderation consistent with the tenor of those instructions. They were not acted upon until I had an opportunity of communicating with the consul at Gothenburg and some of the principal merchants, who appear perfectly satisfied with the indulgence I allowed to the trade of Sweden under the existing circumstances, and the same has been signified to me by the Swedish government who have expressed themselves satisfied with the mildness and consideration I have uniformly acted to the country. I shall therefore feel most sensibly if any unfavourable impression can have been made by misstatements upon any part of my conduct since I came upon this station. There being no immediate appearance of the Russian fleet putting to sea, I propose to remain here some time longer for the greater facility of communication with England as well as accelerating the trade from this rendezvous. I have etc.

123. *Yorke to Saumarez*

Admiralty,

28 June 1810.

Dear Sir, I am to acknowledge the receipt of your (private) letters of the 1st. and 5th. inst., the former announcing the unfortunate and embarrassing event of the prince royal of Sweden's death, as announced by His Majesty's consul at Gothenburg, for which communication being the earliest of an authentic nature which was received by this government, I beg to return you my thanks.

The other letter contains the account of Capt. Pearson's[1] being obliged to quit the *Dictator* in consequence of the state of his health and of the temporary arrangements you had made upon that occasion, and expressing your wish that it might obtain the confirmation of the admiralty.

I am sorry that I am so circumstanced at present as not to be able to give complete effect to the arrangements you have proposed, as I had intended Captain Bradby[2] of the *Calypso* (the only surviving son of my old friend the admiral) for the *first* post vacancy in the Baltic, and he accordingly is directed to proceed from the Nore with the first convoy and will probably be the bearer of this. However, as Capt. Bradby is only to be promoted for *rank*[3] and is not intended to continue in the command of the *Dictator*, Captain R. Williams[4] will have a commission for her which will supersede Bradby; and as it is very much my desire to further *your* wishes for the promotion of Capt. White of the *Ariel* as well as of Lieut. Ross,[5] there will be no objection to your placing Capt. White in the *Ruby* to act till further orders, and Lieut. Ross in the same manner into the *Ariel*; it being my intention afterwards to confirm them in these existing vacancies. Lieut. Henry Weir,[6] who stands first on my list, is commissioned for the *Calypso*; and Mr. Broderick[7] of the *Ardent* is to have the *Alban* cutter till he can be removed to some ship; and it is my intention to appoint Lieut. Thomas[8] of the *Gorgon* to command the *Alban* cutter in his room.

You will have received 'ere this reaches you my former private letter on the subject of the Swedish coasting trade as well as on that of the *reported* detention of ships sailing from the ports of Sweden for England. A good deal of alarm persisted here among the merchants in consequence of the reports circulated on these subjects, which I am inclined to think were much exaggerated, and I have never yet been able to ascertain the facts to which they referred. As for the *coasting trade* it seems evident that your first instructions

[1] Richard Harrison Pearson, the son of Captain Sir Richard Pearson lieutenant-governor of Greenwich Hospital; lieutenant, 1793; captain, 1798.

[2] Matthew Barton Bradby, lieutenant, 1796; captain, 31 July 1810; the son of James Bradby a superannuated rear-admiral.

[3] Yorke was of course acting with an eye to Bradby's seniority on the list of post-captains; but he could not post him without giving him an appropriate, if only temporary, appointment.

[4] Robert Williams (1765–1827) was acting lieutenant of the *Royal Oak* (74) at the battle of the Saints; lieutenant, 1783; captain, 1797; rear-admiral, 1823.

[5] Daniel Ross, lieutenant, 1799; commander of the *Ariel* sloop, 1810; captain, 1816; died, 1827.

[6] Henry Weir, lieutenant, 1794; commander, 1810; captain, 1812.

[7] John Broderick, lieutenant, 29 June 1810.

[8] Samuel Thomas, lieutenant, 1794.

warranted what you are said to have done and that they required explanation. That which they have now received will, I trust, postpone, if not prevent,
an *actual* rupture with Sweden which it is very desirable to avoid if possible.
At the same time I feel for all your difficulties. With every wish for your glory
and success I remain etc.

124. *Nugent*[1] *to Saumarez*

Ystad,

28 June 1810.

Sir, I regret very much not to have the honour of delivering myself the
letter Baron Wessenberg gave me at Berlin. My intention was to pass by
Carlshamn for that purpose, but for want of wind I was forced to land here,
and continue now my journey for Gothenburg where I intend to embark for
England. The account, I got here, that you had left Hanö and sailed northwards prevents my going to Carlshamn by land, which otherwise I would
have done.

Baron Wessenberg desires very much to keep the correspondence with
you, sir, which he considers as useful to both, even for the present, but much
more so for the future. He will send his letters as usual. Mr. Schröder made,
however, some difficulty in giving me his sloop owing, as he told me, to an
order you had given his captain, Gottfried Schwartz, the last time not to
return any more to the fleet.[2] The enclosed letter from him is, I believe, on
that subject. I promised to give him information of your intention in regard
to his further conduct, but not having the pleasure of seeing you, I take the
liberty, sir, of requesting that you may be so kind as to give him an answer
and your instructions by one of your cruisers which could approach the
port of Colberg for that purpose. I need not observe that Mr. Schröder has
Count Wessenberg's confidence, that he showed on all occasions very much
disinterestedness, and was of use to both governments and to all English
who pass this way. Mr. Johnson can speak more particularly on this subject
than I, as I'm going over only for my own affairs. I would not take the liberty
of saying so much if it had not been recommended to me very strongly by
Count W., and if [I] was not convinced that such a communication with the
continent is very useful to you.

[1] Lavall, Count Nugent (1777–1862) was born in Co. Wicklow and as a boy was adopted
by his uncle Oliver, Count Nugent in Austria; was commissioned in the Austrian army,
1793; served on the staff of Archduke John, 1809; possibly made more than one visit tó
Britain, 1810–12; honorary K.C.B., 1815; prince of the Holy Roman Empire, 1816; field-
marshal, 1849; was present at the battle of Solferino, 1859.
[2] This misunderstanding, whatever may have been the reason for it, was quickly cleared
up. Schröder acknowledged the receipt of a passport for Schwartz on 13 July.

I hope, sir, at my return to be more fortunate and to have an opportunity of assuring you personally of the highest respect.

125. *Instructions by the Lords Commissioners of the Admiralty to Saumarez*

9 July 1810.

Whereas we transmitted to the Marquis of Wellesley, one of His Majesty's principal secretaries of state, your letter to our secretary of the 12th. of last month, stating that the Swedish Admiral Krusenstjerna came on board the *Victory*, when off Ystad, by direction of his government, and requested to be informed on particular points relative to the restrictions on the trade of Sweden, and enclosing a copy of the several queries he was directed to propose to you, together with replies from you, and whereas his lordship has by his letter of the 7th. instant acquainted us that it is His Majesty's pleasure, first, that the trade between the ports of Sweden and those of the United Kingdom in Swedish or in any other neutral vessels, not having the property of His Majesty's enemies on board, should not be molested, although such vessels should not have licences on board; secondly, that the coasting trade from one port of Sweden to another port in Sweden in Swedish vessels should not be molested, and that the trade to and from Finland, as far as the River Kemi, should be permitted in open Swedish boats; thirdly, that licences should be granted, or a protection given from the British admiral, to all Swedish packets (the names of which shall be delivered in to him) for the purpose of protecting them on their voyage direct to and from Swedish Pomerania, and the same indulgence to be extended to the boats which convey the Swedish post to and from Germany through the Belt; we do in pursuance of His Majesty's pleasure, signified as aforesaid, hereby require and direct you to order the captains and commanders of His Majesty's ships and vessels under your command not to molest any Swedish or neutral vessels employed in the manner and subject to the regulations abovementioned, and you are to grant licences or protections to all Swedish packets (the names of which shall be delivered to you) to protect them on their voyage to and from Swedish Pomerania and to extend the same indulgence to boats which may convey the Swedish post to and from Germany through the Belt. Given etc.

126. *Croker to Saumarez*

Admiralty,

10 July 1810.

My dear Sir James, I have had the pleasure of your letter of the 20th. June and am very happy to perceive that everything has gone off so well hitherto with regard to Sweden. I never had any doubt that the accounts we received here of your proceedings were unfounded or at least exaggerated and we did you the full justice of believing that you had executed your orders with every degree of moderation.

I give you joy of the success that has attended our first convoys thro' the Belts. Our citizens seem quite aware of how much they are indebted to your care and arrangements for the protection of this great trade. Ever my dear sir, etc.

127. *Saumarez to Yorke*

Victory, Hanö Bay,

25 July 1810.

Dear Sir, I had great satisfaction in receiving yesterday your obliging letter of the 28th. ult., and I beg to return you my sincere thanks for the arrangements you have been pleased to make for the promotion of Captain White and Lieutenant Ross who I have long been solicitous to get advanced in the service. Having received a commission appointing Mr. Broderick a lieutenant of the *Gorgon*, it has given me an opportunity of placing Mr. Rogers[1] in his stead on board the *St. George* with his friend Admiral Reynolds; Mr. Rogers being the only one unprovided for in the list you were pleased to enclose to me. I have appointed Mr. Peter de Lisle[2] acting lieutenant on board the *Ariel* in an invaliding vacancy which I shall be obliged to you to confirm. And having several deserving characters in the *Victory* who have long looked to me for their advancement, I trust you will permit me to appoint them to such vacancies as occasionally may offer, paying due attention to those who you may be desirous to have advanced in preference.

By the latest accounts from the detachment in the Gulf of Finland, I do not find that there is any indication of the Russian fleet being in a state of equipment, with the exception of ten or twelve sail including frigates and sloops. The best understanding is continued to be maintained with the Swedes who seem desirous to afford the supplies of fresh provisions required for the squadron, altho' not openly by the government of the country.

Every possible exertion is used in forwarding the trade to the ports in England. I have paid particular attention to that object, and the supplies of grain from Danzig and other ports will, I hope, arrive seasonably to prevent the apparent scarcity being too severely felt.

I shall always be happy in receiving your commands and I have etc.

---

[1] Probably Francis Rogers, lieutenant, 3 Sept. 1810; died in the wreck of the *St. George*, 1811.

[2] Peter de Lisle was made lieutenant on 8 June 1811.

128. *Johnson to Smith*[1]

London,
27 July 1810.

Sir, I have the honour to inform you that previous to my departure from Prussia I received several letters from Mr. Schröder, Danish consul at Colberg, stating that a vessel belonging to him, the *Gute Bole*, had been detained by a British cruiser in the Baltic in violation of a promise of protection, which he had received from Sir James Saumarez as an acknowledgement and recompense for services rendered by him on various occasions. Mr. Schröder added that in consequence of this event he should no longer continue to furnish, as formerly, intelligence to the British fleet in the Baltic or assistance to such messengers, and other descriptions of Englishmen, as occasionally pass thro' Colberg.

As I was perfectly aware of the services which Mr. Schröder had rendered the British government both during the siege of Colberg and since that period, I did not hesitate to assure him that it was by no means the wish of government that he should experience any loss or inconvenience on its account, and that I should exert myself conjointly with Sir James Saumarez to prevent, if possible, the final condemnation of the detained ship. Mr. Schröder's statement was subsequently confirmed by Sir James Saumarez who expressed regret that circumstances had prevented him from enforcing the order which he recollected to have given, and who, considering the condemnation of the detained ship as inevitable and being of opinion that the past services of Mr. Schröder entitled him to some mark of attention on the part of the British government, agreed with me on the propriety of my making a representation on the subject on my arrival in England.

I have just learned that Mr. Schröder's ship has been condemned by the court of admiralty and has been purchased by Mr. Lindegren, British vice-consul at Ystad in Sweden, for four thousand dollars Prussian. I therefore beg leave to submit to you whether it would not be eligible to indemnify Mr. S. for the loss of his ship by remitting him, thro' the medium of Sir James Saumarez, 4,000 dollars or, according to the present rate of exchange, £800 sterling, which, I think, can in the present instance be provided for with great propriety out of the fund appropriated to secret service.

Sir Richard Keats, Sir James Saumarez and Mr. Thornton, formerly British envoy at the court of Stockholm, will, I believe, be happy to add their testimony to mine in favour of Mr. Schröder. I have etc.

---

[1] Charles Culling Smith was married to Lady Anne Wellesley. He was under-secretary of state for foreign affairs during the tenure of the secretaryship by his brother-in-law, the marquis.

P.S. It may perhaps be proper to add that on my assuring Mr. Schröder that the British government and the commanding officer of H.M. ships in the Baltic were equally desirous of testifying their gratitude for his services, he consented to forward the correspondence between Germany and England *via* Sweden as heretofore.

129. *Saumarez to Croker*

Victory, in Hanö Bay,

27 July 1810.

Sir, I am extremely concerned to have to acquaint you for the information of the Lords Commissioners of the Admiralty that I have received a letter from Captain Honeyman dated the 23rd. instant transmitting the enclosed letter from Captain Ellicott,[1] commanding His Majesty's armed ship the *Hebe*, stating his having fallen in on the 18th. with the *Forward* gunbrig who gave him the account of the trade under the charge of that vessel, bound to Leith and the Long Hope, having been chased by five of the enemy's gunbrigs and two schooners and the whole of them captured.

It appears by the weekly report of the *Ardent* that the *Forward* sailed from Wingo Sound on the 13th. instant in company with the *Solebay*, *Prince William* and *Wrangler*. Not having received any further accounts of this unfortunate disaster but what is contained in the enclosed letter, I must refer their lordships to the Hon. Captain Proby[2] of the *Solebay* and the commander of the *Wrangler*[3] for further particulars of this untoward event. I am etc.

Enclosure:

129a. *Ellicott to Honeyman*

Hebe, Wingo Sound,

22 July 1810.

Sir, I beg leave to acquaint you for the information of the commander-in-chief that I fell in with the *Forward* gunbrig on the 18th. instant off the Naze, who informed me that she had been chased that morning by five of the enemy's brigs and two schooners which surrounded the convoy under his

---

[1] Edward Ellicott (1768–1847) lieutenant, 1794; commander, 1797; captain, 1812; rear-admiral, 1846.

[2] Hon. Granville Leveson Proby (1781–1868) went to sea in 1798 on board the *Vanguard* (74) and was present at the battle of the Nile; commissioned, 1804; a lieutenant of the *Neptune* (98) at Trafalgar; captain, 1806; last employment, 1816; rear-admiral, 1841; vice-admiral, 1851; 3rd earl of Carysfort, 1855.

[3] John Bentinck Pettet, lieutenant, 1797.

charge bound to Leith and Long Hope, consisting of forty-two sail, and unfortunately succeeded in capturing the whole of them. I immediately dispatched the *Forward* to England to acquaint the Lords Commissioners of the Admiralty of this circumstance. I also gave the information to the *Lynx* and the whole of the cruisers which I fell in with in the Sleeve.[1] I have etc.

130. *Nauckhoff to Saumarez*

Stockholm,

29 July 1810.

Your Excellency, I cannot sufficiently express to your excellency my very great thanks for your gracious favour of the 10th. of June in which you show so much kindness to me and to the commerce. Allow me to trespass once more in recommending to you one of my countrymen, Mr. Westfelt, the bearer of this letter who waits on you to ask for a passage to Wismar with a cargo of iron and tar to be disposed there; and the vessel is afterwards to take in a cargo of corn for London.

I also take the liberty of enquiring whether Swedish vessels are allowed to carry corn from Pomerania to Sweden or to the ports of England, Pomerania being at present considered a Swedish province.

My lady presents her compliments to you and I have the honour etc.

131. *Croker to Saumarez*

Admiralty Office,

1 Aug. 1810.

Sir, My Lords Commissioners of the Admiralty having received information that the French have nine or ten sail-of-the-line ready for sea and in a state of activity, I am commanded by their lordships to apprize you thereof, and to signify their direction to you to take the necessary precautions in the possible event of the enemy's destination being for any part of your station.

I am further commanded by their lordships to point out more particularly to your notice the situation of His Majesty's ships in Hawke Road, by whom the enemy would naturally be first observed. It is therefore requisite that you should give directions to the senior officer of the said ships for his guidance in the event of his seeing, or getting satisfactory information of the approach of the enemy.

I am at the same time directed to transmit herewith for your further information an extract of their lordships' instructions to Rear-Admiral Sir

---

[1] The common name among seamen for the Skagerak.

Richard Strachan,[1] dated 4th. June last, under which Sir E. Pellew[2] is now acting. I am etc.

Enclosure:

131a. *Extract of Admiralty Instructions to Strachan*

4 June 1810.

Whereas by our order of the 10th. of last month you were directed to proceed with the squadron under your command off the Scheldt for the purpose of watching the motions of the enemy in that river, you are hereby required and directed, in the event of the enemy's squadron in the Scheldt putting to sea and proceeding to the northward, to send one of the vessels under your orders for the purpose of apprizing Vice-Admiral Sir James Saumarez in the Baltic, as well as such other flag officers and captains employed on that station as he may fall in with on his passage, of the enemy having put to sea and proceeded to the northward; and you are to make the best of your way in pursuit of them and use your utmost endeavours to come up with and to take or destroy them; but should you not get sight of them, you are to push with all possible dispatch off the Scaw or Gothenburg, and if on your arrival there you should receive satisfactory information that the enemy's squadron has not entered the Cattegat, you are to return and cruise between the Naze of Norway and the Holmes [Hanstholm] on the coast of Jutland for such a space of time as should in your judgement, according to the wind and weather, not only have enabled the enemy's squadron to have arrived there, but should make it unlikely that it is intended for that quarter, and then to return to the Downs, for further orders, transmitting to our secretary for our information an account of your arrival and proceedings.

132. *Dixon to Croker*

Ruby, off Sproe [Sprogø]

4 Aug. 1810.

Sir, I beg leave to enclose a duplicate of a letter to Sir James Saumarez, bart and K.B. (stating a convoy for England having passed through the Belt on this day) for the information of my Lords Commissioners of the Admiralty. I have etc.

[1] Sir Richard John Strachan, bart. (1760–1828) was the son of Lieutenant Patrick Strachan, R.N.; lieutenant, 1779; captain, 1783; captured four French sail-of-the-line which had escaped from Trafalgar, 4 Nov. 1805; rear-admiral, 9 Nov. 1805; K.B., 1806; naval commander of the Walcheren expedition, 1809; vice-admiral, 1810.
[2] Sir Edward Pellew, bart. (1757–1833), lieutenant, 1778; captain, 1782; famous as a frigate captain in the Channel fleet, 1793–99; rear-admiral, 1803; commander-in-chief East Indies, 1804–08; commander-in-chief North Sea Fleet, 1810; commander-in-chief Mediterranean fleet, 1811; admiral, 1814; G.C.B., 1815; bombarded Algiers, 1816; 1st Viscount Exmouth, 1816; commander-in-chief Plymouth, 1817–21.

Enclosure 1:

132a. *Dixon to Saumarez*

Ruby, off Sproe,

4 Aug. 1810.

Sir, I have the pleasure to acquaint you that a homeward bound convoy, consisting of 140 sail and under the charge of the *Orion*, passed the Belt in a strong gale from the southward this day; and I have directed the *Ariel*, *Flamer* and *Alban* cutter to see them in safety to England. I have etc.

Enclosure 2:

132b. *List of convoys passed to and from the Baltic through the Great Belt between the 30th. May and 28th. July 1810*

Time when.	No. of vessels.	Where from.	Where bound.	Under whose Convoy
May 30th.	362	England	Baltic	*Princess Carolina*
June 1st.	145	Baltic	England	*Alexandria* and *Sheldrake*
June 4th.	35	England	Baltic	*Pyramus*
June 11th.	76	Baltic	England	*Vanguard* and *Diligence*
June 13th.	5	England	Baltic	*Africa*
June 21st.	150	England	Baltic	*Loire* and *Erebus*
June 27th.	175	Baltic	England	*Solebay* and *Wrangler*
July 12th.	175	Baltic	England	*Lynx* and *Alonzo*
July 23rd.	332	England	Baltic	*Hussar*
July 27th.	220	Baltic	England	*Fisgard* and *Reynard*

Total 1675

133. *Yorke to Saumarez*

Admiralty,

18 Aug. 1810.

Dear Sir, The concluding paragraphs of your letter of the 25 ultimo were extremely satisfactory to the other members of H.M. government to whom I had the opportunity of communicating it as well as to myself and the rest of the board of admiralty; and the apparently intended inactivity of the Russian fleet (which it would seem is not likely to make its appearance in any force this season) as well as the friendly disposition of the Swedes (to be encouraged by all proper means) offer results highly advantageous to H.M. service at this conjuncture.

Under these circumstances, and because the enemy's preparations in the Scheldt as well as the critical situation of affairs in the *Tagus* and at *Cadiz* render an increase of our disposable force at home extremely desirable, it is the intention of the board to desire you to send home such of your line-of-battle ships as can be best spared, as well as to authorize you to take measures for sending back into port before the autumn is too far advanced such further part of your squadron as you may not deem it *necessary* to keep on your station. The *Hero* which is stated to require docking and the *Standard* which is wanted for a particular service, and possibly one or two more, will be called for in a short time.

Tho' a movement of the enemy in the Scheldt on the rear (or western wing) of your squadron is not impossible, but *may be* on their cards, yet is is imagined here not very probable and hardly feasible at a later period. There are 9 off Flushing and 1 more coming down, 2 at Helvout, and 6 or 8 in the Texel and Zuyder Zea [Zuyder Zee]. But there is no fear but *Pellew* will keep a good look-out after them; and should they attempt to come towards your rear, will take the necessary measures to support you.

I am sorry to say affairs in Ireland look very unpleasant, and I think it probable that the preparations in the ports of Holland and Flanders look that way. We shall want by and by a strong squadron of observation (besides all the others) to prevent any possible mischief, *where we ought to leave no opening whatever*. I am etc.

134. *Saumarez to Croker*

Victory, in Hanö Bay,

19 Aug. 1810.

Sir, I have received your secret letter of the 8th. instant enclosing the copy of one from a secret correspondent of the secretary of state for foreign affairs relative to a vessel belonging to Mr. Schröder, the Danish consul at Colberg, which had been captured by one of the cruizers under my orders; and which Mr. Schröder states to be in violation of a promise received from me as an acknowledgement and recompense for his services, and signifying their lordships' directions to report upon the circumstances represented together with my opinion as to the propriety of granting a remuneration to Mr. Schröder.

I beg you will please to inform their lordships that in consequence of the services rendered to His Majesty's government by Mr. Schröder in affording assistance to messengers and forwarding dispatches during the war, I, at his

request and with a view of remunerating him for his trouble, furnished him
with protection for two vessels, the names of which he enclosed to me, to
proceed from Petersburg; both of which arrived in safety at Colberg without being molested by the cruisers. But the vessel alluded to in Mr. Johnson's
letter, not having been furnished with a permit, was captured by the *Alban*
cutter after I had left the station last year, and I find has since been condemned by the court of admiralty in England. The zeal displayed by Mr.
Schröder on various occasions in my opinion entitles him to some remuneration, but it must be left for His Majesty's government to decide how far he is
entitled to the sum proposed.

In my letter to you of the 11th. instant I requested I might be allowed to
furnish Mr. Schröder with licences for two or three vessels trading from
Petersburg, not deeming myself authorized under present circumstances,
without their lordships' knowledge and approval, to allow Russian produce
to enter a port where British commerce is excluded, however desirous I may
be to grant Mr. Schröder this indulgence. I am etc.

135. *Saumarez to Yorke*

Victory, Hanö Bay,

21 Aug. 1810.

Sir, Admiral Krusenstjerna has done me the honour this morning to come
on board the *Victory* with a verbal communication which he has been charged
to make to me from the king of Sweden relative to the election of an heir
apparent to the throne. After expressing to me the regard and confidence of
His Swedish Majesty for my services to Sweden, Admiral Krusenstjerna
signified to me that he was desired by His Swedish Majesty to communicate
to me His Swedish Majesty's intentions to maintain the harmony and good
understanding that subsist between the respective nations, in which the
interest of Sweden is so particularly concerned. In order to the maintenance
of that harmony, as well as for the existence of Sweden, it was indispensable
that the government should be headed by a person who was independent
and not liable to submit to the will of others. He was directed to inform me
that of the four persons who have been proposed to be successor to the
throne of Sweden, the prince of Augustenborg[1] had declined the acceptance
of that distinction in favour of His Majesty the king of Denmark[2] but who,
from political circumstances, was *not* considered eligible. The prince of

---

[1] Frederik Christian, duke of Augustenborg, was brother of the recently deceased crown
prince.
[2] Frederik VI, king of Denmark 1808–38.

Oldenburg[1] had also been mentioned, but insuperable obstacles also arose to prevent the choice fixing upon His Serene Highness. The prince of Ponte Corvo,[2] through the medium of the Swedish minister at Paris, had offered himself a candidate for the high situation, and was the person recommended by the king of Sweden to the diet now assembled at Örebro to be successor to the late crown prince.

Admiral Krusenstjerna was also instructed to signify to me that the prince of Ponte Corvo, in offering himself for this distinction, had professed his firm intentions, as far as depended on him, to maintain the relative situations between England and Sweden, and that his proposing himself was without the participation of Bonaparte. He further mentioned that he was, of all others, the person who would have the firmness to oppose the intentions of Bonaparte or his agents and ministers in the intercourse with other countries.

The admiral was further directed to signify to me that the king of Sweden earnestly hoped that this communication would be acceptable to the king, my august sovereign, and that it would be considered as an additional proof of his earnest wish to preserve the harmony and friendship that have so long subsisted between the two nations.

I requested that Admiral Krusenstjerna would put down in writing the substance of the communication he had to make to me, which he declined being contrary to the instructions he had received. I have, however, stated the particulars of the whole communication as nearly as I possibly can from memory. I have etc.

136. *Saumarez to Yorke*

Victory, Hanö Bay,

7 Sept. 1810.

Dear Sir, Since the letter I had the honour to write to you relating to the election of Bernadotte to be successor to the crown of Sweden, I have received the enclosed document from Admiral Krusenstjerna accompanied with a letter from him, a copy of which I also enclose for your information.

The very injudicious conduct of Captain Acklom, alluded to in the letter, is at this time more particularly unfortunate. I satisfied Admiral Krusenstjerna of my entire disapproval of so great irregularity and signified to him my having recalled Captain Acklom in order to account for his conduct. He

[1] The obstacle to the candidature of Peter, duke of Oldenburg, was that his son and heir George was married to Ekaterina, a sister of Tsar Alexander 1. The house of Oldenburg was thought to be too closely identified with Russian interests.

[2] For a recent scholarly account in a non-Scandinavian language of Bernadotte's election as crown prince and the consequences thereof, see P. Tommila, *La Finlande dans la Politique Europeene en 1809–1815* (Helsinki, 1962).

is a very meritorious officer who has served three years in the Baltic and every former instance acquitted himself in the most judicious manner. I shall delay taking any measures respecting him until I receive the directions of the admiralty in reply to my letter enclosing his statement of the circumstance.

The great embarassment the trade is thrown in by the occupation of French troops of the ports in Mecklenburg and Prussia will, I fear, be severely felt by the merchants in England. They cannot too speedily send directions to their correspondents in Sweden for the disposal of their vessels that have been prevented fulfilling the first object of their voyage.

I am informed that king of Denmark has taken great offence at the deception put upon him by Bonaparte in supporting Ponte Corvo in his election, at the time that he was giving His Danish Majesty the strongest assurances of supporting his claims with all his influence. Mr. Fenwick, formerly consul at Elsinore, informs me that he is well convinced from the intelligence he has obtained that the Danish king and court have lately changed their politics and that the government are disposed to embrace the very first opportunity to vindicate its independence and to break with France.

The late prevailing westerly winds have prevented my receiving any accounts from the Gulf of Finland or any of the ports in Russia. I have etc.

Enclosure:

136a. *Krusenstjerna to Saumarez*

Örebro,

29 Aug. 1810.

Sir, I have the honour to inform your excellency of my arrival at this town on the 24th. and that the following day I was introduced to His Majesty who graciously permitted me to relate before him the contents of the conference with your excellency of which I had the honour the 21st. His Majesty, of whose particular regard I have been entrusted verbally to assure your excellency, expressed to me even on this occasion his most sincere wishes and his firm resolution to maintain, as much as will depend upon him, the moderate system and good harmony which still subsist between our respective nations.

The election of successor to the Swedish throne were executed the 21st. also, three days before my return. I do myself the honour to include for your excellency's information a true copy of the act of election. The obligations therein prescribed the successor to turn over to the religion of this country and to resign all his former titles and employments will, I hope, serve as a farther proof to convince your excellency that no French interest can have directed or imposed upon the free choice of the representatives of this nation. The prince of Ponte Corvo is really, in my private opinion, the only man who at the head of the Swedish government will be capable to oppose the despotic influence of Bonaparte and his agents, to maintain the independence and promote the true interest of the Swedish nation.

The British ship and captain, by whose orders the guns were spiked on board His Majesty's schooner the *Celeritas* the 8th. of this month, are reported by the officer who commanded the schooner to have been Capt. Acklom of the *Ranger* sloop-of-war. His Swedish Majesty are plainly convinced that your excellency will reprimand and prevent such unpleasant accidents for the future. I am etc.

137. *Saumarez to Croker*

Victory, in Hanö Bay,

7 Sept. 1810.

Sir, You will please to inform the Lords Commissioners of the Admiralty that the trade mentioned in the enclosed list, collected since the departure of the *Plantagenet*, sailed under convoy of the *Daphne* on the 30th. ultimo for Dars Head.

Having received information that all the Prussian ports and places of consideration would be garrisoned by French troops and that the commanders of the troops destined to occupy Prussia were nominated and set off for their destination, I have issued orders to the squadron to communicate this intelligence to such of the trade as may be bound to Prussian ports and direct them to repair to this anchorage for orders.

There being several vessels under licence which have been prevented entering the ports of Wismar and Rostock in consequence of their being occupied by French troops, I request that application may be made to the merchants for directions to be sent as speedily as possible for the further proceedings of these vessels and those expected by the numerous convoys that have been so long detained by contrary winds in Hawke Road and Wingo Sound.

In consequence of the insecurity of this anchorage for the trade to resort to at this advanced season of the year, I have directed them to proceed to the harbour of Matvik under the protection of His Majesty's sloop *Lightning* and such other vessels as I shall hereafter appoint until the departure of the last convoy which is fixed for the 15th. of November.

I propose to order Captain Hollis of the *Standard* to proceed with those that are now in readiness, as soon as an easterly wind will enable them to get thro' the Belt. I am etc.

138. *Toker to Saumarez*

Cruizer, off Hanö Island,

11 Sept. 1810.

A statement of the observations on the trade on the south side of the Baltic made on board His Majesty's sloop *Cruizer*:

The *Cruizer* whilst off Jasmünd on the 13th. June boarded the *Amelia* galliot under Papenburgh colours with a cargo of British colonial produce, the master of which vessel stated that he had that morning left Stralsund by order of his merchants in consequence of a rumour that the French intended seizing all produce wearing the appearance of British whether in American or other bottoms which we afterwards found had taken place from boarding an American ship (at anchor under Griefswald island) whose cargo was at that time under the French seal in warehouses at Stralsund, and learnt from another that he had been allowed to discharge his without seizure in consequence of his merchant in Stralsund making it appear that the cargo was actually his and had been shipped as Swedish property at Gothenburg. A third ship stated that by dint of exertion he had conveyed his cargo away by means of land carriage before the French had it in their power to receive intelligence, but was anxious at that time to get clear of the coast fearing they would seize the vessel. July the 7th. we boarded the *Assistance* galliot with British produce prevented from going into Stralsund by his merchants in consequence of the French are sent to Rostock.

August 28th. We boarded the *Junger Ehbert*, under Bremen colours, off Colberg bound for that port from London with a clearance from Baltimore and a cargo of cotton wool, coffee, sugar, etc. She had been at Swinemünde some time and found so much difficulty in landing her cargo that they were then going to try Colberg. Three days after we observed the same vessel apparently returning to the port she came from. An American ship was then laying in the roads which had been boarded by His Majesty's brig *Censor* and had been laying there a week or ten days without a probability of getting clear of the cargo, although actually an American bottom. And from what has passed in conversation with people of various descriptions on the coast of Prussia (since the last date) I cannot draw any other conclusion for their not purchasing produce at this time than that they appear to have a dread of French spies communicating its arrival to the soldiers and that from their being in the neighbourhood that they could not convey it away before the military would put the French seals on it.

139. *Yorke to Saumarez*

Admiralty,
18 Sept. 1810.

Dear Sir, I had the honour of receiving your private letter of the 27th. ult. together with the duplicate of your dispatch marked *most secret*, and the accompanying secret letter detailing what passed between the Swedish Admiral Krusenstjerna and yourself in reference to the late proceedings in the Swedish diet and the election of Bernadotte as successor to the crown of Sweden.

These interesting papers, which confirmed the accounts which had been previously received of this extraordinary transaction, have been communicated to the king's ministers.

I am at present only to express to you my sense of the prudent and proper manner in which you appear to have conducted yourself on this occasion in your conversation with the Swedish admiral, and to acquaint you that the earnest desire entertained by H.M's government of preserving the relations of peace and amity with Sweden as long as possible remains unaltered.

We have made every practicable enquiry of the Archangel merchants and shipmasters respecting the state of preparation of the Russian ships at that port; and it appears from the information hitherto received from them that there is no expectation entertained of their attempting a passage to the Baltic *this season*, and that so late as the 18th. ult. no preparation for that purpose was making or for putting the six ships-of-the-line in a situation to pass the bar, to do which they must, as I understand, take out their guns.

Copies of the information hitherto received have been ordered to be communicated to you; and you will of course use your own judgement as to the retaining a sufficient number of ships in the position of Hawke Roads or at the entrance of the Sound to intercept these Russians in the event of your considering it probable that they will attempt the passage this season. We shall endeavour, if practicable, to have a reserve of 4 or 5 line-of-battle ships ready to go to the entrance of the Sleeve if necessary to form an *outer* line to that composed by the ships of your squadron.

Should you deem it *improbable* that any attempt will be made to pass these ships into the Baltic this year, you will of course take measures for sending in your ships from time to time as you can spare them in order that they may be refitted and got ready for service again as soon as possible.

You will have received official information of the present deteriorated state of the entrance of Yarmouth Roads, (St. Nicholas Gat) which will make it unadviseable for ships-of-the-line to make too free with it, till further researches have been made. Hoseley Bay has been surveyed by Mr. Whedley who reports most favourably of it and as far preferable to Yarmouth at any time. Directions have therefore been given for buoying the shoals and for providing water etc for such ships as may be stationed there in future. I have etc.

140. *Saumarez to Yorke*

Victory, Hanö Bay,

20 Sept. 1810.

Dear Sir, In the letter I transmit with my official dispatch from Admiral Krusenstjerna he lays very particular stress upon the ports in Swedish Pomerania being allowed to trade with the ports in Sweden. He came on board the *Victory* last Monday, and he verbally communicated to me from His Swedish Majesty his particular wish that I should represent to government the great distress and inconvenience that individuals sustained, as well as the country at large, from that trade not being permitted.

As the season is drawing near when it will not be possible to prevent vessels trading from Sweden to the southern coast of the Baltic, granting them the liberty to trade to Swedish Pomerania would be conferring at this time an act of favour to Sweden which would be well received by them, and which it will not be in our power to prevent in a short time. It would also be the means of introducing to the continent colonial and British produce from the ports of Sweden, which is not admitted from other countries.

I have every reason to believe that the government is perfectly well disposed, and that they dread nothing so much as to be in hostility with England. I have received no account relating to Denmark since the letter I had the honour to address to you. I am etc.

141. *Krusenstjerna to Saumarez*

Carlskrona,

20 Sept. 1810.

Sir, In consequence of the orders I received this night with a courier from H.S.M. minister of state for foreign affairs His Excellency Baron von Engeström, I am charged with the honour to inform your excellency of a very unpleasant accident which has taken place in the harbour of Marstrand the 14th. of this month.

The commandant of the castle, who protects the port of Marstrand, has reported His Majesty that from the British frigate, who were cruizing outward the entrance to the harbour, a boat were sent in on the afternoon the

14th. last in which there appeared only two men, the rest being stowed down with their arms.

The sentinels of the castle, believing it to be a fishing boat, took no notice thereof, but soon after a Danish privateer which was anchored in the harbour appeared to be under way and to work himself out. The commandant, who rightly judged that the privateer could not be directed by his own good will to venture to go to sea as long as a British frigate were seen to be cruizing before the port, suspected him instantly to have been surprized and taken by his enemy. He hailed the privateer which he found to be in possession of the English, then very near under the castle, and told him to return to his anchorage. After several repeated intimations the privateer returned, but shaped his course to another sound where the English officer, who commanded on board, run the vessel ashore and tried to set fire thereon. This were, however, prevented by an armed boat sent from the castle in order to retake the privateer and restore him to his former owner. The Brittish officer, judging it equally impossible to destroy as it was to carry away the privateer, took his refuge to the boat wherein he also embarqued the Danish crew; but being chased by the boat from the castle and finding no probability to work his escape, he commenced to fire on the Swedish boat, which returned the fire and forced the Brittish boat to surrender with 2 officers and 17 men who were carried, the former to the tower, the latter to the castle. I am extremely sorry to inform your excellency than an English midshipman are reported to have been killed on the occasion.

His Swedish Majesty, who in the present state of political affairs has done everything in his power to maintain harmony and prevent disturbances between the respective governments, are very sorry that the British cruizers under the command of your excellency shall, as His Majesty presume it, contrary to the intentions of the British government and to the orders they might have received from your excellency, permitt themselves to committ such atrocities against the rights of a friendly nation.

I refer myself to my verbal communication with your excellency, by means of which I had the honour to represent to your excellency His Majesty's just complaints, 1st. of the conduct of Capt. Acklom against His Majesty's schooner, the *Celeritas*, 2nd. the capture of the *Wagram*, French privateer taken in the harbour of Stralsund. Besides this, there has been made several captures within reach of gunshot from the Swedish shore, of which bitter complaints has been communicated His Majesty's ministers from the Danish government. The lately timed unpleasant accident would have comprometted His Majesty with all the ennemys of Great Brittain, who certainly wish no better than to find opportunity for obliging His Majesty to an open rupture, should the commandant of the castle of Marstrand not have been so active and so lucky to recover the capture. His Majesty find also the strongest reason to aprove the conduct of the commandant, but meanwhile presuming that this molestation of His Majesty's rights are strictly contrary to the intentions of the Brittish government, and wishing to testify as well his high regard for His Britannic Majesty as the sincerity of his wishes to prevent every disturbance and maintain the good understanding between both governments, His Majesty has graciously been pleased to ordain that the captured English officers and men, with the boat in which they were taken, shall be released and restored.

His Majesty earnestly wish that your excellency, of whose candour and goodwill for maintaining good harmony His Majesty are plainly confident, would take such efficacious measures, as will be judged necessary, to prevent every future unpleasant accident of this nature.

I embrace this oportunity to renew my assurance of the very high consideration and most faithful attachment wherewith I have etc.

142. *Croker to Saumarez*

Admiralty Office,
26 Sept. 1810.

Sir, I am commanded by my Lords Commissioners of the Admiralty to send you herewith copy of a letter from Messrs. Emes, chairmen of the Baltic merchants, requesting that every possible facility may be given in forwarding and affording every protection to the ships up to such ports as they may be ordered to by their agents and correspondents, and to signify their lordships' directions to you to comply with the request of the merchants accordingly. I am etc.

Enclosure:

142a. *W. and P. Emes to Croker*

London,
25 Sept. 1810.

Sir, In consequence of Mr. Barrow's letter of the 22nd. instant transmitting as an extract of a letter from Vice-Admiral Sir J. Saumarez relative to the vessels under licences being prevented from entering the ports of Wismar and Rostock, we have called a meeting of the merchants interested in the Baltic trade to whom we have communicated the same, but it is impossible for them to give any instructions from hence as to the proceedings of the vessels detained under these circumstances: and the masters will receive instructions from the agents in Gothenburg and Carlshamn of the different merchants who have shipped in these vessels as to the manner in which they are to act and the ports they must proceed to. And we are particularly requested to beg that their lordships will be pleased to send out instructions to Vice-Admiral Sir James Saumarez directing him to give every possible facility in forwarding and affording protection to the ships up to such ports as they may be ordered to by their agents or correspondents. We are etc.

143. *Krusenstjerna to Saumarez*

Carlskrona,

28 Sept. 1810.

Sir, I have the honour to acknowledge the receipt of your excellency's letter of the 24th., the contents of which I have had the honour to transmit for the information of my government.

In reply to the answer your excellency has been pleased to give on the subject complained of in my letter of the 20th. I beg leave to observe that the *Wagram* was fitted and equipped as a privateer in the port of Stralsund long before that place and port were restored under the dominion of His Swedish Majesty.

The depradations of the Danish privateers are too much experienced by the Swedish trade for to find any excuse from the Swedish government, but I think it equally contrary to the rights of nations as it is against the dignity of governments to suffer comittence of hostilities in any of its fortified ports or within reach of gunshot from any defended place of its coasts.

I have no doubt that His Majesty's ministers will return the complaints represented them from the Danish government with a request that this government might put a stop to the molestations which His Majesty's subjects and neutral vessels has suffered under the Swedish coast from the insolence of Danish privateers.

I am most perfectly persuaded that my royal sovereign will enjoy the greatest satisfaction in accepting the assurance your excellency has been pleased to communicate of His Britannic Majesty's intentions to preserve the harmony and good understanding that exist between both nations: intentions which, for the benefit and prosperity of both nations, it has been an object for His Swedish Majesty's earnest wishes and most studious endeavours to inspire in the British government. The zealous support which your excellency has been pleased to give for promoting this great interest intitle your excellency to that gratitude of the Swedish nation and the most distinguished regard from its sovereign.

It is with sentiments of the most perfect esteem and consideration that I have etc.

Apostille: By a letter which I in this moment received from His Excellency Baron von Engeström, I am charged to assure your excellency of His Swedish Majesty's most sincere regard and his very high satisfaction with the answer and explications that I have received from your excellency on the subjects complained of in my letter of the 20th.

His Majesty has also graciously charged me to express his wish that the affair with the *Celeritas* may drop without any further inconvenience for Capt. Acklom than the reproaches he already has received from your excellency.

144. *Barrow to the Senior Officer of H.M. ships at Gothenburg*

Admiralty Office,

5 Oct. 1810.

Sir, I am commanded by my Lords Commissioners of the Admiralty to signify their directions to you to provide a passage as soon as possible in an armed vessel for Mr. J. M. Johnson, who is about to proceed to the continent on His Majesty's service, from Gothenburg to Colberg or to any other neighbouring port on that coast at which he may be safely disembarked. I am etc.

145. *Saumarez to Croker*

Victory, in Hanö Bay,

8 Oct. 1810.

Sir, You will please to inform the Lords Commissioners of the Admiralty that I have directed Rear-Admiral Reynolds to proceed with the *St. George* and *Formidable* to the Downs and that I have also ordered the *Edgar* and *Alonzo* to that anchorage and the *Gorgon*, hospital ship to North Yarmouth.

I have directed Captain Sir Archibald C. Dickson of the *Orion* to give instructions to the homeward-bound trade assembling in Matvik harbour, and to proceed with them under his protection and some of the smaller vessels under his orders to see them in safety to the ports of England.

I shall proceed in the *Victory* to Wingo Sound making such further arrangements in passing the Great Belt as I may find circumstances to require; and I hope on my arrival off Wingo to receive their lordships' orders for my further proceedings.

Conformable to my letter to you of the 14th. ultimo I propose to leave Captain Eyles[1] of the *Plantagenet*, with the *Minotaur* and *Africa* under his

[1] Thomas Eyles, lieutenant, 1790; captain, 1795; rear-admiral, 1814.

orders, for the protection of the last convoy to leave the Baltic on the 15th. of November; and previous to my leaving Hanö Bay I shall adopt such further measures for the protection of the trade that circumstances will admit, according to the state of the season after the departure of the last convoy. I am etc.

146. *Saumarez to Croker*

Victory, off Hanö Island,

12 Oct. 1810.

Sir, You will please to inform the Lords Commissioners of the Admiralty with my having sailed from Hanö Bay this morning having left Captain Barrett of His Majesty's ship *Minotaur* at that anchorage; and I herewith enclose for their lordships' information a copy of my orders to him to repair to Matvik for the protection of the trade. Sir A. C. Dickson in the *Orion* is in that harbour, having received my orders to sail on the 15th. instant with the trade that may have assembled there at that time; and I have left orders for Captain Ryves of the *Africa* to sail with the subsequent convoy on the 29th.

I am in daily expectation of seeing the convoy that I am informed sailed from Wingo Sound for the Baltic on the 8th. instant. By a messenger which has just arrived from Gothenburg I have received your letter of the 22nd. ultimo respecting the island of Anholt to which I shall pay every attention on my passage thro' the Belt. I am etc.

Enclosure:

146a. *Instructions to Barrett dated 11 Oct. 1810*

You are hereby required and directed to repair in His Majesty's ship under your command to Matvik harbour and remain there for the protection of the trade of His Majesty's subjects under licences, which may from time to time assemble there, until the 15th of November next, when, taking under your command His Majesty's ships and vessels named in the margin [*Loire, Erebus, Ariel, Censor, Cheerful*], you are to proceed with as little delay as is consistent with the safety of the convoy thro' the Great Belt, and on your arrival off Wingo Sound take the trade that may be in readiness to avail themselves of your protection, and, after being clear of the enemy's ports in the Sleeve, detach the trade bound to the northern ports and repair with the remainder off Yarmouth where, having seen them in safety, you are to proceed with the *Minotaur* to the Downs, reporting your arrival to the secretary of the admiralty for the information of the Lords Commissioners, and transmitting to me a report of your proceedings under cover to John Barrow, Esq., their lordships' secretary.

On the arrival of His Majesty's ship *Africa* you are to deliver to Captain Ryves[1] the enclosed order directing him to proceed with the homeward bound trade, that may have assembled there on the 29th. instant, the first favourable wind and weather afterwards, placing under his order His Majesty's bomb vessel *Fury* and the vessels named in the margin [*Tartarus*, *Lightning*, *Woodlark*].

During your stay at Matvik you are to transmit to me a weekly report of your proceedings and the number of convoy assembled, agreeable to the form you will receive herewith, to be forwarded by post to Messrs. Schmidt and Co. of Carlshamn under an envelope to John Smith, Esq. Gothenburg, also giving me an account of any alteration in the state of His Swedish Majesty's ships in the port of Carlscrona, and also transmit to Rear-Admiral Dixon, stationed in the Great Belt, any information you may deem of importance for his knowledge.

During your stay in the Baltic you are to be particularly cautious not to give any ground of offence to Sweden, nor to permit any of the officers to be absent from their respective ships except when the service may require it.

Until the time appointed for your leaving the Baltic you are to keep some of His Majesty's sloops or vessels under your orders constantly cruising off the Utklippers, in Danzig Bay and off the Eartholmes for the protection of the trade of His Majesty's subjects. Given etc.

147. *Saumarez to Croker*

Victory, in Wingo Sound,

18 Oct. 1810.

Sir, I have received your letter of the 22nd. ultimo signifying to me the directions of the Lords Commissioners of the Admiralty to furnish you for their lordships' information with a detailed opinion on the advantages to be expected from keeping possession of the island of Anholt, both in a military and a commercial point of view.

I request you will be pleased to inform their lordships that I consider the possession of the island of Anholt to be of the utmost importance to His Majesty's service inasmuch as it affords a constant supply of excellent water for the squadron stationed in these seas, and which is not attainable on any

---

[1] George Frederick Ryves served on the West Indian and American stations during the American revolution; lieutenant, 1779; captain, 1798; appointed to command the *Africa* (64) in March 1810, his last employment.

of the small islands off Gothenburg during the summer months, and very partially in the spring and autumn. It also affords an anchorage for the trade of His Majesty's subjects when totally excluded from the Swedish ports; and the advantage of the lighthouse greatly tends to the safety of convoys passing to or from the Baltic. From the present restrictions of the trade with the continent, it may in a certain degree serve as a depot for colonial produce and British merchandize which may be exported from thence to the coast of Jutland, to Zealand and the islands in the Belt, and find its way from thence to the coasts of Holstein and Mecklenburg.

The garrison has been ordered to be augmented to 500 men which Captain Maurice,[1] governor of the island, considers as a sufficient force to repel any attack the enemy may make against it after the works constructing for the defence of the island are completed.

Their lordships will further appreciate the advantages derived from the possession of Anholt when they are pleased to consider that on the event of the political relations with Sweden being entirely abandoned, there is no other place in the Sleeve or Cattegat where the trade can be protected from the innumerable gunboats and armed vessels, nor where a supply of water can be obtained for the use of His Majesty's fleet. Neither is there any place within the Baltic nearer than Gatska Sandö, the entrance of the Gulf of Finland, where that essential and important article can be procured. I have etc.

148. *Saumarez to Yorke*

Victory, Hawke Road,
23 Oct. 1810.

Dear Sir, I have the honour to acquaint you that yesterday I received a letter from Mr. Fenwick informing me that the new crown prince landed at Helsinborg from Zealand on the 19th. instant. I understand he dined with the king of Denmark the day preceding without making any stay at Copenhagen.

The orders I have received to permit the trade from Sweden to the Swedish ports in Pomerania will afford great satisfaction to this country without, I trust, being prejudicial to us. It evidently appears to be the disposition of Sweden to keep upon terms of friendship with England, but what effect the arrival of Bernadotte may make is very doubtful.

[1] James Wilkes Maurice (1775–1857), lieutenant, 1797; distinguished service in defence of Diamond Rock, 1805; captain, 1809; governor of Anholt, Aug. 1810–Sept. 1812; no further employment; retired rear-admiral, 1846.

I sincerely congratulate you on the glorious success of Lord Wellington in repelling the attacks of the French army under Massena.[1] I have etc.

149. *Saumarez to Yorke*

Victory, Wingo Sound,

5 Nov. 1810.

Dear Sir, Owing to the *Folkestone* lugger having unfortunately proceeded to the Belt without calling off this anchorage I had not the honour to receive your letter of the 19th. ult. before yesterday evening. Not being aware of the probability of the enemy's force in the Scheldt being destined for these seas[2] in the event of their being enabled to elude the vigilance of Sir Edward Pellew's squadron, I detached to England most of the largest line-of-battle ships conformable to the directions I had previously received on that head; and after having made the final arrangements for the security of the last convoy I was proceeding with this ship to the Downs. I expect the *Resolution*, *Saturn* and *Africa* from the Belt which, with the *Victory* and *Ardent*, I trust will enable me to check the progress of the enemy's squadron should they attempt to enter the Cattegat, or, (should they be in too great force) to effect a junction with the remaining five under Admiral Dixon which will defeat their object of attacking our convoy, altho' it may not be in my power to prevent their getting to Copenhagen.

Since my departure from Hanö Bay I have had no communication whatever from Copenhagen or any intimation of what may have been the result of Bernadotte's visit on his way to Sweden. It is understood that at Helsinborg he expressed himself in terms strongly favourable to the commercial intercourse between Sweden and England, but it must be supposed so long only as he considers it to the interest of the former.

If it were possible for us to go on without any trade to the Baltic, I am convinced it would soon reduce Russia to the necessity of making peace and also prevent Sweden having it in her power to annoy us.

I beg to observe that the date of the latest letters are to the 19th. ult., four mails being due tomorrow. I have etc.

[1] André Massena (1758–1817) made his reputation in Italy, 1796–97; marshal of France, 1804; duke of Rivoli, 1808; prince of Essling, 1809; commander-in-chief in Spain, 1810–11.

[2] No movement of the enemy fleet from the Scheldt to the Baltic was intended.

150. *Yorke to Saumarez*

Admiralty,

13 Nov. 1810.

Dear Sir, I have to acknowledge the receipt this morning of your letters of the 5th. 6th. 7th. inst. which are this moment arrived. The telegraph from Yarmouth last evening announced the arrival of the *Tartarus* with the unfortunate king of Sweden on board.[1] The necessary directions have been forwarded for permitting him to land, and for his being received with all due respect.

I am concerned to hear that the officer commanding the *Folkestone* lugger had not the good sense to call off Hawke Roads to ascertain whether you were there or not before he proceeded to the Belt. The matter however is now of the less consequence as I trust that by the time this reaches you the *Harwich* (tho' long detained by adverse winds in Yarmouth Roads) will have reached you with the board's letter of the 5th. inst. apprizing you that the enemy's squadron had retired up the Schedlt, supposed for the winter, and that you were at liberty to make your arrangements for immediately returning home with your squadron.

I embrace this opportunity of expressing the high approbation of the board as well of the steps you have taken for receiving and sending to England the king of Sweden (Count Gottorp) as of those for collecting such a force in Hawke Roads, as your means then afforded, for the purpose of checking the enemy in the event of his entrance into the Sleeve, along with preventing any accident happening to the convoys then collecting.

I am happy to add that H.M. is considerably better than he was and that no doubt is entertained of his recovery. The accounts from Lisbon are likewise highly encouraging, and Massena's army appears to be involved in serious difficulties. I remain etc.

151. *Saumarez to Yorke*

Victory, Wingo Sound,

20 Nov. 1810.

Sir, I have the honour to acquaint you that I have this moment received a private communication from Count Rosen,[2] governor of Gothenburg, that

---

[1] Gustavus's travels in 1810 brought him to Riga whence he took a passage on board a British man-of-war to Wingo. Saumarez, much to the relief of the Swedish government, sent him to Britain where he was courteously received as Count Gottorp. He returned to the continent in 1811 by way of Yarmouth and Heligoland.

[2] Axel Pontus, Count von Rosen (1773–1834) Swedish soldier and statesman; appointed deputy-governor of province of Varmland, 1805; governor, 1808; governor of Gothenburg, 1809–34; entrusted by the Swedish government with the delicate task of explaining its policy to Saumarez for the information of the British cabinet, 1810–12.

he has been informed by his government that Bonaparte has peremptorily demanded that Sweden shall adopt the same system against the commerce of England as the other powers on the continent in alliance with France, and that all British and colonial produce shall be forthwith confiscated, also that measures of hostility shall be immediately pursued towards England.

In making this communication to me in a confidential manner, Count Rosen hopes that as these measures are perfectly contrary to the sentiments of the Swedish government, and particularly to those of the crown prince, and as they are to be acted upon in the most modified manner and only confined to the sequestration of British produce, that I shall abstain from any offensive measures against Sweden.

This has been intimated to me by Mr. Parish, an eminent merchant of Hamburg, who is come on board the *Victory* accompanied by Mr. Johnson, who is on his way to the continent on the service of His Majesty's government. They also mention that [Alquier], French envoy at Stockholm,[1] has intimated having received orders from Bonaparte to quit Sweden should these measures not be adopted, and that it was expected he would leave the country, as well as the French consul at Gothenburg named Randchoup. It is added that in consequence of the early communication made by the Swedish governor in Gothenburg, it is expected that very little loss will be incurred to the British merchants, having had time to make their necessary arrangements.

I further beg to acquaint you that Count Rosen has signified to me that a person was to be immediately sent to England by the Swedish government. I have etc.

152. *Saumarez to Yorke*

Victory, Downs,

3 Dec. 1810.

Dear Sir, I have great satisfaction in acquainting you with my arrival in the Downs this afternoon after six days passage from Gothenburg. The evening previous to my departure Mr. Johnson came on board this ship, from whom I received the interesting communication, of which the enclosed is a copy for your information. I had partly decided on remaining in Wingo Sound until further accounts had reached me from England, but the strong assurances given by the Swedish government that no acts of hostility were

---

[1] Charles Jean Marie, Baron Alquier (1752–1826) was an experienced diplomat, the object of whose mission in Stockholm was the coercion of Sweden. He arrived in Stockholm on 17 Sept. 1810 and left on 2 Nov. 1811; ambassador to Denmark, 1812–14.

intended to be pursued, I considered it most adviseable at the advanced season of the year to avail myself of a favourable wind to repair to England.

As I hope to find my leave for going to London has been sent to Admiral Campbell, I shall be able to explain to you more particularly any circumstances on which you may be desirous to have further information. I have etc.

Enclosure:

152a. *Copy of a Communication made to Vice-Admiral Sir James Saumarez by Mr. Johnson*

The governor of Gothenburg has read to me the letter which he received from Mr. de Iverta communicating the declaration of the Swedish government with respect to England which declaration is not founded on any alleged grievances, but is stated to be rendered necessary by the amicable relations existing between Sweden and France. As far as I can judge from the translation, somewhat confused and imperfect, of the governor, the relations between England and Sweden will continue nearly the same as they have been for the last six months, as the new declaration appears to me to have principally in view the enforcing of municipal regulations which were enacted on a former occasion.

1. The Swedish government declares war, it is true, against Great Britain, but it is not said that any measures of active hostility are to be had recourse to.

2. Should it be found that there are any British merchantships in Swedish ports they are to be *detained* (no mention is made of confiscation or even of sequestration). It will be recollected that the declaration of the 24th. April prohibited the entry of British vessels, and I believe there are none in Swedish ports.

3. It is declared that as there is a sufficient quantity of colonial produce now in Sweden for the internal consumption of the country, no more shall be allowed to be imported, nor shall any be exported from Sweden *to the continent*, but nothing is said of the trade with the islands or with America, nor is it stated that a fresh supply shall not be imported when the stock at present on hand is consumed; and I apprehend that it will be difficult to fix precisely the quantity necessary for home consumption without leaving any surplus for exportation.

It is understood that the communication with England by packet boats is to continue, but as it is necessary that this should be done with caution, it is recommended by the governor of Gothenburg that only one packet should be dispatched weekly from Harwich for Gothenburg, and that those from

England should land their passengers and deliver their mails on parts of the coast which shall be pointed out to Mr. Smith.

I have the pleasure to inform you on the authority of Mr. Smith, late British consul here, and others that the British merchants trading to Gothenburg will not sustain any loss in consequence of the Swedish declaration.

I have also great satisfaction in being able to inform you that Count Rosen, governor of Gothenburg, has, by instructions from his government, taken every possible precaution to prevent British subjects from sustaining any loss, and, as I have already observed, these precautions have been attended with all the success that could have been desired.

On communicating to me the determination of the Swedish cabinet, Count Rosen informed me that he was instructed by his government to give the strongest assurances to His Majesty's government and to Vice-Admiral Sir James Saumarez that it was by no means the intention of the Swedish government to follow up its declaration by any act of hostility.

153. *Saumarez to Croker*

Victory, in the Downs,

3 Dec. 1810.

Sir, You will please to inform the Lords Commissioners of the Admiralty of my arrival in the Downs with His Majesty's ship *Victory*, having sailed from Wingo Sound on the 27th. ultimo, leaving Captain Honeyman of the *Ardent* with the sloop and cutter named in the margin [*Raleigh*, *Swan*] under his orders for the protection of the trade of His Majesty's subjects, and to prevent vessels arriving with British produce from proceeding to Gothenburg. I also left Captain Dundas[1] of the *Ganges* with orders to remain there until the arrival of the convoy expected from the Baltic under the protection of the *Plantagenet* and *Minotaur*.

The only Swedish naval force in Gothenburg consisted of two brigs-of-war ready for sea and thirty-three gunboats, the latter dismantled and hauled up. There appeared no disposition on the part of Sweden to adopt any hostile measures, but on the contrary the strongest assurances were given by Count Rosen, governor of Gothenburg, that no act of hostility was intended to be pursued against this country.

I enclose for their lordships' further information a copy of my orders to Captain Honeyman together with the copy of a secret letter to Captain Dundas or the senior officer in Wingo Sound. I am etc.

[1] Thomas Dundas, lieutenant, 1793; captain, 1798; commanded the *Naiad* (36) at Trafalgar.

Enclosure:

153a. *Saumarez to Dundas*

Victory, in Wingo Sound,
27 Nov. 1810.

Sir, Having received information that the Swedish government has been compelled by the present ruler of France (Bonaparte) to enter into the continental system, and that a declaration of war against England is in consequence thereof to be expected, although, as I have been informed, without any intention on the part of the Swedish government to adopt any measures of hostility, I have to desire you will hold yourself in readiness with His Majesty's ship under your command and the vessels placed under your orders to oppose any attack that may be meditated against you; but you are not on any account to commence hostilities against the Swedish flag or the trade of that country until you receive orders for that purpose. I am etc.

PART IV

1811

PART IV

INTRODUCTION

Dixon commanded the squadron in the Belt, Reynolds that in Hanö Bay, which had been established in 1810 as the rendezvous for ships from the upper Baltic ports bound for Britain. Saumarez spent the campaigning season off Gothenburg, assisted for part of the time by Rear-Admiral Durham. The campaign began on an uncertain note. There was talk of combined Franco-Russian naval movements in the Baltic, which the admiralty felt obliged to take seriously (doc. 157). On top of this came news of ships, laden on British account, being detained at Karlshamn; which, in spite of the assurances offered unofficially by the Swedish government, aroused anxieties in London concerning the intentions of Sweden. On the other hand, Saumarez found no obstacles placed in the way of a continued correspondence maintained by unobtrusive channels (doc. 167). His attention was also drawn to the growing interest of Bernadotte in the acquisition of Norway (doc. 164). It was clear, however, that no lead could be expected from Sweden in encouraging any growth of anti-Napoleonic sentiments in the north. The rising of the northern powers against Napoleon was foreshadowed in the late summer; firstly by the receipt of reports from Russia sufficiently encouraging to prompt the offer, prematurely as it turned out, of arms to the tsar (docs. 172, 181) and secondly by the dramatic turn of events in Prussia where the war party headed by Blücher and Gneisenau appeared to be in the ascendant. A selection from this interesting correspondence is printed here. Arrangements for the defence of trade were much the same as those of 1810. The importance of the possession of Anholt in this context was underlined by the Danish attempt to retake this island in the spring. Most of the documents dealing with trade protection are focussed upon the trials and tribulations of the last homeward convoy which culminated in the loss by shipwreck of the *St. George* (98), *Defence* (74) and *Hero* (74) and the deaths of nearly 2,000 men.[1] They illustrate the hazards of winter in the northern seas and the problem of reconciling the requirements of commerce with the safety of the great ships in waters distant from their bases.

---

[1] See my article, 'The Melancholy Fate of the Baltic Ships in 1811', *Mariner's Mirror* (vol. 1, 1964), pp. 123–34 and Commander W. E. May's valuable comment thereon, *ibid*, p. 282.

154. *Croker to Saumarez*

Admiralty Office,
22 March 1811.

Sir, I have it in command from my Lords Commissioners of the Admiralty to send you herewith the copy of a letter which I have received from the chairman of the Baltic trade relative to convoys to and from thence in the coming season and to signify their direction to you to govern yourself in the arrangements you may make for the protection of the said trade this year conformable to the system therein proposed as far as circumstances will permit. I am etc.

Enclosure:

154a. *W. and P. Emes to Croker*

London,
21 March 1811.

Sir, In order to prevent any misunderstanding on the points agreed upon yesterday with yourself and Vice-Admiral Sir James Saumarez for the regulation of the convoys to and from the Baltic this season, we beg leave to state the arrangement which our P.E. considered as finally settled.

In the first place with respect to the outward bound convoys, they are to sail the same as last year, viz. every fortnight from the Nore, the Humber, Leith and Long Hope Sound, the first convoys to sail on the 15th. April next, the last convoys to sail on the 15th October; and in case of the ships being dispersed in the North Sea or Kattegat, the rendezvous to be considered at Wingo Sound from whence convoys will be forwarded through the Belt up the Baltic, as they arrive there, provided the weather will admit of it.

The homeward bound vessels to rendezvous at Hanö Bay, the same as last season, and to be protected and forwarded from hence at least once a fortnight, or more frequent provided a sufficient number (say 30 vessels) are collected in a shorter space of time, and that circumstances will in any way admit of it. And as much will depend upon the line of conduct which the Swedish government may pursue, whether decidedly hostile to the trade or otherwise, it was suggested by Sir James Saumarez and fixed that the last convoys should sail from Hanö Bay for this country on the 1st of October, on account of the impossibility of remaining there later, but that provided the Swedes did not show that hostile disposition and allowed the vessels to rendezvous at Matvik, without interruption as they had done last autumn, in that event or any other favourable circumstance that might occur, it was left discretionary with Sir James Saumarez to continue the convoys from thence until the 1st of November which is at all accounts to be the latest period of their sailing from the Baltic. These we conceive to be the principal points as settled yesterday, and shall be obliged by your confirming the same in order that the merchants may be enabled to act accordingly. We are etc.

155. *Mills[1] to Saumarez*

Berlin,
24 Mar. 1811.

Sir, The name of the commander-in-chief of His Majesty's naval force in the Baltic not having yet been made known to me, I am ignorant whether I have the honour to address Admiral Saumarez or his successor on that important station. Allow me, sir, to request your attention to any persons who shall wait upon your excellency with letters bearing the signature of Franz Schmidt; and should any packets to that address or to the addresses of Gottlieb Muller, Ferdinand Grose or Mr. Tentsch be sent to your excellency I have further to request that you will have the goodness to direct their being forwarded either under cover to Monsieur Schröder, consul of His Danish Majesty at Colberg, or to Königsberg, but in the latter case they must be under double enclosures: the first directed to Mr. S. Marks[2] and the envelope to Mr. James Phillips.

When I have the honour to address your excellency, my letters will be directed as last year to W. D. Fairman and always signed Franz Schmidt. Under that name your excellency will address me if you should do me the honour to write; and in order to avoid risk in the event of having something of importance to communicate directly to His Majesty's commander-in-chief in the Baltic I will make use of an inverted alphabet[3] as on the other side. I have etc.

---

[1] George Galway Mills, a former M.P. resident in Berlin, was the most brash and indiscreet of the British agents in Germany.

[2] The alias of Alexander Gibson, who was an agent of both the house of Solly (see doc. 171) and the British government.

[3] A very simple code: $N=A$; $O=B$; $P=C$; and so in rotation through the alphabet.

156. *Saumarez to Yorke*

32 St. James Place,

9 April 1811.

Dear Sir, It was not until this moment that I have been enabled to obtain from Dr. Jamison[1] the extract of the letter to which I alluded yesterday. The writer[2] is known to be a staunch friend of this country, and equally inimical to the French party in Sweden. I cannot help expressing my firm conviction that the intention of Bonaparte is to get his fleet from the ports of Holland, if possible, to Copenhagen, and to intimidate the Swedes to fit out their fleet and to act hostilely against this country. The possession of the island of Zealand could next to amount to our exclusion from the Baltic, but even should they reach Copenhagen it would require a double force in order to guard both entrances of the Sound. I am etc.

Enclosure:

156a. *Extract from a private and confidential letter from Sweden dated 17th. Mar. 1811.*

You will no doubt become acquainted through the medium of your public prints with the afflicting state of health of our feeble-minded royal sovereign,[3] which really requires that his mind should not continue to be perplexed with the critical juncture of our political state of affairs at this moment. He has therefore prudently retired, I hope only for a short interval, and charged our *royal crown prince* to decide on the great political commotions which Bonaparte continues to agitate our country with. Notwithstanding the weak understanding of our king, yet him and his ministers were sufficiently alive to the real interest of the country to preserve *pax in bello* with dear England.

You are well acquainted with the censure I implicitly suffered by examining the body of late beloved crown prince. However, it sometime happens that out of evil good arises, if I may call this so, as the blame attached to me on that occasion has lately made me appear favourable to the French interest. I cloak myself under this mask without betraying myself, but you know the sincerity of my friendship for you and my unalterable attachment to your dear country. A few days ago in confidential confab with our bishop who is a confident of Count C. and a firm adherent to French principles I learned that

---

[1] John Jamison obtained his warrant as a naval surgeon in 1799; surgeon of the *Agamemnon* (64) at Trafalgar; physician to the Baltic fleet, 1808; K.B., 1813; died, 1844.

[2] The internal evidence strongly suggests the correspondent to have been Professor Engelhart of the university of Lund who performed the autopsy on the body of the crown prince in May 1810 immediately after his death in Scania.

[3] A reference to the increasing senility of Charles XIII, hastened by a recent stroke.

it was whispered among the French party that you were not to be masters of the Baltic Sea this campaign, as the Walcheren fleet was expected at Carlscrona with troops on board to man the forts and to give energy to the equipment of our fleet, with which and the Russians united you were or are to be driven from our shores.[1] Such I give you as the delusive whispers of the French party. And should our king not recover soon, I have great reason to tremble for the fate awaiting my poor country. Our crown prince, on first entering this kingdom acquired great popularity, but from no other reason than his supposed private hostility to France and his disposition to attend to the dearest interest of the country, that of preserving an intercourse with England. But the subjects begin now to watch him with a jealous eye; and should he, by vile artifice or treachery, depart from the principles he first adopted and asserted, *long life to him*, and God grant him forgiveness in time. You know how well disposed the landholders of Sweden are, and how brave and capable they are of serving their country, and how ready and capable they are to punish perfidious guilt. I lament to think their hitherto tranquil minds appear now disturbed and roused into suspicions, and I may say party work is now begun, and the friends of England are numerous among our best subject. The moderation and contempt you have shown to our unwilling declaration of war has increased your party greatly.

157. *Instructions by the Lords Commissioners of the Admiralty to Saumarez*
12 April 1811.

Whereas it appears by intelligence we have received that the enemy's ships in the Scheldt, the Texel and at Helvout are in a state of forwardness for service at sea, and having some reason to suppose that it may be their intention to put to sea, provided they can escape the vigilance of our several blockading squadrons, with a view, in the present state of affairs in Sweden and Denmark, of reaching Copenhagen or of passing into the Baltic, you are hereby required and directed to put to sea with such ships and vessels as have been placed under your orders and as may be ready for sea, and proceed the moment the wind and weather will permit to Wingo Sound, where you are to take up a safe anchorage and such as may be most convenient for carrying on the various services under your charge and protecting the trade to and from the Baltic agreeably to former orders and instructions, and, at the same time, stationing your cruisers in such a manner as to give you timely notice of the approach of the enemy's squadron, should its object be that of

[1] This was a rational speculation, nothing more. There is no evidence that Napoleon intended to risk the Scheldt fleet on an expedition to the Baltic. See *Correspondance de Napoléon*, vol. xxi, pp. 394, 462; vol. xxii, pp. 48, 259 ff.

passing the Sleeve, in order that you may intercept and use your utmost endeavours to take or destroy the same. With this view, you are to retain in Wingo Sound till further orders as many of the largest ships-of-the-line under your command as can possibly be spared from the service in the Belt or in the Baltic, detaching such frigates and other vessels up the Baltic, in addition to those employed for the protection of the trade, as may be necessary to keep you informed from time to time of the state of preparation, and other movements, of the line-of-battle ships and frigates in Carlscrona and Cronstadt, and using every other means of gaining intelligence of any operations that may be carrying on in either of the abovementioned ports, which you are to take care to communicate to us for our information by every opportunity.

And whereas the admiral, whom we have appointed to command a squadron of His Majesty's ships to be employed on a particular service in the North Sea, has been directed, in the event of the enemy's ships escaping from the Scheldt and proceeding to the northward, to send a frigate or sloop with all possible expedition to Wingo Sound for the purpose of gaining intelligence, and to proceed with the squadron under his orders to a rendezvous from ten to fifteen leagues S.W. of the Naze of Norway, you are hereby further required and directed to give instructions to the cruisers under your orders in the Sleeve, the Cattegat or on the coast of Norway, in the event of their falling in with the enemy, to convey to you immediate intelligence thereof and to push directly to the rendezvous abovementioned to communicate the same to the admiral who on his part has been ordered to instruct the commander of the frigate or sloop, which he shall send to Wingo Sound for intelligence, in the event of gaining such intelligence and falling in with any of your cruisers to communicate the same to their captains or commanders, who (whatever their rank may be) are to be considered responsible for conveying the information to you with the utmost possible despatch; and you are therefore to take care to furnish them with corresponding directions. Given etc.

158. *Saumarez to Croker*

London,

15 April 1811.

Sir, You will please to inform the Lords Commissioners of the Admiralty that I have directed Rear-Admiral Reynolds to proceed to Wingo Sound with His Majesty's ships named in the margin [*St. George, Hero, Courageux, Vanguard, Defence, Loire, Ethalion*], and have ordered His Majesty's sloop

Rose and *Censor* gunbrig to cruise in the Sleeve; and directed the rear-admiral to leave orders on board the *Vigo* for such ships as may not have arrived to proceed and join him in Wingo Sound. I am etc.

159. *Saumarez to Yorke*

Victory, Wingo Sound,

3 May 1811.

Dear Sir, I have the honour to acquaint you with my arrival here yesterday morning after a short passage of only four days from the Downs. Admiral Reynolds, with the detachment from Hoseley Bay, arrived here two days before, and Admiral Dixon yesterday evening.

The weather proving unfavourable I have received no communication from Gothenburg except by a letter from Mr. Smith informing me that on his having signified my arrival to the governor, he immediately dispatched a courier to Stockholm agreeable to orders he had lately received from thence, and that when the courier reached Stockholm it would determine the commander-in-chief Count Essen's[1] journey to Gothenburg which had been postponed until the account of my arrival was received.

The consul adds that everything was very quiet and tranquil hitherto and that I should see him soon on board the *Victory*. I have received letters from Mr. Fenwick informing me that the Danes are fitting out more than double the number of privateers and armed vessels than they had last year, intending, if possible, to obstruct the passage of convoys thro' the Belt. This is a service that I fear will be attended with much hazard and difficulty if the trade is carried on to any considerable extent.

The island of Anholt is threatened with a second attack, and will require a stationary force for its protection.[2] I have etc.

160. *Saumarez to Croker*

Victory, in Wingo Sound,

4 May 1811.

Sir, You will please to inform the Lords Commissioners of the Admiralty

[1] Hans Henrik, Field-Marshal Count von Essen (1755–1824) was responsible for the Swedish coastal defences in 1811. He entered the army, 1768; colonel, 1792; major-general, 1795; governor of Stockholm, 1795–97; governor-general of Swedish Pomerania, 1800–07; signatory of the treaty of Paris, 1810; governor of Norway, 1814–16; governor of Scania, 1817.

[2] A Danish force of about 1,500 men, supported by twelve gunboats, had invaded Anholt on 27 March. Aided by the timely arrival of the *Tartar* (32) and the *Sheldrake* (16) the garrison beat off the invaders. There was no second attack in 1811.

with the arrival of Rear-Admiral Durham[1] in His Majesty's ship *Ardent* with the *Dictator* yesterday evening. I propose to detach Rear-Admiral Reynolds in the *St. George* with the *Hero*, *Plantagenet* and *Tremendous* to Hanö Bay, together with such of the small vessels as can be spared, for the protection of the trade and the interception of the enemy's privateers in the Baltic. The rear-admiral will also be directed to afford convoy to the home-ward bound trade from Carlshamn and other Swedish ports; and under-standing there are several vessels laden with colonial produce for the southern ports of the Baltic that are desirous to proceed thither, and there being also several from Gothenburg, I request their lordships' directions respecting them, being unwilling to risk so much British property to the ports that are actually occupied by the enemy. I have etc.

161. *Krusenstjerna to Saumarez*

Carlskrona,

6 May 1811.

My dear sir, I am requested by the commander-in-chief of this station Admiral Baron Puke, and the governor Baron Håkansson[2] to assure your excellency, that they in consequence of orders received from their govern-ment has authorised the bearer of this Mr. John Lindegren, on the one side, to solicit, that your excellency would be pleased to communicate, either verbally to him or by private letter to me, the intentions of the British government respecting the Swedish trade during the present forced situation of war between our respective governments; on the other to assure your excellency, that the Swedish government are willing to do everything in its power (without compromize itself) for to maintain the same good under-standing which so happily existed last year, in case your excellency should be authorised to act against us in the same generous manner. Everything can be furnished to the fleet by means of trusted agents and boats from the country, but to prevent suspicion and malicious observations Baron Puke requests that your excellency would be pleased, not to permit any British boats or vessels to approach or land at the places where detachments of our troops are stationed, which on this coast is Hellavill, Puttavill, Sölfvitsborg and Matvik. The letters which your excellency should wish to have forwarded to England, if laid under cover to any of your agents in Gothenburg, can be conveyed to the post office at Sölfitsborg in any for that purpose hired fishing

---

[1] Philip Charles Henderson Calderwood Durham (1763–1845) survived the sinking of the *Royal George* in Portsmouth harbour, 1782; lieutenant, 1782; captain, 1793; com-manded the *Defence* (74) at Trafalgar; rear-admiral, 1810; K.C.B., 1815; vice-admiral, 1819; admiral, 1830; G.C.B., 1830; commander-in-chief Portsmouth, 1836–39.

[2] Anders, Baron af Håkansson (1749–1813) was governor of Blekinge.

boat, but the officer or trusted persons who are charged to deliver the parcel of letters to the post office ought however not to be dressed in uniform. Mr. Lindegren will at the next settle or arrange with your excellency respecting the furnishments of water, vegetables and cattle, which latter is to be transported in open hired boats or smaller vessels from the province of Skåne.

I avail myself of this favourable opportunity, to present your excellency with my earnest wish, that your excellency would be pleased to regard me, never as an enemy, but as a true friend of the British nation, and as a constant most sincerely attached admirer of your excellency's noble heart and great qualities; for avoiding ever to act against my friends, I have requested leave from service for a year which His Majesty has graciously granted me. I have purchased a small country seat in the S.W. part of the country which I intend to be my future abode. The transport of my household cannot be executed by land, I am also obliged to embark all my effects in a vessel, which I would send to Gothenburg, but as I dare not so to do without being provided with a licence from your excellency, I humbly request that your excellency would be pleased to inform me, if any licence for the said purpose can be granted me, in which case I beg your excellency will permit me in a next letter to assign the name of the vessel and master for which I should wish to receive such a licence.

My wife and family request me to present your excellency with their very best compliments and also to assure you of their warmest and most sincere wishes for your constant health and prosperity. I beg your excellency will be pleased to present Captain Hope, Captain Dumaresq,[1] Doctor Jamison and my good friend Mr. John Ross with my very best compliments.

It is with the highest consideration and most unfeigned attachment that I have etc.

162. *Saumarez to Yorke*

Victory, Wingo Sound,

11 May 1811.

Dear Sir, I received two days since the enclosed from Mr. Fenwick informing me of the unloading of the cargoes on board the neutral vessels at Carlsham, and that the British goods and colonial produce had been conveyed up the country. Altho' Mr. Fenwick appears under very considerable alarm at the circumstance I do not believe it to have been with any hostile

[1] Philip Dumaresq, commander of H.M.S. *Victory*, 1808–12, went to sea with Saumarez at the beginning of the war; lieutenant, 1799; flag-lieutenant to Saumarez in the actions of 1801; commander, 1803; captain, 1806. The Dumaresq and Saumarez families were related. In all probability Philip Dumaresq was a cousin of the commander-in-chief.

view against our commerce, altho' it certainly requires explanation; and I have written to Mr. Smith upon the subject.

I expected to have received some communication from Stockholm in consequence of the courier which was dispatched upon my arrival, but nothing has yet reached me. This is rather a dubious crisis, and I trust soon to be better informed of the sentiments of the Swedish government towards us. At the same time I have no reason to believe they are more hostile than last year. I have etc.

Enclosure:

162a. *Fenwick to Saumarez*

4 May 1811.

Dear Sir James, I this day communicate to the senior officer of His Majesty's ships the alarming intelligence that the cargoes of British goods and colonial produce at Carlshamn are ordered by the governor of Carlscrona to be discharged and conveyed up the country. As I am not in the secret of the actual understanding between the governments I wish that this measure may prove a mask only to the real sentiments of the Swedish court towards Great Britain, but the facts are such as make me apprehend the worst. Admiral Puke has ordered three of the largest merchant vessels to be fitted as blockships for the defence of Carlshamn which is an additional bad omen.

As your arrival at Gothenburg will either already have taken place or may daily be expected, I sincerely wish that these circumstances may soon be favourably developed. In the meantime I have etc.

163. *Instructions by the Lords Commissioners of the Admiralty to Saumarez*

16 May 1811.

Whereas the Marquis Wellesley, one of His Majesty's principal secretaries of state, hath by his letter of the 15 instant, represented to us that intelligence has been received, by which it appears that during the course of the last autumn, several merchant vessels of different nations, and among them several vessels which either belong to British subjects, or have been insured in this country, had, by stress of weather been forced on the coast of Sweden, that similar accidents having happened on the opposite coasts of the Baltic, the governments of Prussia, Denmark and Mecklenburgh, in compliance with orders from France, had confiscated all Swedish and other vessels which were at that period thrown upon the coasts of their powers respectively, and had also committed other acts which are considered by Sweden as derogatory to her commercial interests, and that the Swedish government had therefore determined to make reprisals.

And whereas his lordship has at the same time represented that information has been received that the ships belonging to British subjects, and the cargoes which have been insured to a considerable amount in this country, as above stated, will probably form a part of the reprisals ordered by the Swedish government against the vessels of Prussia, Denmark, Mecklenburg and other states, and signified the pleasure of His Royal Highness the prince regent, acting in the name and on the behalf of His Majesty, that you should be directed to remonstrate strongly against measures so deeply affecting the interests of His Majesty's subjects, and that should the Swedish government persevere in acts of this injurious nature, after such remonstrances shall have been made, you should declare to the Swedish government that you cannot permit proceedings which (under whatever pretext they may be disguised) are calculated to injure the interests of His Majesty's subjects in the most serious manner, and that you should be empowered to exercise your discretion in determining on the spot, whether the conduct of Sweden may not require an alteration of that indulgent course, which is now pursued by the British forces in the Baltic, conformably to the commands of His Royal Highness the prince regent, signified to us by his lordship's letter of the 17 ultimo; we do in pursuance of His Royal Highness's pleasure signified as aforesaid, hereby require and direct you to remonstrate strongly to the Swedish government against the measures above-mentioned, and should the said government persevere in acts of this injurious nature after such remonstrances shall have been made, you are to declare to the Swedish government that you cannot permit such proceedings, and you are hereby required and empowered to exercise your discretion in determining on the spot, whether the conduct of Sweden may not require an alteration of that indulgent course, which by an order of the 18th of last month, you were directed to pursue. Given etc.

164. *Saumarez to Yorke*

Victory, Wingo Sound,

17 May 1811.

Dear Sir, I have transmitted some information relating to Christiansand brought by an officer who has been some time a prisoner in Norway. Should an attack be determined upon, I think it probable they would consent to give up the armed vessels and flotilla in the port for the purpose of saving the town which would otherwise run great risk of being destroyed.

You will perceive, sir, that the Swedes are very intent for the possession of

Norway either by negotiation or other ways. How far it may be thought adviseable to allow Sweden the possession of so great an extent of territory, it is not for me to judge; but I consider that if Norway could be rendered independent of Denmark or any other country it would be highly favourable to Great Britain. And I do not think it improbable that the inhabitants of Norway, with the support of our government, would accede to proposals to that effect, holding out to the advantage of trade, supplies, etc.

The ships from Spithead have not yet made their appearance. Should they not shortly arrive, I propose to detach Admiral Dixon to the Belt, trusting that the squadron off the Dutch coast will keep the enemy in their ports. I have etc.

165. *Saumarez to Croker*

Victory, in Wingo Sound,

20 May 1811.

Sir, You will please to inform the Lords Commissioners of the Admiralty that Rear-Admiral Dixon with His Majesty's ships and vessels named in the margin [*Vigo, Plantagenet, Dictator, Mercurius, Woodlark, Fly, Snipe*] sailed this morning for the Great Belt together with the trade assembled at this anchorage bound for the Baltic, a list of which I herewith enclose. The rear-admiral will be joined off Anholt by the *Vanguard, Diligence* and *Safeguard*.

Having received information that a considerable number of the enemy's gunboats and armed vessels were laying in the harbour of Collendburg [Kalundborg], I have directed the rear-admiral to use his best endeavours for reconnoitring that port and, in the event of finding they may be attacked without risk and danger to His Majesty's ships under his orders, to do his utmost to take and destroy them.

Rear-Admiral Reynolds having been directed to detach one of the line-of-battle ships under his orders, with some smaller vessels, with the trade collected at Hanö Bay intended for England to see them to the entrance of the Great Belt until they fall in with Rear-Admiral Dixon, I have directed him to see them in safety as far as the island of Anholt, leaving Captain Eyles of the *Plantagenet*, with the *Woodlark* and *Fly* under his orders, to occupy the station between Dars Head and the island of Femeren to intercept the enemy's armed vessels and privateers and to cut off the communication with Zealand.

Rear-Admiral Dixon, after having seen the convoy as far as Anholt and completed his water, will repair to the station off Nyborg with the *Vanguard* and *Dictator*. I have etc.

166. *Yorke to Saumarez*

Admiralty,
21 May 1811.

Dear Sir James, I had the honour to receive your letters of the 3rd., 4th. and 11th. inst. and am glad to hear that the first division of your squadron had so favourable a passage to their rendezvous in Wingo Sound. The four ships with Linzee,[1] which have been ready for some days, have been detained by the strong easterly winds and, tho' they sailed from St. Helens the day before yesterday, I should not wonder to hear that they have put back again. *Impetueux* is getting forward, and we shall send her to you as soon as we can spare her from the reserve. *Fisgard* ought to be ready, but is to call at Deal for Mr. de Bezerra,[2] minister from Portugal to Russia, whom you will have the goodness to land as well as you can at Gothenburg, that he may find his own way forward.

I think we ought not to listen for a moment to any Swedish projects on *Norway*. My own opinion is that Bernadotte is playing us false, and at any rate I for one should dread to see a *consolidation* of the Swedish and Norwegian power, such as it is, in his, or indeed in any hands. Since the arrival of the accounts of the landing of the cargoes at Carlshamn and the accompanying measures considerable distrust appears to prevail here about the ultimate views of the Swedish government; a little more time will develop their play in all probability. In the meantime it seems very desirable that the bulk of your at present force should remain where it is (in the Sleeve) to be ready to receive the requisite orders. Admiral Young[3] has taken his station off West Capel and has 15 sail-of-the-line. Enemy, 11 in the Scheld, 3 in Texel, 2 at Helvout. When the *Impetueux* joins you will have 18, which is as many as we shall be able to give you, for some time at least.

The public letters will have apprized you of the order of the board of trade and of the government in the several points in which it was important that you should be informed. The Swedes should be *gently* but *steadily* convinced that it is in our power to resent their ill-usage and to turn the consequences of perfidy on the executors, but the evil day should be postponed as long as possible and every practicable chance should be given them of remaining in the right path.

[1] Samuel Hood Linzee, a nephew of Admiral Lord Hood; lieutenant, 1790; captain, 1794; rear-admiral, 1812.

[2] Joao Paulo Bezerra de Seixas (1756–1817), one of whose functions was to encourage the anti-French party at St. Petersburg.

[3] William Young (1751–1821), lieutenant, 1770; captain, 1778; rear-admiral, 1795; board of admiralty, 1795–1801; vice-admiral, 1799; commander-in-chief Plymouth, 1804–07; admiral, 1805; commander-in-chief North Sea fleet, 1811–14; K.B., 1814; G.C.B., 1815.

Accounts from Oporto via Bristol in 8 days received this morning give us reason to suppose that Massena has had a good beating near Almeida[1] on the 3rd., 4th. and 5th. inst. and obliged to return towards Salamanca with the loss of 4,000 killed and 700 prisoners. The British loss is stated at 1,200. It is very probable, as when the last accounts came away, a battle was shortly expected. I have etc.

167. *Saumarez to Yorke*

Victory, Wingo Sound,

28 May 1811.

Dear Sir, I have received the honour of your letter of the 20th and I beg to assure you that I shall pay particular attention to that part of it which relates to the measures to be pursued with this country. With the exception of the affair at Carlshamn, which took place previous to my arrival, nothing has occurred to cause any interruption to the same intercourse as was held last year. The usual supplies are continued and the places pointed out where they can be most readily received.

There certainly appears great prevarication in the part of the Swedish government relative to the property landed from neutral vessels at Carlshamn and in an object of so much importance I beg to suggest the expediency of one or two persons duly authorized by the merchants and underwriters concerned in the Baltic trade repairing to Stockholm for the purpose of asserting their claims and seeing how far this government may be disposed to indemnify them for the property sequestered.[2] The sooner such a measure is adopted the better as, should it be delayed and any alteration takes place between the two governments, the whole may be lost. From what passed between Baron Tawast and myself I have reason to believe that Sweden would accede to this proposal.

In my letter to the board I have recommended that the two bomb vessels that were intended for this station should be expedited. Their appearance alone would have the best effect in intimidating the Swedes to a compliance with our just demands.

I am in hourly expectation of seeing the ships from Spithead. The addition of the *Impetueux* will I hope make us sufficiently strong in line-of-battle ships, but two or three good frigates are much required.

[1] An allusion to the battle of Fuentes d'Onoro where Wellington managed to prevent the relief by Masséna of the fortress of Almeida.

[2] Appropriate compensation for British underwriters with an interest in the cargoes of the Karlshamn ships was finally arranged in March 1812 after long and complicated negotiation in Stockholm conducted by two representatives of Lloyd's, Messrs. J. Atkins and Adalbert.

I beg to offer you my sincere congratulations on the continued success of the army under Lord Wellington and I trust the accounts from Spain will prove equally splendid. I have etc.

168. *Yorke to Saumarez*

Admiralty,

14 June 1811.

Dear Sir, I take the opportunity of the *Impetueux* sailing to join your flag to acknowledge the honour of your letters of 17, 19, 24, 28 and 31 ultimo, the 3 latter of which only reached me in the course of last week.

On the subject of Christiansand you will have been informed that the board (under all the circumstances stated and having no land forces or marines adequate to the attempt upon that place at present at their disposal) do not think it at present adviseable to make any attack upon it, which can have the effect of committing any considerable part of the force under your orders.

With respect to the transactions at Carlsham, they certainly appear of an extraordinary and dubious nature. I am not at this moment enabled to inform you of the decision of H.M. government upon the subject, altho' I can rather imagine that your suggestion of sending proper persons out for the purpose of making good the claims of the merchants and underwriters to the sequestered property and of obtaining an adequate indemnification for it is likely to be adopted.

The bomb vessels are now ready and waiting to be paid at Spithead, but it is deemed adviseable to keep them a little longer in *reserve*. They will be forwarded to you, however, as soon as there is any probability of their being wanted either for *demonstration* or *actual service*. With regard to your demand of frigates, I am sorry to say that there are really none whatever that can be spared at this time from other very pressing services.

You must therefore do the best with what you have, which now amount to *six large* besides the *Daphne*. The *Grasshopper* is under orders to join you, and you will be so good as to send home a sloop of equal force in exchange for her.

It is considered best for the present that you should continue to act under the existing orders of the board by keeping with you in Wingo Sound and in the Sleeve as many of the largest and most efficient line-of-battle ships of your squadron as can be spared from other services in order to be ready to check the enemy's fleet from Flushing (now 15 or 16 of the line) in case of their attempting to come that way or to be in readiness to receive such orders for your future proceedings as circumstances may render proper.

I am very sceptical on the subject of the various reports from Russia and Prussia. Matters are hardly ripe as yet for any decisive alterations, and the French have too strong a hold on Germany and Poland. Nothing effective can be done till the Germans and Italians decide on imitating the Portuguese and Spaniards by making a *national* war on the French determined to *conquer* or perish *altogether*. I am etc.

169. *Wilkinson[1] to Saumarez*

Hanö,

20 June 1811.

Sir, I had the pleasure of receiving here on the 10th. inst. the letter wherewith you were pleased to honour me under the 6th. and am so sensible to the obliging disposition under which it was written that I feel extremely anxious to obviate the possibility of anything occurring in any part of my correspondence that might wear even the semblance of encroaching on your indulgence. It is with this desire that I could wish to establish a distinction betwixt my situation as a private individual and my capacity as a merchant, in which latter it will become an incumbent duty on me to lay aside those considerations in point of delicacy, which I trust I shall never be wanting in proper respect scrupulously to observe in the other, and indeed perhaps you will not apprehend that in making such an explanation, I shall ever intentionally transgress on your time or patience. In furtherance of this desire I shall take the liberty, with your permission, to address all my applications on matters of business through the medium of Mr. Champion,[2] leaving it to his discretion to submit them to you or to withhold them.

As yet our communications from the continent have nothing of novelty in them. The measures adopted at Hamburg against the intercourse with Great Britain and which, under the eye of Davout,[3] extend up to Königsberg are enforced with the most barbarous severity. In the neighbourhood of the former place scarce a family anyways formerly employed in the British trade is free from apprehension. Several have been transported in chains to Paris, and many have abandoned their home from the insinuations they have received of their names being upon a list of prescription, whilst at the latter some recent arrestations have occurred. The French are clandestinely augmenting

---

[1] W. D. Wilkinson, a merchant whose activities are amply explained in doc. 232a.

[2] Samuel Champion, secretary to Saumarez.

[3] Louis Nicolas Davout (1770–1823) became a marshal of France in 1804; was conspicuous in the battles of Austerlitz, Auerstädt and Wagram; governor of Warsaw, 1807–09; duke of Auerstädt, 1808; prince of Eckmühl, 1809; governor of the Hanseatic towns, noted for his rigid enforcement of the measures against British trade, 1810. He was Napoleon's minister for war during the Hundred Days.

their forces through the north of Germany and resort to every subterfuge to assign any other than the real object of their reinforcement. From Russia we have accounts of a war with France being extremely popular throughout the whole of that empire, and that the nobles and others have intimated the most earnest disposition to make voluntary contributions for its support in which Moscow, we understand, has taken a very distinguished part. The inhabitants throughout the opposite states are kept in a state of complete ignorance of the glorious events in Spain, but I have begged a few papers from Admiral Reynolds (my own not having yet reached me) detailing the late battles, which I have got transmitted to Memel to an officer there in high command, and unless you see any objection I purpose to continue this method of communicating our successes, and of throwing a proper light on the example so happily established for the emancipation of the north.

You may rely, sir, upon my paying that respect to your communication in regard to the business at Carlshamn due to the honour and deserving of the confidence in which it was imparted, and that in every instance I shall study to prove myself worthy of it. I am etc.

170. *Saumarez to Yorke*

Victory, Wingo Sound,

26 June 1811.

Dear Sir, If I could have had any further doubts upon my mind relative to the sincerity of the intentions of this government they have been perfectly removed by the conversation I had yesterday with Count Rosen who came aboard the *Victory* by desire of the crown prince in consequence of my remonstrance upon the affair at Carlshamn, as will appear by my public letter. Count Rosen assured me that it was the earnest desire of the crown prince to render Sweden independent of France, whenever he can do so consistent with her security; but they are so apprehensive that in the event of the differences between Russia and France being settled that Bonaparte will bring that country to act against Sweden, they dare not openly avow their sentiments.

I informed Count Rosen that, so long as Sweden acted up to the system he mentioned to be intended towards England, I had every reason to believe that His Majesty's government would be satisfied with it, but that if it should be deviated from I had the authority and, they might be assured, I would exert the utmost in my power to resent any aggression on the part of Sweden, with which he was perfectly satisfied, and informed me that he would communicate to the crown prince precisely what I stated to him.

There has been very serious commotions in Scania on account of the conscription, wherein several of the peasantry have lost their lives, and about three hundred have been made prisoners. A strong body of troops have been ordered to that province to restore order.

I have had the honour to receive your letter of the 13th. by the *Impetueux*, and since that one of the 8th. with a commission for Mr. de Lisle, for which I beg to return to you my sincere thanks. I have etc.

171. *Croker to Saumarez*

Admiralty,

2 July 1811.

Sir, I have it in command from my Lords Commissioners of the Admiralty to send you herewith a copy of a letter which I have received from Viscount Chetwynd[1] enclosing six licences[2] from the lords of His Majesty's most honourable privy council to enable Messrs. Solly and Sons to execute the contract entered into by them for supplying naval stores, and to signify my lord's direction to you to fill up the blanks in the manner therein mentioned before the said licences are delivered to Mr. Gibson of Königsberg, the agent of Messrs. Solly with whom you are to communicate on the subject. I am etc.

Enclosure:

171a. *Chetwynd to Croker*

Council Office, Whitehall,

1 July 1811.

Sir, Referring Mr. Fawkener's[2] letter of the 14 Ultimo to you stating that the lords of the council would grant to Mr. Solly six licences on the terms mentioned in the said letter, I am therefore directed to transmit to you the said licences in order that the same may be forwarded to Sir James Saumarez to be by him filled up with the names of the vessels, the names of the masters the tonnage and the ports where the cargoes are to be taken on board before the same are delivered to Mr. Gibson of Königsberg, the agent of Mr. Solly who will furnish Admiral Sir James Saumarez with all the particulars above stated. I am etc.

[1] Richard, 5th Viscount Chetwynd of Bearhaven (1757–1821) was clerk to the privy council.
[2] William Fawkener, clerk to the privy council; died, 26 June 1811.

172. *Yorke to Saumarez*

Admiralty,
16 Aug. 1811.

Dear Sir, I have had the honour of receiving your letter of the 29th. of July. The affair of the Carlshamn cargoes is considered here a matter of much more nicety and difficulty than at first appeared in consequence of the political situation in the north of Europe. From circumstances which have lately occurred it seems highly desirable to gain as much time as possible and to avoid coming to any rupture with Sweden as long as there is any chance of a favourable turn of affairs in that quarter. For this reason, and altho' we cannot altogether entertain (at least to the same extent) the favourable opinion you appear to possess of the fair and amicable intentions of the Swedish government, in this occasion it has been thought adviseable to frame the instructions which you will receive officially by the same convey-ance with this letter. It has not been thought expedient for several reasons to employ Mr. Foy[1] nor to acquiesce in the terms suggested by M. d'Engeström; and alternately it will be expected that the Swedes should restore all that can be proved to be British property in order that the agents and consigners may either return to England or dispose of it on the spot, as may turn out most for their advantage. In the mean time, there will be no difficulty about allow-ing any of the persons interested in these cargoes to proceed, if they so will, into Sweden for the purpose of taking care of their own concerns.

You will find that your conduct in restricting the coasting trade of Sweden between Gothenburg and Strömstadt has been approved.

I am glad to find that *Grasshopper* and convoy were arrived and proceed-ing to their destination.[2] Further advices from Russia are anxiously looked for; and before it is long a person will probably present himself to you charged with a mission of importance to that quarter.

Prince Lubomirski[3] does not appear to have been provided with any express *credentials*.

Reports state that the French fleet are gone up the Scheldt and landed the *garnisons de vaisseaux*; but it is not quite ascertained. We shall reckon on your holding in readiness the six sail-of-the line ordered, in case we should want them on this side.

I am sorry to say the good old king continues in a very anxious state, tho' no immediate danger is apprehended. I am etc.

[1] George Foy, an agent in Stockholm of the British government.
[2] The *Grasshopper's* convoy was made up of transports laden with arms for Russia, the sending of which was prompted by reports that a Franco-Russian war was imminent. But the offer was premature and the convoy was turned away.
[3] Prince Casimir Lubomirski was sent to London by the tsar in July to explore privately the possibilities of a reconciliation with Britain.

173. *Barrow to Saumarez*

Admiralty Office,

19 Aug. 1811.

Sir, I am commanded by my Lords Commissioners of the Admiralty to send you herewith a copy of a petition from Messrs. Friedman and Co. stating that the Prussian vessel *Moritz* dispatched by them for a port in Prussia had been ordered by you to proceed to a port in Russia, and to signify their lordships' direction to you, if this statement is correct, to permit this vessel to return with a cargo although the licence is for a port in Prussia. I am etc.

Enclosure:

173a. *Petition of B. J. Friedman and Co.*

London,

13 Aug, 1811.

To the Lords of His Majesty's Privy Council, the humble petition of B. J. Friedman and Co. of London, merchants for themselves and others, sheweth that your humble petitioners expedited in the month of October last the Prussian vessel *Moritz*, Captain John Schulenberg, with a cargo of British manufactures and colonial produce to the Baltic under British licence and bound to a Prussian port, at which time your humble petitioners, availing themselves of the encouragement extended to the merchants by order in council, applied to [for] and obtained a license for the importation of a return cargo, that the British commander on the Baltic station deemed it, however, necessary to refuse permission to the said ship to proceed to a Prussian port and, ordering her to proceed with convoy to Russia, rendered thereby nugatory the licence your petitioners had previously obtained for the importation of a cargo, the produce of Prussia. Your humble petitioners therefore beg your lordships will be pleased to grant them a new licence for the importation in the said ship of a cargo of such articles, the produce of Russia, as are by law permitted to be imported into this kingdom. And your petitioners shall ever pray etc.

174. *Saumarez to Yorke*

Victory,

2 Sept. 1811.

Dear Sir, You will have been pleased to observe by my public letter of this date that I have received indirect information of the intentions of Bonaparte to attack Colberg and of the king of Prussia having ordered a strong body of troops for the protection of that fortress. Altho' I do not place implicit reliance on this information, I think it very probable that some occurrence may have taken place to give rise to the report. It is well known that General Blücher,[1] who commands the Prussian troops in the vicinity of Colberg, has always expressed his determined resolution to defend the place to the utmost of his power.

According to the best information I can obtain there are not more than eighty pieces of heavy artillery in that garrison, and that at least one hundred and eighty pieces are required for the defence of the different fortifications. The Prussian troops are also in want of powder and ammunition. It is of importance that I should be instructed how far I am authorized to supply the forces of His Prussian Majesty on the event of his actually being at war with France, application being made to me for that purpose, and to what extent I may be allowed to grant such supply from the means the squadron in the Baltic may be enabled to furnish. I have etc.

175. Gneisenau[2] to Saumarez

Berlin,
8 Sept. 1811.

Admiral, Mr. Johnson, the agent of your government at Vienna, informs you in the attached letter of the motive which leads me to address to you these lines, the bearer of which is Colonel Baron Ompteda to whom I request you will accord your full confidence in all that pertains to the affairs of Prussia.

Our government, threatened by France with the loss of its independence, is resolved sooner to risk the most dangerous of conflicts than to yield dishonourably. We will endeavour to rouse all the available population and to prepare a vigorous resistance; but we lack arms and ammunition for that purpose. Rumour has it that your government, forseeing an early rupture between France and Russia, has taken steps to put aboard your fleet an abundant stock of weapons. If this be so, we count upon the generosity of your nation not to refuse to furnish the means of defence against the most

---

[1] Gebhard Lebericht von Blücher (1742–1819) entered the Prussian army during the Seven Years War; fought against France in 1793–94 and 1806; lieutenant-general, 1801; held the chief command in Prussian Pomerania and was an ardent advocate of resistance to France, 1809–11; field-marshal and prince of Wahlstadt, 1813; commanded the Prussian army in Belgium, 1815.

[2] August Wilhelm Anton, later Count Neithardt von Gneisenau (1760–1831) achieved distinction by his defence of Colberg in the Franco-Prussian war, 1806–07 and was ap- appointed a member of the commission for the re-organization of the Prussian army. He advocated war with France in 1811; chief-of-staff to Blücher in the Waterloo campaign.

heinous tyranny to a people firmly resolved to sell their liberty and independence dearly. Be so kind, Admiral, as to honour me with a reply on this important issue.

In the event of your being able, sir, to afford assistance with fire-arms and ammunition, the point of debarkation, which is at once the most certain and the most within a convenient range for us, would be Colberg, our fortress on the Baltic which is beyond attack.

All this I have the honour, sir, to reveal to you and to entrust to your discretion and your loyalty. Our request must for the moment be shrouded in secrecy, the preparations for the insurrection not having reached the stage at which the mask can be thrown off.

Accept, sir, the assurances of the high consideration with which I have etc.

Enclosure:

175a. *Johnson to Saumarez*

Vienna,

29 Aug. 1811.

Sir, As some communications recently made to me by my friends in Prussia lead me to expect that the government of that country will in a short time adopt and avow a line of policy very different from that which we have had reason to apprehend, I conceive it probable that it will make some application to you for assistance in the contest with the French army in which it appears to be on the point of engaging; and as it is probable that such application will be made to you thro' the medium of Colonel Gneisenau, with whose reputation I believe you are already acquainted as the brave and successful defender of Colberg, I beg leave to recommend him to you, not only as a very distinguished officer, but as a man of patriotic principles and unsullied integrity. I have for some time been honoured by his friendship, and can assure you that he possesses, in a very eminent degree, all those qualities that entitle him to your esteem and confidence. I have etc.

176. *Barrow to Saumarez*

Admiralty Office,

14 Sept. 1811.

Sir, I am commanded by my Lords Commissioners of the Admiralty to enclose for your information and guidance the copy of a letter which the Marquis Wellesley has addressed to their lordships; and I am to call your attention particularly to the latter paragraph of the said letter and to signify to you their directions that you keep always in view, in the case specified, the not risking His Majesty's fleet in the Baltic at too late a period of the year, the keeping it in a sufficiently effective state in point of military stores and the effectual protection of trade. I have etc.

Enclosure:

176a. *Wellesley to the Lords Commissioners of the Admiralty*

Foreign Office,

13 Sept. 1811.

My Lords, Intelligence has been received which renders it probable that war may break out between Prussia and France and that Prussia is likely to solicit the assistance of Great Britain, and especially the immediate support of His Majesty's fleet in the Baltic towards the defence of the Prussian fortresses on the coast of that sea.

In the event of any request of this nature being made from the Prussian government or from the officers in command of any of those fortresses, it is the pleasure of His Royal Highness the prince regent that every practicable assistance, consistently with the safety of His Majesty's ships, should be afforded by the officer in command of His Majesty's naval force in that quarter. I am therefore commanded by His Royal Highness the prince regent, acting in the name and on behalf of His Majesty, to desire that your lordships will instruct Sir James Saumarez to use every endeavour to establish a communication with the most important points of the Prussian coasts, especially Colberg, and that your lordships will further detail Sir James Saumarez to afford every practicable aid to the Prussian government or any of its officers in resisting the power of France.

It is, however, to be clearly understood by the officer in command in the Baltic that it is not intended that any proceeding on the part of His Majesty's forces should precede the actual commencement of hostilities between Prussia and France or the direct resistance which it is stated that Prussia purposes to make against the further assaults of the French power. I have etc.

177. *Dörnberg[1] to Saumarez*

Colberg,

19 Sept. 1811.

Sir, I have the honour to inform you that we were landed yesterday at this

[1] Wilhelm Kaspar Ferdinand, Baron von Dörnberg (1768–1850) was active throughout the wars of 1793–1815 in regular and irregular warfare. He was at the head of the abortive anti-Napoleonic conspiracy in Hesse, 1809 and then became associated with the Black Legion of the duke of Brunswick; escaped to Britain and was employed as a military agent in Prussia and Russia, 1811–12.

place by the zeal of Lieutenant Lucas[1] of the *Censor*, and to whom I most humbly beg you may be pleased to charge with the protection of the further communication, as there is certainly no officer more fit for this service, having a thorough knowledge of the coasts and persons and being very discreet and indefatigable. I have taken the liberty to request the same of Admiral Reynolds, to whom I have also more fully stated the particulars of our landing.

General Blücher, who is extremely sensible of your kind remembrance, presents his most respectful and affectionate compliments. He has received full powers from the king of Prussia to act as he thinks best for the defence of Pomerania at large, and more particularly of Colberg, in case of being attacked, but ordered by no means to begin hostilities. The works at Colberg are carried on with the greatest activity. About 10,000 men are to work at it, but the great object is to find provisions enough to maintain an army from 20 to 30,000 men for at least four months. And General Blücher therefore requests if you would be pleased to direct the cruisers on this coast that the coasting vessels laden with corn may be allowed to enter Colberg freely, and particularly requests, if it was possible, to allow to the ships mentioned hereafter to come to this place, viz., the *Friendschaft*, Captain Ludwig Wilcke, with corn from Riga; *Young Henry*, Johan Haabas, with corn from Libau; *Concordia*, Gottlieb Neitzel, with iron from Stockholm. They all belong to Mr. Schröder who is charged with victualling Colberg. The iron is also very much wanted for the ordnance.

Mr. Schröder has English licences for the said ships to bring them to England, but, as in the present circumstances, it would be extremely desirable to bring them to this place, but Mr. Schröder would not venture to do it without your permission; and should you not be able to grant it, these ships are to go to England according to their licences. And he wishes therefore to be informed of your intentions as soon as possible. General Blücher also intended to request you to send him arms, but I have prevented it by telling him I was sure you had none on board your fleet. If I am mistaken, I beg your pardon; but I thought it would be better not to mix different things, and shall mention it to government.

There is another circumstance which General Blücher is very anxious to have stated to you under the right view. An officer of the marines and 6 sailors belonging to the *Courageux* have been driven somewhere here on shore, and are still detained here. But the greatest care is taken of them, and they will be sent back to the fleet as soon as General Blücher has an answer

---

[1] Mark Robinson Lucas, lieutenant, 1799; promoted commander in 1831, three years before his death.

from Berlin. Colonel Ompteda,[1] who will have the honour of remitting you this letter, will be able best to explain General Blücher's reasons for acting so.

I hope you will pardon this horrible scrawling and my bad English, which I hope you will be able to understand. Should you be pleased to favour me with an answer, or on any further occasion write to me, I beg [you] to address them to Mr. P. Müller under cover to Mr. Schröder at Colberg. It is with the greatest respect I have etc.

178. *Saumarez to Gneisenau*

Victory, in Wingo Sound,

28 Sept. 1811.

Sir, I have received the letter which your excellency has done me the honour to write to me, with the one enclosed from Mr. Johnson, by Colonel Baron d'Ompteda; and I entreat your excellency will be persuaded of my perfect readiness to use my utmost endeavours in promoting the success of the glorious cause in which Prussia is likely to be so soon engaged.

It will afford your excellency some satisfaction to be informed that I have received intimation from my government that two vessels actually laden with arms and ammunition have been ordered to join me without delay, and that I shall lose no time after their arrival to forward them to Colberg under a proper escort.

I have to regret that the advanced state of the season will not permit me more effectually to co-operate with the forces of His Prussian Majesty and to fulfill the views of His Royal Highness the prince regent of England, whose magnanimous intentions in favour of the cause of the continent have already been so strongly evinced. I request your excellency to receive the assurances of the high and very distinguished consideration with which I have etc.

179. *Saumarez to Dörnberg*

Victory, in Wingo Sound,

28 Sept. 1811.

Sir, I have had the honour to receive your letter of the 19th. instant informing me of your arrival at Colberg; and it has afforded me particular pleasure to find that you are so well satisfied with the exertions of Lieutenant Lucas

---

[1] Christian Friedrich Wilhelm, Baron von Ompteda (1765–1815), colonel in King George III's German Legion; formerly of the Hanoverian army; employed on a confidential mission to Germany, 1811; killed at Waterloo. He was the elder brother of Ludwig Karl Georg von Ompteda (1767–1854), once of the Hanoverian diplomatic service, who resided at Berlin and acted as an intermediary with London.

than whom no officer is better qualified for carrying on the communication, so long as the squadron will be enabled to remain in the Baltic.

By the same opportunity that brought from England the packet which I forwarded to you thro' Admiral Reynolds, I received intimation from government that two vessels, laden with arms and ammunition, were ordered to join me for the purpose of being conveyed to Colberg in the event of hostilities having taken place between Prussia and France. The quantity of small arms that could be furnished from the squadron is too inconsiderable, or I should otherwise have readily complied with General Blücher's wishes upon that subject.

I enclose to Mr. Schröder the licences for the three vessels named in your letter, and I shall direct the commanders of the cruisers to admit vessels laden with corn to enter Colberg without molestation.

I request you will do me the honour to present my best respects to His Excellency General Blücher. I am too well persuaded of his noble and ex- alted sentiments not to be fully convinced that the officer and six men belong- ing to the *Courageux*, who have been detained at Colberg, will have been treated with due attention and that directions will be given for their being released as soon as circumstances will admit.

In my letter to government I have stated the great service that might be derived in two of the gunbrigs being left during the winter months at Colberg, which I shall be happy to have complied with. I shall feel myself honoured in any communication you may be pleased to make to me; and I only regret that the present advanced state of the season will not permit me to contribute, so essentially as I wish, towards the success of the noble cause in which Prussia is likely to be so soon engaged. I have etc.

P.S. It has given me great pleasure to be enabled to furnish a vessel for the conveyance of Colonel d'Ompteda to England. He has sailed this afternoon. Have the goodness to address any letters you are pleased to favour me with under a cover to Mr. Smith at Gothenburg.

180. *Croker to Saumarez*

Admiralty Office,

5 Oct. 1811.

Sir, I have received your several dispatches up to the 28th. ult. No. 229 and have read the same to my Lords Commissioners of the Admiralty, and Mr. Yorke having laid before the board your private letter to him of the 28th. Sept. I have received their lordships' commands to signify their approval of your having permitted corn and other articles to be carried into Colberg, and to convey to you the following additional instructions.

The departure of the last homeward bound convoy from Hanö Bay is on no account whatever to be delayed beyond the 1st. of November (the latest period fixed upon by the trade previous to your departure and stated in Messrs. Emes's letter of the 21st March last, a copy whereof was transmitted to you in my letter of the 22nd.); and on the appearance of this convoy off Wingo Sound, you are to appropriate an adequate force to see the trade in safety to the respective ports of its destination.

It is their lordships' further direction that you then proceed with the ships-of-the-line to Spithead, except the two 64-gun ships named in the margin [*Ardent, Dictator*] which you will detach to the Nore; and you will direct the captain of any ship-of-the-line which you may have attached to the convoy to proceed, after having performed that service, to Spithead or the Nore according to the preceding distribution.

Their lordships, having taken into consideration those parts of your several dispatches which report the appearances of approaching hostilities between France and some of the Baltic powers, have commanded me (in addition to my former letters on the subject to which I beg again to call your attention) to authorize you to make such a disposition of the frigates and smaller vessels under your orders as may appear to you most advantageous with the view of affording assistance to any such power in the event of actual hostilities between it and France, as long as the state of the season and a due regard to the safety of His Majesty's ships will permit.

With respect as well to the frigates and smaller vessels, which you may thus for a certain time direct to remain behind, as to which you may attach to the homeward bound convoy, or those others which you may return under your immediate command, their lordships direct you to order to such as may stand in need of repair to proceed to the Nore, and the rest to repair to the Downs for further orders.

Their lordships, being aware that the time is not distant when such even of His Majesty's ships as you may order to stay the latest must leave the Baltic, and deeming it at the same time possible that political affairs in that quarter, and particularly on the coast of Pomerania, may have assumed an aspect of decided hostility to France and that presence of some of His Majesty's ships or vessels at Colberg may be required by the governor of that fortress as a means of increasing his powers of resistance to the common enemy, their lordships command me to authorize you, in the event which I have just stated and if you shall be of opinion that the probability of their being effectively useful is sufficient to warrant the risk, to leave two or three of the gunbrigs under your command to winter at Colberg for the purpose of the co-operation beforementioned.

If circumstances should induce you to avail yourself of this authority, you will, no doubt, select those brigs which may be best adopted for the general purpose in view, but which at the same time, if any accident were to happen to them, would be of the least loss to the public service. And you will take care that the last ships which leave the Baltic shall complete the stores and provisions of the brigs that are to remain to the full extent of their capacity.

If you should determine on carrying this measure into execution, their lordships feel the necessity of entrusting it to an officer of a rank superior to those in the command of gunbrigs; and they therefore direct you to select from the commanders under your orders one in whose prudence, activity and talents you can most confide, and who may be in a greater degree acquainted with the coast and languages of the country to whom you are to entrust the command of the gunbrigs, directing him to hoist on board such one of them as he shall think fit a distinguishing pendant; and their lordships, confiding in your local experience, have no doubt that the arrangements which you will make and the instructions which you will give to this officer will be the best adopted to the circumstances of this important service.

I need not here repeat to you their lordships' intentions with regard to the several transports laden with military stores, including the lead and powder ships, which may have joined or on their way to join you. You must already have received my former letters conveying to you their lordships' authority and directions to employ these stores in any manner which, in the event of actual hostilities between any of the Baltic powers and France, may best contribute to the assistance of the former.

Nor do their lordships doubt that you will, previous to your departure, turn your attention to the state of the island of Anholt, supplying it with such stores and provisions, and taking such other measures as may be in your power to place it in the best state of defence for the ensuing winter. You will also direct the last ships that are to leave the Baltic to communicate with Captain Maurice up to the latest possible period; and you will instruct this officer to take every opportunity of communicating with me during the time His Majesty's fleet may be absent from the Baltic. I am etc.

181. *Yorke to Saumarez*

Admiralty,

5 Oct. 1811.

Dear Sir, I take the opportunity of the *Briseis* sailing from Yarmouth direct to Wingo Sound to acknowledge the honour of your private letters of 30th August and of the 1st. 2nd. 6th. 14th. and 18th. of Sept. all of which reached me between the 13th and 28th of that month, as well as of your letter of the 28th. ult. by the hired cutter which arrived this day.

I am obliged to you of keeping me so well informed of what is passing within the limits of your command, tho' considerably mystified and disappointed at finding that the intelligence you first communicated of the favourable reception of the transports under the charge of *Grasshopper* did not turn out to be correct. The public and secret communications from the board which you will receive by this conveyance as well as by former opportunities in the course of the last three weeks (and which I trust you will 'ere this have received safe) will render it unnecessary for me to reply at any length to most of the topics which are touched upon in your letters, and the Marquis Wellesley has assured me that *Mr. Thornton* who is to embark in the *Briseis* on a secret mission to the court of Sweden[1] will receive definitive instructions to negotiate and conclude that *perplexing* business of the Carlshamn cargoes. You will of course hear from Mr. Thornton the outline of what relates to the view taken by H.M.'s government of the present political situation of the north. It is a most anxious consideration; and I trust that, if Prussia is actually obliged to have recourse to hostilities, Russia will not and cannot suffer her to be crushed without making every possible effort to relieve her. This may afford a favourable opportunity both for Sweden and Denmark to break the French yoke; and one may justifiably entertain the opinion that a *cordial union* of the four powers for that purpose may be successful considering how matters stand in the peninsula.

You will find by the board's order that you will receive by this conveyance that we shall be anxious for the arrival of yourself and the large ships-of-the-line at Spithead as early in November as circumstances will admit as it is intended to refit that part of your fleet with all expedition and to keep it in reserve at Spithead off St. Helens ready either to assist in cutting off the Scheldt fleet should they attempt to push down channel or to sail for the Tagus, should the exigencies of the scene require it.

Should you decide on leaving the gunbrigs to assist in the defence of Colberg, it occurs to me that Capt. Fanshawe[2] of the *Grasshopper* from his intimate knowledge with Russia and his general activity and intelligence would be a very proper officer to select for this service. In this case the *Grasshopper* would have an acting commander during his absence on this special service. I hope the *Helder* will have arrived safe at Anholt with the

---

[1] Thornton arrived Wingo Sound on 17 Oct. and went on to Åmal where he had talks with the Swedish diplomat J. I. Netzel. In the still unpredictable state of Franco-Russian relations, however, the Swedish government drew back from purposeful negotiations for peace.

[2] Henry Fanshawe, the son of General Robert Fanshawe of the Russian army, began his career in the Russian navy; entered the Royal Navy at the age of twenty, 1798; lieutenant, 1805; prisoner-of-war, 1811–14 following the loss of the *Grasshopper* (doc. 196); captain, 1814; retired, 1846.

stores etc. We must endeavour to secure it for the winter by all practicable means. I have etc.

182. *Dörnberg to Saumarez*

Colberg,

Oct. 1811.

Sir, I have the honour to acknowledge the receipt of your letter of the 28th. ult. in which you do me the honour to inform me of the intimation you received of two vessels laden with arms and ammunition being sent to your fleet. As I am at a loss how to act with respect to these arms, I shall endeavour to explain to you the real state of things at the present moment, which is rather a critical one.

The silence of Russia on account of her real intentions towards Prussia has occasioned some wavering in the bold measures which the Prussian cabinet had begun. Their very great exertions for arming in every part of the kingdom having excited the suspicion of Buonaparte, he first asked that the works for the formation of fortified camps, begun near almost all the Prussian fortresses, should be left off. In compliance with this demand, an order was given to stop all these works, but was accompanied by a private hint to carry them on. And, as particularly General Blücher was very active in completing them and in training a number of young soldiers, new threats came, and the demand to recall General Blücher. This demand has also been complied with in order to gain time, and General Count Tauentzien[1] has been sent here to take the command during the absence of General Blücher who is gone to Berlin. But General Tauentzien has declared to the commandant of this place, to the chief engineer and the officer commanding the artillery that General Blücher had acted according to the king's private order, that the whole was a mask to gain time and that the works are to be carried on as ordered by General Blücher, though with great caution and to hide as much as possible from the French. This, I am sure, is quite impossible as they are too well served in spies; and I suppose we shall see them here ere long. They perhaps only wait for the departure of your fleet. I therefore take the liberty of must humbly requesting you to leave a few gunbrigs, as well as the aforementioned vessels with arms, as long as possible in the Baltic. These ten thousand firelocks will give as many more defendants to this place, who are fully trained and only want arms.

[1] Friedrich, Count von Tauentzien-Wittenberg (1766–1824) began his military career in 1775 and became an aide-de-camp to Prince Henry of Prussia; posted to St. Petersburg on a diplomatic mission, 1793; major-general, 1796; badly wounded at Jena; lieutenant-general and commander-in-chief of the 4th. Prussian army corps, 1813–14.

I hope the officer and six men have happily reached the *Courageux* as they have been sent off, I believe, the 27th. or 28th. of September.

Be pleased, sir, to accept my most hearty thanks for the kindness with which you have granted my request to give the three licences to Mr. Schröder and to order your cruisers to allow vessels laden with corn to enter this place. I have etc.

183. *Saumarez to Yorke*

Victory, Wingo Sound,

13 Oct. 1811.

Dear Sir, I received the honour of your letter yesterday by the *Briseis*, by which conveyance I was also happy to receive secret instructions for my guidance on the close of the station.

No accounts from Prussia have reached me since my last dispatch, but as I expect Baron Dörnberg will be here very soon, I hope to be then enabled to decide upon the measures to be adopted relative to the transports laden with stores etc., and upon the expediency of leaving armed vessels to assist in the defence of Colberg. Permit me in confidence to observe that Captain Fanshawe appears by no means calculated to be entrusted with a service of so much importance.[1] The officer, who of all others appears the best qualified is Captain Acklom of the *Ranger* who is a very intelligent officer, and from the intercourse and experience he has had the last four years with Prussia I have every reason to believe that he would give every possible satisfaction, should it be found adviseable to leave any of the armed vessels to winter at Colberg.

I was deeply mortified to find that I had been so much deceived in the information which I transmitted of the favourable reception of the four transports at Revel, but the intelligence which was communicated to me appeared to come from so good a source as left no room to doubt its authenticity. I enclose an extract of the letter received from an eminent merchant for your information.

This station which has been to me a most anxious one during all the summer is becoming still more so as it draws to its close. My utmost endeavours will be continued for its favourable termination; and I trust my exertions will be found to merit the approbation of government, I have etc.

[1] Saumarez's attitude was grounded upon a complaint from Bezerra that Fanshawe by his deplorable lack of discretion, when off Revel with the *Grasshopper* and convoy, had acutely embarrassed the Russian government.

184. *Saumarez to Croker*

Victory, in Wingo Sound,

18 Oct. 1811.

Sir, Having taken into my particular consideration your most secret letter of the 7th. instant signifying the directions of the Lords Commissioners of the Admiralty, in the event of my finding a greater force than what is mentioned in your letter of the 5th. can be usefully employed in co-operating with any of the powers in the north of Europe which may take a decided part against France, to add one or both of the ships named in the margin [*Dictator, Ardent*] or, in case I should consider the frigates and smaller vessels adequate to the service, to direct Rear-Admiral Hope to hoist his flag on board one of the ships to be left upon this service, with the command of the whole force which I may judge it expedient to remain upon my leaving the station, having always due regard for the safety of His Majesty's ships; I request you will please to inform their lordships that I do not consider it to be adviseable, consistent with the safety of His Majesty's ships, that any force should be left within the Baltic to a later period than the state of the weather at this advanced season of the year will admit, to be judged of by the senior officer left with the command of the division of frigates and small vessels directed to remain in the Baltic after the departure of the last convoy appointed to sail the first of November from Matvik. Which service I proposed to have entrusted to Captain Dashwood[1] of the *Pyramus*, with directions to remain in Hanö Bay or Matvik as long as he finds he can do so consistent with the safety of His Majesty's ships, leaving the two gunbrigs to assist in the defence of Colberg should circumstances render it adviseable.

But, as it may be expedient that two of the line-of-battle ships should occupy the station in Wingo Sound until the arrival of the ships under the orders of Captain Dashwood from the Baltic, I propose, should it meet their lordships' approbation, to direct Rear-Admiral Hope to hoist his flag on board one of the two-decked ships and to remain in Wingo Sound accordingly, placing under his command the frigates and other vessels stationed in the Sleeve and Cattegat, and for maintaining the communication with Sweden and the ports of Prussia until their lordships' pleasure is signified.

You will please to inform their lordships that, in view of the obvious defects, I have ordered her [*Plantagenet*] to proceed to the Nore. I have etc.

---

[1] Charles Dashwood served in the West Indies, 1780–82; lieutenant, 1794; captain, 1801; regularly employed until 1825; rear-admiral, 1830; K.C.B., 1840; vice-admiral, 1841.

185. *Saumarez to Dörnberg*

Victory, in Wingo Sound,

29 Oct. 1811.

Sir, I had the honour yesterday evening to receive both your letters, one dated the 13th. inst., the other without any date. As in the latter you have been pleased particularly to request that the gunbrigs, as well as the transports laden with arms and ammunition, should be left as long as possible in the Baltic, I have sent the two transports to Hanö Bay, and I have given orders to Captain Dashwood of H.M. ship *Pyramus*, in the event of the supply of arms and ammunition being required by the Prussian government, to send them to Colberg in the manner that will be pointed out. Permit me to observe that, as the transports draw too much water to enter the port of Colberg, they will require small vessels to unload them, and it may be adviseable to have them in readiness for that purpose.

Captain Dashwood has also received orders to leave two gunbrigs to assist in the defence of Colberg should he receive any application to that effect; and I have entrusted Captain Acklom, an officer of great merit, with that important service, with orders to hoist a distinguishing pendant on board one of the gunbrigs and to co-operate to the utmost in his power with his excellency the governor of Colberg against the common enemy.

As the season of the year is so far advanced as to make it extremely dangerous for His Majesty's ships and the transports to continue in the Baltic, I have most earnestly to request that Captain Dashwood may be informed as speedily as possible whether the supply of arms and ammuntion will be required, in order that he may proceed to England conformable to his orders and before running great risk of being impeded by the sea on his arrival in the Cattegat. I have etc.

186. *Saumarez to Croker*

Victory, in Wingo Sound,

29 Oct. 1811.

Sir, Since my letter of yesterday's date I have received two letters from Colonel Dörnberg, copies of which I enclose for the information of the Lords Commissioners of the Admiralty. As Colonel Dörnberg particularly requests that the gunbrigs and the vessels laden with ammunition should be left as long as possible in the Baltic, it is my intention to place them under the orders of Captain Quilliam[1] of the *Crescent* with directions to proceed

---

[1] John Quilliam entered the navy as an impressed seaman and rose from the lower deck; lieutenant, 1798; first lieutenant of the *Victory* at Trafalgar; captain, Dec. 1805. He died in 1829.

as soon as the state of the weather will permit to Hanö Bay, detaching also the *Vigo* and *Orion* for their protection thro' the Belt, giving orders to Captain Dashwood, senior officer of His Majesty's ships in the Baltic after the departure of Rear-Admiral Reynolds, to take them under his protection and send the supplies in the best manner he can to Colberg, should they be required, or return with the transports to England.

I have also written to Colonel Dörnberg acquainting him that the transports are ordered to Hanö Bay, and requesting he would be pleased to communicate with Captain Dashwood on the best means of the stores being conveyed to Colberg, should they be wanted by the Prussian government. I am etc.

187. *Saumarez to Dashwood*

Victory, in Wingo Sound,
10 Nov. 1811.

Dear Sir, Although I most truly hope that the ordnance stores intended for Prussia will not be required by that government and that I shall very soon receive information from you to that effect, I have thought it most adviseable to order the transports to join in the event of their being wanted. You will observe by the copies of my letters to Baron Dörnberg (under the name of Mr. P. Müller) that I have urged him as much as possible to signify to you the determination of Prussia with regard to those stores, in order that you return with the transports as speedily as possible through the Belt. It will be adviseable for you also to communicate with Colonel Dörnberg, and represent to him the necessity of its being decided without delay whether the supplies will be required or not.

The wind is too far to the southward to admit the convoy to sail from Wingo Sound; and I yet hope to receive some satisfactory information from you previous to their departure. Independent of your public dispatches, I wish you to write, if possible, by every post either by Carlshamn or by Solvitzborg, even though nothing very interesting has occurred. I have enclosed my latest papers which may be acceptable. Believe me etc.

188. *Saumarez to Yorke*

Victory, Wingo Sound,
13 Nov. 1811.

Dear Sir, Having waited with considerable impatience to hear from Colonel Dörnberg, I received yesterday evening a letter from him, of which the enclosed is a copy, written on board the *St. George* in Hanö Bay, and wherein he informs me of his intention to go to Ystad for the purpose of carrying on the correspondence. As it is of the utmost importance that something should be speedily decided with respect to the eleven transports laden with ordnance stores, I have sent off an express to Colonel Dörnberg requesting him, if possible, to come to Gothenburg for the purpose of making some decisive arrangement upon that important subject and also relative to the gunbrigs proposed to be left at Colberg.

Admiral Dixon sailed this morning with the transports and trade under his protection for the Belt; and I have directed Captain Dashwood, in the event of his receiving intimation from Prussia that the stores are not required, to detach the *Ethalion* with the information to Admiral Dixon, in order that the transports may return under his convoy to England. By what I can infer from Colonel D[örnber]g's letter, he expects that Prussia will be attacked after the departure of the squadron from the Baltic. No time should therefore be lost in coming to a determination whether the stores are to be received, provided the advanced state of the season will admit the practicability of their being landed; which must be considered as very doubtful.

I have not heard from Mr. Thornton since the day he left Gothenburg, but expect to receive letters from him hourly. The wind has proved favourable for the convoy under Admiral Reynolds, and I expect his arrival off the Wingo very soon, but I consider it of so great consequence that I should, if possible, have an interview with Colonel Dörnberg that I shall remain here for that purpose, and detach the other line-of-battle ships with the rear-admiral to England. I have etc.

Enclosure:

188a. *Dörnberg to Saumarez*

Hanö Bay,
8 Nov. 1811.

Sir, My friends at Colberg, fearing that the French have some notice of my being there, advised me to leave it for a time, which I accordingly did intending to stay some time at Ystad from whence I will be able to carry on the correspondence quite as well as from Colberg itself.

When I left Colberg (the day before yesterday), things were still in the same uncertain state, Bonaparte was expected at Hamburg and Marshall Davout was gone to Magdeburg where the French assemble a large body of troops, so that I have very little doubt but they will attack Prussia as soon as they think your fleet has left the Baltic.

I hope, sir, you will excuse this scrawl, but I am still not able to write on board as on shore. But wherever I am, it is always with the greatest respect that I have etc.

189. *Dashwood to Saumarez*

Pyramus, Matvik harbour,

21 Nov. 1811.

Sir, The official letter, which I have had the honour of addressing you and which accompanies this, will acquaint you that the messenger I had dispatched to Ystad with letters to Mons. Müller had returned but without any answer, Mr. Müller having set out for Gothenburg about two hours before his arrival, but that they were immediately forwarded; and 'tis more than probable he would have received them before his arrival at Gothenburg, By this unfortunate circumstance, I am still left in total ignorance whether the stores will be required by the Prussian government or not. I should imagine, however, that you must have seen Mr. Müller before this, and I trust I shall very soon be honoured with your further commands on this subject; but I still hope the transports have not quitted Wingo, for I see but little possibility of our succeeding in any mode or shape whatever at this advanced season of the year.

I have also sent you a list of Admiral Reynolds's convoy that have returned to Matvik.[1] They are all entirely without a single bower anchor or cable and are now riding within the inner harbour, some made fast to trees or rocks, others with their streams or kedges. All their masters are necessarily absent, some at Carlshamn and others at Carlscrona, to endeavour to get their wants supplied, but which, I fancy, will be found very difficult. I understand it will take 16 or 18 days to bring anchors and cables from Carlscrona as they must come by land, and the roads are very bad. There are not above 10 at Carlshamn, and 'tis very doubtful whether so many can be purchased at Carlscrona.

It is not for me to know, or even to guess, whether they will be safe, were they to pass the winter in a Swedish port, as those that arrive at Carlshamn are put under an embargo. It is however evident they cannot proceed on their voyage without anchors and cables. Therefore, under all the existing circumstances, I shall remain here until I have the honour of receiving your further orders on this subject. For my own part I do not see how they can be got ready and, if they could, how we are to convey them thro' the Belt and Cattegat at that advanced season of the year. On the other hand, should they be obliged to winter at Carlshamn, I should think they would not run much risk of condemnation as the principal merchants consider the embargo as a matter of precaution, as vessels under similar circumstances last year were

---

[1] Reynolds with the convoy left Hanö Bay on 9 Nov. and was hit by a gale on the night of 15–16 Nov., during which the *St. George* was severely disabled and the convoy scattered. See Ross, ii, pp. 252 ff.

given up after being detained several months. I entreat you will have the goodness to give me your future and, I trust, final commands as to when I shall leave the Baltic, and whether I may expect the transports or not, and also what directions I shall give to the masters of the ships that apply to me for protection.

I hope you will not be displeased at my presuming to write to you so strongly. I can only plead in my excuse that I am actuated by the best of motives, being with great personal esteem and respect etc.

190. *Saumarez to Croker*

Victory, in Wingo Sound,

24 Nov. 1811.

Sir, You will please to inform the Lords Commissioners of the Admiralty that Colonel Dörnberg, who I had stated in my most secret letter of the 13th. instant to have requested to come to Gothenburg, arrived on board the *Victory* yesterday evening. Finding from him that no determination could as yet take place whether the ordnance stores would be required by the Prussian government or not, and having represented to him the great dangers and risks of the transports being exposed at this late season of the year in the Baltic, after due deliberation it has been thought most adviseable that Colonel Dörnberg should repair to Matvik harbour; and should he not receive communications from Colberg that the supply of ordnance stores was required, Captain Dashwood was to proceed without further delay thro' the Belt with the transports.

Colonel Dörnberg was fully aware of the necessity of taking immediate measures in providing for the safety of the transports at this advanced state of the season, and expressed himself satisfied that every practicable means had been adopted for furnishing Prussia with the supplies intended by His Majesty's government, if circumstances had but admitted of their being received. I am etc.

191. *Saumarez to Croker*

Victory, Wingo Sound,

2 Dec. 1811.

Sir, you will please to inform the Lords Commissioners of the Admiralty of the arrival here yesterday morning of Rear-Admiral Reynolds in the *St. George* with His Majesty's ships named in the margin (*Hero, Cressy, Defence, Dictator, Rose*) and 72 of the convoy which sailed from Matvik on the 9th. ultimo.

Most of the line-of-battle ships are very short of bread and spirits. The moment the weather moderates, I shall equalize those articles to each of the ships which will complete them to six weeks' bread at two-thirds allowance and five weeks' spirits, leaving a supply of about three months to the *Ardent* and *Dictator*. The *Vigo* and *Orion* expected from the Belt with Rear-Admiral Dixon have nine weeks' bread and seven weeks' spirits; and the detachment under Captain Dashwood have about three months for the ships and vessels under his orders calculating the whole at two-thirds allowance of bread.

It now blows a hard gale of wind at south-west which prevents the possibility of any communication.

I herewith enclose the defects of the *St. George*. She is fitted with a Pakenham rudder[1] and topmasts erected for jury masts. I shall appoint the *Cressy* and *Defence* to accompany her to the Downs, giving charge of the convoy to Captain Newman[2] of the *Hero*, a list of which I herewith enclose. I am etc.

192. *Dashwood to Saumarez*

Pyramus, Matvik harbour,

5 Dec. 1811.

Sir, I have received your very obliging letter of the 27th. Nov. this very moment. My official letters up to this day will have communicated to you that every hope of sending the stores on shore had been given up, and that I only waited for a favourable wind to take my final departure. I am glad, however, that the communication was kept up with Colberg to the latest moment, viz., until Nov. 30th. at 11 o'clock in the morning when the *Earnest* stood close in shore, and they might have communicated if they thought proper.

We are still with our yards and topmasts struck and three anchors down; blowing very hard from the S.W. I regret most exceedingly the utter impossibility of the *Ethalion's* sailing to communicate the intelligence to Admiral Dixon. She has had orders ever since the morning of the 1st., but it has blown a continual gale of wind ever since. She will most certainly depart the instant it is possible; and I shall follow with the convoy as quick as I can.

I am truly gratified my humble efforts have been honoured with your high approbation. It is more peculiarly gratifying when it proceeds from an officer of so high and distinguished a character, and to whom I have the

---

[1] An artificial rudder created by the inventive Edward Pakenham, lieutenant, 1777; captain, 1790; killed in the destructive explosion on board the *Resistance* (44), 24 July 1798.

[2] James Newman Newman (1767–1811) a post-captain of 1794; died in the wreck of the *Hero* (74) off the Texel, 24 Dec. 1811.

honour to be but so little known. In all situations in life I shall endeavour to merit a continuance of your good opinion. I have etc.

193. *Yorke to Saumarez*

Admiralty,
8 Dec. 1811.

Sir, This will go by the *Fawn* which is ordered to proceed immediately from the Nore with as much bread and spirits as she can stow for your ships in Wingo Sound, which have been detained together with the last convoy from the Baltic so much longer than was expected. We are accordingly anxious about you, relying at the same time on your making the best use of your time and trusting that in any case you are safe at anchor in a good road-stead during the present icy temperatures and persevering bad weather. The latest letters from you are of the 18th. ult., since which we have not heard anything of what is going forward in your quarter which adds not a little to our solicitude.

I received your private communications of the 7th., 9th., and 13th. ult. which I should have acknowledged sooner, but as they did not reach me till between the 19th. and 21st. I was in daily expectation of hearing of your arrival in the *Victory* either in the Downs or at Spithead. All your measures, as detailed in these letters, appear to me to have been judiciously arranged for the purpose of fulfilling the intentions of government with a view to rendering the utmost practicable assistance to Prussia that circumstances might admit of in the event of their being forced into hostilities. It is greatly to be regretted, however, that her government has not been more explicit with *you* and has delayed so long to apprize you whether it was or was not her intention to receive the stores etc. which have been offered for her use. I fear nothing was to have been expected from Count Dörnberg's emigration to Sweden. The last accounts we have of him is his arrival at Ystad; and we are in total ignorance of everything that may have passed since.

The French fleet are gone up the Scheldt out of our sight and there is reason to believe that they are gone up to Antwerp to be laid up for the winter, but we have no positive advice of this. Admiral Young accordingly remains in the Downs with 10 sail-of-the-line in momentary readiness, and five are with Durham between Hollesley Bay and the Texel. These have been dispersed in the late gales.

Matters here remain in the *statu quo*. I have etc.

194. *Narrative of the loss of the 'St. George' and 'Defence' by Saumarez*

On the 1st. of November 1811 Rear-Admiral Reynolds (as appears by his letter of this date) got the convoy in Matvik under weigh. On the 4th. he mentions that as it was late in the evening of the 1st. before many of the convoy arrived off Hanö, and several having remained behind, he made the signal to anchor; and as in the night the wind came round to the southward with a heavy swell and in the morning of the 2nd. increased, many of the merchantmen were obliged to slip and to return to Matvik with the *Pyramus*, where they all arrived in safety.

By his letter of the 19th. the rear-admiral states that he sailed from Hanö with the convoy on the 9th. and anchored in the evening of the 10th. between Moen Island and Dars Head. On the 12th. they weighed and came to anchor off Nystadt [Nysted]; and during the night of the 15th. the furious gale of wind came on, during which a large ship of the convoy driving athwart hawse of the *St. George*[1] parted her cable and after drifting into shoal water obliged her, with the loss of her rudder, to cut away her masts; which misfortune unhappily led to the subsequent calamitous loss of that ship and the *Defence*. On the 19th. the *St. George* had her jury masts rigged, Pakenham rudder fixed and was in all respects fit to proceed on her passage. She arrived at Wingo Sound on the 1st. of December from whence, after further securing her jury masts and rudder and completing her water and provisions, she sailed on the 17th. in company with the *Victory* and ships named in the margin [*Vigo, Dreadnought, Orion*], besides the *Defence* and *Cressy* which were placed under the rear-admiral's orders and directed to stay by and accompany the *St. George* to England. The *Hero*, which had charge of the homeward bound trade, sailed at the same time; but the wind proving too scant for the merchant vessels to weather the Scaw, the signal was made from the *Victory* for them to bear up again for Wingo Sound. On the 19th. the *Bellette* sloop was placed under the rear-admiral's orders; and on the 20th., early in the morning, the *St. George* with the ships and sloop parted company.

It appears by Captain Pater's narrative that on the morning of the 21st. they were close in with Salö Beacon and it was proposed to anchor in that harbour the ensuing night. But a strong breeze springing up at N.N.E. about noon they made sail to the westward and continued their course all night thro' the Sleeve, the *St. George* steering and sailing very well about 5 knots per hour. At 11 a.m. on the 22nd. the land about the Holmes [Hanstholm] bore S.S.W., distance 7 leagues. The squadron stood to the westward with moderate weather all night, wind about N. by W. On the 23rd. at nine in the morning Captain Pater asked permission to take the *St. George* in tow, which

---

[1] Across the stem of the *St. George*.

was negatived. At 10 came on to blow very strong. At 11 the *St. George* took in her topsails and courses, standing to the N.E. with a view to open the Sleeve. The whole of this day she drifted so much to leeward as to oblige the *Cressy* to bear up three or four times in a watch to keep up to leeward of her; and at ½ past 10 at night Captain Pater, seeing no possibility of clearing the land on the larboard tack, wore ship and by carrying a press of sail had the good fortune to weather Horn Reef. At the time the *Cressy* wore, the *St. George* and *Defence* were left with their heads on shore E.N.E. under storm-mizzen staysail and trysail, with the land to the southward of Bovenbergen [Bovbjerg] upon their lee beam and drifting on shore at the rate of three miles per hour.

195. *The Loss of H.M.S. 'Defence' by a survivor*

We sailed from Salö in company with H.M.S. *St. George* and *Cressy* without anything worthy of notice occurring until the 23rd. when a hearty gale sprang up from the W.N.W. At 1 took in the foretopsail and at 2 split the maintopsail in taking it in. Unbent it and got a foretopsail on deck in readiness for bending when the weather moderated. Having no other topsail on board, Captain Atkins[1] would not allow it to be bent for fear of losing it. Hove to under storm staysails and reefed foresail. The captain being at ½ past nine o'clock informed that the *Cressy* had wore and stood to the southward under storm staysails and reefed foresail ordered Mr. Baker (first lieutenant) to see all clear for wearing, but told him if the *St. George* had not wore we should continue on the same tack as long as possible, At 12, the watch and idlers were turned up to wear ship, at which time the *St. George* burnt a blue light. Captain Atkins asked Mr. Baker, if the admiral had wore; and on his telling him she had not, he said 'we will not call the watch'. At ½ past twelve we hauled down the fore and main staysails and lay to under a storm mizzen. At quarter past six the hands were turned up to wear ship. The first lieutenant ordered me into the fore-top to attend the backstays and to take four hands with me to overhaul the fore buntlines etc. But just as I got in the top she struck lightly and I then saw the breakers on the lee bow. Almost immediately after the ship fell into the trough of a sea and struck very heavy fore and aft. I then ordered the men out of the top. As I was going down the rigging I heard the masts ordered to be cut away and as I stepped in the forecastle, the main mast, mizzen mast and fore topsail yard fell into the sea. In the course of a few minutes the foremast followed. At this period the sea was making a fair trench over us. Dismal cries were heard throughout the ship from many people having their legs and arms broken or jammed by the guns and other

[1] David Atkins, lieutenant, 1784; captain 1798; died 24 Dec. 1811.

articles of the ship breaking adrift. About this time our sheet anchor by the violence of a sea and a list of the ship was hove in upon the forecastle and killed a great many men. Our boats were then laying by the gangway which was on a level with the water's edge. The next sea washed the boats overboard with about twenty men in the pinnace which was turned bottomupwards, at which time the ship parted by the chess-tree[1] and gangways, the sea then making a fair breach between the poop and forecastle. Myself and all who stood amidships were forced overboard. When I recovered, I saw at least one hundred men on a raft of one side of the booms. I then made the best of my way towards it by swimming to the mizzen top, at which time a sea swept the raft of all hands except two who came on shore with me. I and a few more reached the raft a second time; but only six got on shore, one of whom died as soon as he landed. When nearly on shore I observed the poop and forecastle part from the hull and almost instantly upset, by which the remainder of the crew were overwhelmed into the sea. We were humanely treated by the Danes who assisted us in getting off the raft and took all possible care of us. After we recovered we were informed the body of one of our officers was washed on shore; which on examining we found to be that of our captain. He was buried on the 29th. and on the 13 of January taken up again and buried with the honour of war at (I believe) Shelton Church. We were about two miles from the *St. George*.

196. *Narrative by a person on board the 'Grasshopper' of the circumstances attending the loss of that vessel and the 'Hero'*

On Wednesday the 8th. [18th.] December 1811, we sailed from Wingo Sound in company with H.M. ships *Hero, Egeria* and *Prince William*, armed ship, with a convoy of 120 sail or upwards. The *Egeria* and *Prince William*, with the greatest part of the convoy, separated from us in the tremendous weather we had shortly after leaving the Sleeve; and on the 23rd. inst. we found ourselves in company with the *Hero* and about 18 sail, mostly government transports. At half-past eleven that day, Capt. Newman made signal to come within hail; when he told us, as he conceived we were near about the Silver Pits, he should steer S.W. after noon, which was accordingly done. And at the close of day we were steering that course, running at the rate of nine knots per hour. At about ten o'clock the night signal was made to alter course to port two points, which was repeated by us. At this time only four of the convoy were in sight, and they were shortly loss sight of in the heavy squall of snow and sleet. At half-past three the hands were turned up, the

---

[1] A piece of oak fastened with bolts on each topside of the ship for boarding the main tack to.

ship being in broken water. We found we were on a small sandbank, the pilot imagining it to be Smith's Knoll. The captain instantly ordered the brig to be steered S.S.E. thinking to get out to sea; but she continued striking so hard for a length of time that we had almost given up for lost, when suddenly and very fortunately we fell into three fathoms water, upon which the captain caused an anchor to be let go, when we perceived the *Hero* again (as we then thought) also at an anchor, though she fired several guns and burnt blue lights. But alas, when the day broke we had the mortification of witnessing a most horrid scene: the *Hero* was totally dismasted and on her larboard beam ends, with her head to the N.E. about a mile from us upon the Haeck's [Haake] Sand, as we then found we were inside of it, off the Texel Island. The ship's company were all crowded together on the poop and forecastle. As soon as daylight appeared, she hoisted a flag-of-truce and fired a gun, which we repeated; and very shortly after saw a lugger, two brigs and several vessels plying out of the Texel to our assistance; but owing to the flood tide having made and the wind blowing a perfect gale at N.N.W. the lugger was only able to come within two or three miles of us by two o'clock in the afternoon. In the meantime we hoisted out our boats and made an attempt to get near the *Hero*, but the surf was so high that it was all ineffectual; and we were under the cruel necessity of seeing so many of our brave countrymen perishing, without being able to render them an assistance. The *Grasshopper* at the same time was constantly striking very hard, though everything had been thrown overboard to lighten her except the guns, upon which it was feared she would have bilged. The master was then sent to sound in every direction for a passage to make our escape by, though I have since found that an escape was totally impossible. But quarter less three and two fathoms and a half were the only sounding he could meet with. The captain therefore, with the opinion of the officers, agreed that we had no chance of saving ourselves but by surrendering to the enemy, who were at this time, as I have before mentioned, coming to our assistance and that of the *Hero*, from whose wreck I am sorry to say not one soul has been saved. . . .

197. *Dashwood to Saumarez*

Pyramus, Spithead,

10 Jan. 1812.

Sir, I have the very great pleasure to acquaint you of my arrival here yesterday, having disposed the ships under my orders, as far as circumstances would permit, in obedience to directions given me by Adml. Hope. As I was latterly under the orders of Adl. Hope, I conceived it more correct that I should report my arrival and proceedings to him, which I did yesterday addressed under cover to the admiralty with a request that should the *Ardent* not have arrived, he would lay it officially before the board. I trust that I have not acted wrong in not writing officially to you, but if I have, I fervently hope you will believe that it has originated from a misconception and not from an intentional error. I cannot, however, refrain from the pleasure of writing you privately, and to hope that my conduct, since I had the honour of being under your command, will meet your approbation. Believe me, I have done everything to the best of my poor judgement. In my official letter to you, and which I gave Adml. Hope, you will learn that I succeeded in carrying the men-of-war and convoy thro' the Malmö without any accident whatever, aided and assisted by Capt. Acklom. I am convinced, had I persevered in attempting the Belt, the whole of the convoy and some of the men-of-war would have been lost in the very severe gale of wind we encountered in Elsinore Roads. I have therefore great satisfaction that all the convoy have safely arrived. I entreat you to believe that I am etc.

P.S. Altho' I date this from the ship yet I am, thank God, safe with my family for a day or two on private leave from Sir Roger Curtis.[1] Mrs. Dashwood begs you and Lady Saumarez will accept of her best thanks and respect.

[1] Admiral Sir Roger Curtis, commander-in-chief Portsmouth, 1810–12.

PART V

1812

PART V

INTRODUCTION

Dixon, who was appointed to the command of the South American station, and Reynolds were succeeded by Rear-Admirals Martin and Morris. Morris resorted to Hanö Bay where he supervised convoy arrangements. Martin, after going off Anholt to observe the state of that island, sailed towards Danzig, entered into correspondence with the military governor of Riga and complied with his request for naval assistance. Martin's part in the defence of Riga, as also his other proceedings in 1812, is amply documented in the second volume of the *Journals and Letters of Admiral of the Fleet Sir Thomas Byam Martin* edited by Sir R. Vesey Hamilton for the Navy Records Society in 1898. It has not, therefore, been found necessary to print many documents dealing with the defence of Riga, though a good number of Saumarez's letters to Martin, valuable for the light they throw on the commander-in-chief's perplexities, are included. Indeed the impression given in the editorial introduction to the Martin papers, where excessive claims are made for the navy's contribution to Napoleon's defeat in Russia, must be modified.[1] Despite Martin's activities at Riga, the role of the fleet was essentially passive. The commander-in-chief's correspondence reveals how little it was in his power to take the initiative in operations against the enemy. The proposed offensive against Denmark could not be launched without the co-operation of Russia and Sweden, both which powers for its own reasons held back. 1812 was in fact for Saumarez a tedious and frustrating year. His exasperation with the apparent reluctance of the opponents of France to seize the moment runs through the correspondence. The command of the Baltic was secure, but its further exploitation in the war against Napoleon was impossible without a striking change in the distribution of power on the continental mainland. There was no hint of the catastrophic outcome for France of the Russian war when Saumarez quitted the Baltic, having set in train the arrangements for the flight to Britain of the Russian fleet. Only in the last letter of the volume with its news of the passage of the Beresina by the retreating Grand Army is the note of victory sounded. Saumarez did not return to the Baltic. Nor did he ever again hold a sea-going command; though he did serve as commander-in-chief, Portsmouth between 1824 and 1827. He was belatedly raised to the peerage in 1831, five years before his death in October 1836. The delay was resented by Saumarez and is indeed difficult to explain. A possible explanation is that the formal disapproval of his letter to the tsar in September 1808 was treated by members of successive governments as an obstacle to his elevation.

[1] Vesey Hamilton, *op. cit.*, p. xii.

198. *Barrow to Saumarez*

Admiralty Office,
18 March 1812.

Sir, I am commanded by my Lords Commissioners of the Admiralty to send herewith for your information an extract of a letter from Gothenburg containing intelligence relating to the enemy's force in Norway. I am etc.

Enclosure:

198a. *Intelligence from Gothenburg*

Gothenburg,
6 March 1812.

The number of Danish cruisers now in Norway seems to require a greater caution, and this was the cause I desired the *Carl Johan* to be delayed with you until she could come under the protection of a British convoy, but if this convoy is not stronger than those of last year, it would be better for her to run it as a single ship. The Danes have now in Norway besides a new 40-gun frigate[1] (which got there from Copenhagen the other day in spite of three British frigates cruising to intercept her), 4 fine cutter brigs and a good many gunboats. They know exactly the force, strength and numbers of the convoys and are informed of the time of their sailing. Thus if an armed vessel[2] is to protect a convoy, it is very probable they will make a number of prizes.

199. *Saumarez to Croker*

Tunbridge Wells,
20 March 1812.

Sir, I request you will please to inform the Lords Commissioners of the Admiralty that in consequence of their directions signified to me in your letter of yesterday I have directed Captain Dashwood to order the *Daphne* and a sloop-of-war to remain off Anholt for the protection of the island and to repair in the *Pyramus* with the remaining force to Wingo Sound, putting to sea at such times as the weather permits to keep in check the enemy's frigate and armed vessels upon the coast of Norway and for the protection of

---

[1] A reference to the passage from Copenhagen to Christiansand of the *Naiad* (40).
[2] A ship privately equipped for warlike proceedings, furnished with a letter of marque and employed by the admiralty.

the trade of His Majesty's subjects. Should it meet their lordships' approval, I propose to detach Captain Quilliam of the *Crescent* with the *Ethalion* under his orders upon that service, directing Captain Dashwood to repair to the Nore for the purpose of being paid and to complete with stores and provisions. I have etc.

200. *Croker to Saumarez*

Admiralty Office,

21 March 1812.

Sir, I am commanded by my Lords Commissioners of the Admiralty to transmit for your information the accompanying copy of a letter which their lordships have received from Lord Castlereagh, His Majesty's principal secretary of state for foreign affairs,[1] signifying the prince regent's pleasure that instructions be given for watching the coast of Norway with a view of intercepting troops (whether French or Danish) and any description of arms and military stores which the enemy may attempt to throw into that country; and that as many of the lighter vessels destined for service in the Baltic, as can be spared from convoy or other services, may be sent thither as soon as possible. And I have their lordships' commands to signify their direction to you to take immediate measures for carrying into execution the instructions pointed out in Lord Castlereagh's said letter. I am etc.

201. *Croker to Saumarez*

Admiralty Office,

8 April 1812.

Sir, I have it in command for my Lords Commissioners of the Admiralty to send you herewith copy of a letter which I have received from the chairman of the Baltic trade relative to convoys to and from thence during the ensuing season and to signify their direction to you to appoint a convoy for the protection of the trade from the Nore to Gothenburg on the 13th. instant, and to govern yourself in the arrangements you may make for the protection of the trade to and from the Baltic conformably to the system proposed in the abovementioned letter, as far as circumstances will permit. I am etc.

[1] Castlereagh was appointed foreign secretary in March 1812.

Enclosure:

201a. *W. and P. Emes to Croker*

London,

6 April 1812.

Sir, In consequence of the conversation we had the honour of having with yourself and Sir James Saumarez upon the subject of the Baltic convoys this morning, we request that you will be pleased to submit for the consideration of the Lords Commissioners of the Admiralty what we deemed most advisable to be adopted for the season ensuing:

That a convoy be appointed to sail from the Nore for Gothenburg on the 13th. instant.

That the first convoy for the Baltic be appointed to sail from the Nore on the 20th. instant, and from Gothenburg into the Baltic on the 10th. May, and that this convoy return from Hanö Bay the first favourable wind with whatever vessels may be collected there, at Carlscrona and adjacent Swedish ports.

That the last convoy from Gothenburg thro' the Belts sail the first favourable wind after the 15th. Sept. and the last convoy from Hanö Bay downwards the first favourable opportunity after the 1st. Oct.

That the last convoy from the Nore bound to Gothenburg only sail from thence upon the 15th. Oct. or at the latest upon the 1st. Nov., and that the last convoy from Gothenburg be left to the discretion of the commander-in-chief on that station.

The other intermediate convoys to be as hitherto. We are etc.

202. *Croker to Saumarez*

Admiralty Office,

18 April 1812.

Sir, I have it in command from my Lords Commissioners of the Admiralty to send herewith for your information copy of a memorial from Messrs. J. C. Splitzbergen and Co. of London, requesting protection for the vessels therein mentioned from Hanö Bay to the entrance of the ports of their destinations; and I am to signify their lordships' directions to you to adopt such measures herein as you may judge expedient under the circumstances of the several cases. I am etc.

Enclosure:

202a. *Memorial of J. C. Splitzbergen and Co.*

Church Court, Walbrook,

6 April 1812.

The memorial of Messrs J. C. Splitzbergen and Co. of the city of London, merchants, humbly sheweth that your memorialists having shipped on board the following vessels, viz. the *Flora*, Captain Sierach, the *Anne Charlotte*, Captain Frahm, the *Elbing*, Captain Girard, and the *Dorothea*, Captain Dodt, under Prussian colours, sundry colonial and British manufactured goods to the amount of £90,000 sterling in order of introducing into and being disposed of at a Prussian port or ports between Swinemunde and Libau.

Your memorialists therefore humbly pray that your lordships will appoint a suitable convoy for the said vessels from Hanö to the roads or entrances of the ports of their respective destinations to guard them against capture by French privateers, or until such vessels may be taken possession of by military belonging to either the Prussian or Russian governments, as it is utterly impracticable to obtain any insurance against capture and seizure by French privateers, a great number of which are constantly cruising off the very ports to which the goods are intended to be sent.

203. *Saumarez to Croker*

Victory, in Wingo Sound,

2 May 1812.

Sir, You will please to inform the Lords Commissioners of the Admiralty of my arrival in Wingo Sound this morning with His Majesty's ships *Courageux*, *Orion* and *Reynard*, and found laying here Rear-Admiral Morris[1] with the ships and vessels named in the margin [*Vigo, Mars, Dictator, Nimble, Hebe*].

The packet for England being under sail, I herewith enclose the disposition of the squadron and the state and condition of such of His Majesty's ships and vessels as I have been enabled to collect; which you will please to lay before their lordships. I am etc.

---

[1] James Nicol Morris (c. 1763–1830) was the son of Captain John Morris, R.N. killed in the attack on Sullivan's Island, 1778; lieutenant, 1780; captain, 1793; commander of the *Colossus* (74) at Trafalgar where he was badly wounded; rear-admiral, 1811; K.C.B., 1815; vice-admiral, 1819.

204. *Fenwick to Saumarez*

Engelholm [Ängelholm],

3 May 1812.

Dear Sir James, Altho' the winds have of late been so adverse that I have no hopes of your being arrived off Wingo, still as it now seems to be drawing to the westward I have the honour of addressing you by the present lines, which will I trust soon be handed to you there, to express how welcome the intelligence will be to me of your presence in these seas and at the same time to ask your commands. I beg leave most heartily to congratulate you on the very favourable turn which the political system of this country has taken and which cannot fail to afford you the greatest satisfaction, as it is beyond doubt that the conciliatory measures you have pursued during the unfortunate space of time which is now happily passed have operated powerfully on the resolution which this government has taken to maintain its independence and to shake off the trammels of Bonaparte.

Having kept up a regular and frequent communication with Captain Dashwood during his stay on this station and, since his departure, with Captain Pipon and as those officers have no doubt in their reports to you mentioned anything that may have appeared worthy of your notice in my correspondence I will not trouble you with a repetition thereof. In adverting to Captains Dashwood and Pipon I cannot refrain from expressing how greatly I feel gratified by their acquaintance and obliged to them for the very polite and friendly manner in which they have on every occasion facilitated my endeavours to perform the pleasant duty of rendering this squadron any service in my power, which has until the present moment necessarily been conducted with all the former circumspection.

As you will be in possession of much more authentic and recent information as to what passes at Örebro[1] than I am able to give you from public report, I will not intrude with any further observations thereon than that the states appear to have the fullest confidence in the measures recommended by the prince royal and are disposed to give him every authority in the government, not only during any future indisposition of the king but also whilst his health enables him to ostensibly hold the reins of government. There is a party which is supposed to be adverse to the present system. It consists of persons who took the most active part in the dethronement of King Gustavus Adolphus, but their votes in the committee of the states were only 9 against a majority of 52. Any object they may have had in view has therefore for the present been defeated. I have, however, seen a letter from Örebro which

---

[1] The *riksdag*—the Swedish parliament—met at Örebro in 1812. Negotiations for peace between Sweden and Britain were also conducted there.

expresses an opinion that this party will gain strength in the progress of the diet.

Another letter from the same place states that the first information which the Emperor Alexander received concerning the horrible conspiracy[1] which has so happily been defeated came from the crown prince here. General Armfelt appears to have taken an active and successful part on the same side of the question; and it is very remarkable that, altho' it is not many months since he was sent away from Stockholm in disgrace, his conduct towards Sweden at the Russian court has been such as to reconcile this government to him entirely.

I wish it were in my power to state any favourable news from Denmark; but the government of that country either from the perverseness, which has been so long fatal to it, or from an improper view of its own interests seems to be getting daily more deeply into the whirlpool which must inevitably one way or other draw it to destruction and, what is worse, in the meantime form a serious obstacle to the good effect which a contrary system would have in the great contest which seems now on the point of commencing. There seems to be a strange mixture of weakness and an occasional attempt at firmness in that government. On the one hand it is stated that the king of Denmark has absolutely refused to furnish troops to Bonaparte and that the army, which is now collected in Holstein, is there for the purpose of protecting that province against any aggressions of the French; whilst on the other the Danish cabinet is certain that this and the other continental provinces will fall ultimately and neglects the present, and probably last, opportunity that will ever offer for permanently regaining its independence.

You will have been informed by Captain Pipon that the French privateers in the Sound commit all sorts of outrages and that this has led to the capture of one of them by the Danish armed vessels. She has, however, since been released; and it is said that M. de Rosenkrantz,[2] the Danish minister for foreign affairs, told M. Alquier that this liberation was an act of grace only and that rather than submit to the insults of these privateers His Danish Majesty was prepared to renounce the French alliance altogether. Altho' M. Alquier is generally disliked by both the cabinet and the people at Copenhagen, he seems to have a decided influence there or the French privateers, whom he has taken under his immediate protection, could not possibly maintain their ground. The Swedish ships that were lately captured by them

---

[1] The supposed pro-French sympathies of Alexander's reforming minister Mikhael Speransky (1772–1839) led to his dismissal from office and exile from St. Petersburg in March 1812. Bernadotte certainly warned Alexander about the existence of a group which favoured good relations with France, but the source of the opposition to Speransky was the resistance of leading aristocrats to his proposed reforms.

[2] Niels Rosenkrantz (1757–1824) succeeded Christian Bernstorff as Danish foreign minister in 1810.

off Höganäs were principally destined for Denmark so that the owners of the property will have the mortification of seeing it condemned in their own ports. A custom house order has, however, lately been issued to prohibit the clearance inwards of all goods coming from abroad except grain and provisions; and this may form an obstacle to the French in selling their prizes.

There is at present in Denmark considerable apprehension that some part of the Danish states will be attacked this year by Sweden in conjunction with England. It is said that they have received an intimation of this kind from Paris and that, in the event of Zealand being the object, 10,000 French troops will come over to that island.

I now beg leave to ask the favour of your commands in any respect that you may think my services can be useful either along the coasts of this province or neighbourhood of Hanö. I am of course quite ignorant of the arrangements that you may consider it expedient to make respecting the passage of the convoys to and from the Baltic, but as public conjecture and opinion are in favour of the channel of the Sound, provided that the Swedish is a friendly coast, and as in the case of this passage being adopted pilots for the Malmö Channel will be required, I beg leave to submit to you that, there being no regular ones to be met with on the coast north of Malmö and only four at the latter place, the fishermen at the village of Rå about three miles south of Helsingburg are in case of need the most eligible persons to employ on this service. The situation is very favourable for going off to ships as they can meet them near Helsingburg without causing any detention to the convoys; and I know by experience that they are very zealous and expert in whatever they undertake. Having in the course of the winter had an opportunity to learn their sentiments on this subject, I found that they were willing to send up their boats before the convoys that might pass to the northward and be there as marks on the shallows in the channel. Any orders that you may be pleased to give me on this subject shall be executed without delay.

The number of gunboats at Elsinore is 8. This is the utmost that the harbour there can contain. But there is another harbour lately constructed at Hummelbek about 4 miles south of Elsinore which will contain 12 gunboats; and it is said that should the convoys pass thro' the Sound that number will be stationed there. The Danish gunboats will, I am informed, be provided with rockets which they pretend are an improvement on those of Colonel Congreve[1] and carry 15,000 feet. There are now 4 Swedish gunboats at Malmö, 6 at Landscrona and two at Höganäs. The Swedish frigate *Camilla* and *Swallow* brig were two days ago off Landscrona preparing to sail with a

---

[1] William Congreve (1772–1828), the inventor of rocket warfare. See Christopher Lloyd (ed.) *The Naval Miscellany*, vol. iv (N.R.S. vol. xcii).

convoy from thence. The last Swedish convoy that went towards Cattegat saluted the fortress of Cronenburg at passing and received a great number of guns in return. The gunboats were at the same time firing at the French privateers.

In the hopes of soon hearing of your arrival at Gothenburg, I have etc.

205. *Thornton to Saumarez*

Carlslund near Örebro,

6 May 1812.

My dear Sir James, I must inform you after congratulating you most sincerely on your arrival here that things are going on fast, though not so fast as the cause perhaps demands, towards their maturity. I regard the peace as made, though in truth it is not signed for we wait for more from England.

Between Russia and this country a treaty of alliance offensive and defensive is signed and ratified in which is an article (separate) stipulating to invite our accession. The thing therefore is advanced, you see, with Russia also; and though I have no reason to think that I shall put the finishing hand to that business (which must be settled with and in Russia) I am labouring hard to bring out something decisive.

I must inform you, but this, as indeed all this, is in entire confidence that when peace is made, this government mean to present you with a mark of their gratitude for the distinguished kindness you have on all occasions shown them, with which I assure you it is impossible to be more affected than they are. Baron d'Engeström mentioned this to me, and, as I understood him, it is to be a sword, the hilt ornamented with precious stones. You have, my dear Sir James, still more brilliant ornaments on your sword; but these marks so deserved will serve to perpetuate them to your childrens' children.

I am extremely satisfied with the prince royal. He is, I am persuaded, perfectly sincere, loyal, and is the life of the good cause here and in Russia. His influence on Alexander is prodigious; and, I am sure, he more than any other has brought Russia to the stand where it is.

Pray offer my kindest and most affectionate remembrances to Captain Dumaresq and Mr. Champion, and to all my shipmates, Captain Pipon and Mr. Gamble, who allow me a place in their remembrance.

When things are a little more settled, I will endeavour to run down to Gothenburg and perhaps in the course of the summer you may have a more distinguished visitant. I am etc.

206. *Saumarez to Thornton*

Victory, Wingo Sound,

10 May 1812.

My dear Sir, I have received with the greatest pleasure your obliging letters of the sixth and truly rejoice that the important object of your mission is so soon likely to be brought to a favourable termination. I shall also be happy to find that after having so well succeeded in this country, you will be permitted to extend the olive branch and that Russia will renew her former terms of friendship and alliance with us. I shall give particular directions on the subject of your public letter. Previous to the receipt of it I had ordered the ships appointed to convoy the trade to the entrance of the Gulf of Finland to return immediately to Hanö Bay in order not to give any interruptions to the operations of Russia against the common enemy.

The consul with Count Rosen did me the honour to dine on board here yesterday. And I was in hopes to have had Mr. Zee Bermudez's[1] company also, but the packet being under sail with a favourable wind, he embarked on board of her immediately. There is not the smallest risk in the Sleeve from the number of cruizers I am obliged to keep there to prevent supplies getting to Norway.

The *Plantagenet* arrived last evening in ten days from the Downs, having had constantly easterly winds which accounts for the non-arrival of the packets. I inclose to Mr. Smith the only two papers received by her to be forwarded to you. I have also entrusted the consul with a case of St. Michael's oranges of which I request your acceptance.

I am much flattered at the distinguished manner in which it is intended to notice the attention I have invariably wished to show to the Swedish government, and it will be the greatest happiness of my life if my endeavours have any way tended to establish a fixed and permanent alliance between our respective nations.

You will be glad to hear that Admiral Martin who distinguished himself so highly in the *Implacable* is placed under my orders. I daily expect him with his flag on board the *Aboukir*. Captains Dumaresq and Pipon and all friends on board send their respects and are thankful for your kind remembrances of them.

---

[1] Francisco Zea Bermudez, the unofficial representative of Spain at St. Petersburg where he worked in the anti-French interest.

207. *Lindegren to Saumarez*

Carlscrona,
24 May 1812.

Your Excellency, It is a source of great pleasure to me again to be permitted to wait on your excellency under more agreeable prospects than those which have existed the two preceding years, and beg your excellency will accept of my sincere and respectful congratulations on this happy change. And as His Britannic Majesty's ships will meet a friendly reception at this port, I hope of having the pleasure of seeing some of those under your excellency's command here this season; and I trust your excellency is perfectly assured that my best services shall be at all time devoted to His Britannic Majesty's ships and services. Your excellency's commands will always be punctually attended to by me and my house; and I have etc.

208. *Morris to Saumarez*

Vigo, Hanö Bay,
27 May 1812.

Dear Sir, I fear you will think me remiss in not having before acknowledged your obliging letter by Mr. Wilkinson whom, on your recommendation, I shall have great pleasure in showing attention to. The fact is Mr. Wilkinson, when I first saw him, had not your dispatches with him and did mention having a letter of introduction from you, but he did not send it with the dispatches; and I only received it last evening on his coming to Hanö Island in expectation of the convoy's arrival, which my public letter reports. I beg of you to accept my thanks for the communications you are pleased to make me, and assurances of my desire to meet your wishes in everything.

I have today had some conversation with Mr. Donaldson (Mr. Fenwick's clerk) and by interrogating I learn from him that he heard Mr. Fenwick say it is believed to be the desire and expectation of the Swedish councils to preserve a neutrality and not to enter into any alliance before the Russian resistance to Bonaparte shall prove successful. This does not appear reconciliable with their fitting out eight sail-of-the-line and having five frigates, besides brigs, actually at sea protecting their trade. I trust our envoy's sanguine hopes for the success of his own negotiation will not induce him to forget that a maritime power equipping its navy can never be considered a mark of neutral intentions; and until I see the Swedish squadrons employed in assisting our convoys through the Sound or acting in equal numbers in conjunction with us, I cannot help feeling very jealous of their movements. I have etc.

209. *Saumarez to Martin*

Victory,
3 June 1812.

Sir, The Lords Commissioners of the Admiralty having signified their direction to me to make or cause to be made an actual inspection of the island of Anholt and to transmit a detailed report of the state of the island, and more particularly with regard to its defences, I have to desire you will take the first favourable opportunity of proceeding to that island for the purpose of carrying their lordships' orders into execution; signifying to me for their lordships' information your proceedings therein, holding yourself in readiness to proceed thro' the Great Belt on the appearance of the convoy under the charge of Captain Pater of H.M. ship *Cressy*. I have etc.

210. *Instructions by Saumarez to Martin, dated 6 June 1812*

Having directed Captain Pater of His Majesty's ship *Cressy*, with the *Crescent* and *Briseis* under his orders, to proceed with the trade from this anchorage bound to the ports in the Baltic and on falling in with you off Anholt to put himself and the said ships and vessels under your command and follow your orders for their further proceedings; you will please to take them under your command accordingly and proceed with as little delay as is consistent with the safety of the convoy thro' the Great Belt. And having seen them clear of the south end of Langeland, you are to leave them in charge of Captain Pater and repair in the *Aboukir* with the *Censor* gunbrig without delay to Hanö Bay, and follow the orders you will receive upon your arrival at that anchorage.

You are to direct Captain Pater after having seen the convoy in safety to the eastward of Hanö Island to repair to that anchorage and follow the orders of Rear-Admiral Morris, detaching the trade bound to the Russian ports in the Gulf of Finland under the charge of Captain Quilliam of the *Crescent* to see them as far as Dagerort, when he is to return to Hanö Bay and put himself under the orders of Rear-Admiral Morris, having also placed the trade bound for Libau and Riga under the charge of Captain Ross of the *Ariel* and *Briseis* and then repair to join you or the senior officer of His Majesty's ships and vessels in the Bay of Danzig. Given etc.

211. *Saumarez to Morris*

Victory, Wingo Sound,

8 June 1812.

Sir, Herewith I enclose for your information and guidance the duplicate of an order I have received from the Lords Commissioners of the Admiralty authorizing me to permit until the 1st. of August next vessels bearing any flag, except French, to export from Carlshamn the cargoes which have been condemned there, under the limitations specified in the copy of Mr. Buller's[1] letter also herewith enclosed; and you will be pleased to govern yourself accordingly. I have etc.

Enclosure:

211a. *Buller to Cooke*[2]

Council Office, Whitehall,

25 May 1812.

Sir, The Lords of His Majesty's Most Honourable Privy Council having had under their consideration the copy of a letter from J. Atkins, Esq., transmitted in yours of the 21st. inst., praying for the adoption of a more convenient mode of issuing licences with respect to the produce of the Carlshamn cargoes, and for an extension of the duration of such licences; I am directed to acquaint you for the information of Viscount Castlereagh that their lordships see no objection to Sir James Saumarez's being authorized to permit vessels bearing any flag except the French to export from Carlshamn the cargoes which have been condemned there, provided he shall be satisfied that the cargoes so to be exported shall consist wholly and entirely of the articles so condemned or which shall have been imported into that port from some port of the United Kingdom.

Their lordships are also of opinion that Sir James Saumarez should be further instructed to withhold the granting such permission after the first day of August. I am etc.

212. *Morris to Martin*

Vigo, Hanö Bay,

11 June 1812.

Sir, The commander-in-chief having signified to me that a communication has been made to him from Örebro that eight sail-of-the-line and five frigates,

---

[1] James Buller was clerk to the privy council.
[2] Edward Cooke was Culling Smith's successor as under-secretary of state for foreign affairs.

with probably smaller vessels, will be ready to sail from Carlscrona in about one day from this time for the purpose of cruising along the southern shore of the Baltic, the island of Rugen and adjacent coasts; this communication having been made to him by desire of the Swedish government thro' Mr. Thornton in order to prevent the possibility of any collision or misunderstanding between them and any of His Majesty's cruisers in the Baltic, it is his direction that in the event of your falling in with the Swedish squadron or any detached ships you pay due attention to his secret letters upon that subject dated 5th. April last.

It has also been represented to him through the same channel that, in consequence of this country suffering considerably from the scarcity of grain, that contracts have been entered into by the government with individuals for a considerable quantity, principally rye from the Russian ports of the Baltic. And as Swedish vessels so laden will for the most part be escorted by Swedish convoy to Stockholm and other ports, but there being a number of vessels of this description at the port of Revel, and no convoy being intended to proceed so far up the Gulf of Finland, it is his direction that you allow Swedish vessels furnished with Swedish licences and laden with grain to proceed from the Gulf of Finland without convoy to the port of Stockholm *only*, taking care that they do not deviate from that tract.

There is also a vessel called the *Uriel* at the port of Revel, laden with Russian brandy for the Swedish government, which he directs may be likewise allowed to proceed to Stockholm without molestation. These directions you will be pleased to communicate to His Majesty's ships and vessels under your orders. I am etc.

213. *Saumarez to Croker*

Victory, Wingo Sound,

12 June 1812.

Sir, It was with the greatest surprize that I yesterday received a letter, herewith transmitted, from Admiral Morris with its accompanying enclosures from Captain Wilkinson[1] of the *Courageux* and Captain Watts[2] of the *Woodlark* relating to a Swedish frigate with a convoy of merchant vessels which had entered the Belt avowedly bound for Kiel. And in requesting you will please to lay the same before the Lords Commissioners of the Admiralty, I

---

[1] Philip Wilkinson, lieutenant, 1790; captain, 1794; rear-admiral, 1813.
[2] George Edward Watts, lieutenant, 1804; served in the expedition to Copenhagen, 1807; commander 17 Sept. 1807; captain, 1814.

beg you will inform their lordships that, having always considered the introduction of Swedish produce to the canal of Kiel to be ultimately intended for
the ports of the enemy in Holland and the Scheldt, I have uniformly refused
all applications that have been made to me for licences permitting vessels to
enter that port. I have, therefore, written to Mr. Thornton at Örebro to
make a strong remonstrance to the Swedish government upon the subject,
expressing my great surprize at a convoy having been allowed to sail for an
enemy's port without previous intimation having been made to me of such
intention and also expressing my hope that a similar circumstance might not
occur again.

In the existing state of affairs with Sweden I hope their lordships will approve of Captain Wilkinson not having warned the convoy from proceeding
to their destination. It is at the same time to be regretted that he did not
inform himself more particularly of the nature of the cargoes on board and
the ports where they were loaded, although I have no reason to suspect they
were from ports belonging to Denmark. As Captain Serrell[1] of the *Helder*
with the *Bellette* are stationed between Kiel and the south end of Langeland,
it is possible he may have been more exact in his examination of the convoy.
I enclose a copy of my letter to Mr. Thornton relating to the circumstance;
and as soon as I receive his reply I shall transmit the same for their lordships'
information. I have etc.

Enclosure:

213a. *Saumarez to Thornton*

Victory, in Wingo Sound,

10 June 1812.

Sir, Having had the honour to apprize your excellency of my having
stationed His Majesty's cruisers on the coast of Pomerania and also off the
coasts of Mecklenburg and Holstein with the view of preventing supplies
being conveyed to the enemy's forces occupying those coasts, your excellency
will judge of my extreme surprize at receiving a letter from Rear-Admiral
Morris transmitting to me the information that a frigate belonging to His
Swedish Majesty, escorting a convoy of 15 sail of merchant vessels, entered
the Belt on the 2nd. instant avowedly destined for Kiel.

I herewith enclose to your excellency the documents that have hitherto
reached me of so unexpected a circumstance; and as I have not obtained any
information from His Majesty's ships immediately stationed off Kiel, I am
unapprized of what measures the senior officer may have thought proper to

---

[1] John Serrell, lieutenant, 1793; commander, 1800; captain, 1803.

adopt. But I trust that your excellency will lose no time in making such representations to the Swedish government as will prevent similar occurrences in future, as I consider it indispensable for the furtherance of the good cause in which we are engaged to prevent supplies entering the ports that are known to be occupied by the troops of the enemy. Having desired Mr. Consul Smith to transmit this letter by express to Örebro I hope to receive your excellency's reply without delay. I have etc.

214. *Saumarez to Martin*

Victory, Wingo Sound,

17 June 1812.

My dear Sir, The very unaccountable neglect of Mr. Champion in having enclosed the orders intended for you by the *Cressy* to Admiral Morris would have been attended with the greatest inconvenience, had it not been for the very judicious manner in which you carried into effect what you considered to have been my intentions; and I return you my sincere thanks for preventing the service sustaining any injury from so great a mistake.

The very rapid run of the convoy through the Belt will have prevented the orders sent by a courier meeting you on your arrival off Hanö. I however hope that they will not have been long delayed and that you are by this time proceeding to your station, whence I shall be most anxious to receive favourable accounts. My last letters from Örebro are so late as the 14th. when Mr. T. formed every expectation that the peace with Russia would very soon be signed. I trust that nothing will have intervened to prevent it and that I shall in a very short time have the pleasure to communicate to you so desirable an event.

We are still without letters from England of later than the 5th. Two mails are at present due, which I hope will arrive in time to enclose what letters there may be for you to be transmitted with the present dispatch. I shall be most happy to find that an efficient administration has at last been formed and that the country will no longer remain in the state of anarchy it has been in since the lamented death of Mr. Perceval.[1]

My son[2] begs to write in best remembrances and I have etc.

---

[1] A reference to the recent assassination of the prime minister Spencer Perceval.

[2] James, later the Reverend Baron De Sausmarez, was the eldest son of the commander-in-chief. He accompanied his father to Gothenburg and later made a tour of the northern capitals, rejoining the flagship in October.

215. *Morris to Puke*

Vigo, Hanö Bay,
23 June 1812.

Sir, I have the honour to acknowledge the receipt of your excellency's letter of the 22nd. instant informing me that His Swedish Majesty has been pleased to direct that no convoy shall henceforth be given to vessels for Kiel and other places in Holstein or foreign places in the Baltic except Russian ports, and that arrangements have been made with my royal master's envoy that some vessels now laden at Kiel with wine and medicines should return to Sweden; and further doing me the honour to communicate to me your excellency's intention of sending His Swedish Majesty's frigate *Jarramus* to convoy those vessels.

I have the honour in reply to acquaint your excellency that the captains and commanders of His Britannic Majesty's ships are ordered on meeting with those of His Swedish Majesty to show them every friendly attention and assistance; and to assure you that the *Jarramus* will consequently meet with it from any of our detachments she may fall in with on her intended voyage. Our orders for preventing supplies of any kind going to ports in the power of the enemy remain in force; and from the present circumstances of the war carried on by the French our attention is particularly called to a strict compliance with them; and for which purpose Rear-Admiral Martin is cruising with a squadron on the southern shore of the Baltic. I beg leave to assure your excellency of the satisfaction I shall receive in manifesting upon all occasions the friendly disposition directed in my orders from my commander-in-chief and of the respect and high consideration with which I have etc.

216. *Croker to Saumarez*

Admiralty Office,
1 July 1812.

Sir, I have it in command from my Lords Commissioners of the Admiralty to send herewith for your information copy of a letter and its enclosure which I have received from the Master of Lloyd's Coffee House relative to the detention for want of protection of upwards of 250 sail of vessels at Wingo Sound bound to the Baltic, and also copy of my letter to him of this day's date in reply; and I am to express to you their lordships' hope that the convoy did sail on or immediately after the 22nd. of last month, as they observe that you had the *Dictator* with you and the *Zealous* at hand. I am etc.

Enclosure 1:

216a. *Bennett*[1] *to Croker*

Lloyd's,

30 June 1812.

Sir, I am directed by the committee for managing the affairs of Lloyds to send you the enclosed copy of a letter just received relating to the detention for want of protection of upwards of 250 sail of vessels at Wingo Sound bound to the Baltic, a circumstance much to be regretted as it will occasion their homeward voyage to be late in the season. The committee request that you will be pleased to lay this communication as early as possible before the Lords Commissioners of the Admiralty in order that their lordships may adopt such measures which they may consider proper on this occasion of so much importance to the mercantile interest, and prevent a recurrence of the accumulation of so large a convoy to go through the Belt at one time, unless unavoidably detained by contrary winds or bad weather. I have etc.

Enclosure 2:

216b. *Oswell Selby & Co., Todd Mitchell & Co., Stephen Thornton Bros. & Co. to Lloyds*

London,

30 June 1812.

Gentlemen, It has been reported to us on the authority of letters from Gothenburg and from several captains at Wingo Sound dated the 22nd. instant that above 250 sail bound to the Baltic were waiting convoy. This fleet has been accumulating for some time, and must have consisted of:

The fleet from Long Hope	—	*Hebe*	—	46 sail
do.	Nore	—	*Persian*	— 70 sail
do.		—	*Providence*	— 33 sail
do.	Leith	—	*Snake*	— 10 sail
do.	Humber	—	*Prince William*	— 13 sail
				172 sail,

besides a convoy from Heligoland and several ships from Gothenburg. The letters state that the admiral thought that a convoy for them might be expected in about eight days, but the fact is that there were no large vessels at Wingo, and the admiral was waiting for the convoy from the Baltic. When this may arrive is doubtful, for the downward convoy had not left Hanö on

[1] John Bennett junior was secretary to the committee for managing the affairs of Lloyd's.

the 20th. June, and it seemed the opinion of the best informed captains that the convoy at Gothenburg would not sail before the middle of July. We do not communicate the intelligence with a view to censure the admiral who, it appears, cannot send the convoy forwards without line-of-battle ships, but that the lords of the admiralty may be informed of the disadvantages attending the passage of a large fleet through the Belt, and may enable the admiral to dispatch them more frequently. We are respectfully etc.

Enclosure 3:

216c. *Croker to Bennett*

Admiralty Office,

1 July 1812.

Sir, I have received and laid before my Lords Commissioners of the Admiralty your letter of yesterday's date enclosing copy of a letter which the Committee at Lloyds had received relating to the detention for want of protection of upwards of 250 sail of vessels at Wingo Sound bound to the Baltic in order that their lordships might adopt measures to prevent a recurrence of an accumulation of so large a convoy to go through the Belt at one time; and I have their lordships' commands to acquaint you for the information of the committee that on the 8th. of last month a convoy of 130 sail was passed up the Belt, and that in the usual course of endeavouring to dispatch the convoys every fortnight, no convoy would be due until the 22nd. of last month, the very date of the complaint, so that in truth there was no accumulation of the trade that the admiral could be expected to prevent, and as their lordships see no occasion why the admiral should not have dispatched the convoy immediately after the 22nd., he having a sufficient force at hand for that purpose, they suppose that he has done so, and therefore hope that the apprehensions expressed on this subject will be found altogether groundless. I am etc.

217. *Thornton to Saumarez*

Carlslund, near Örebro,

5 July 1812.

Sir, I lose no time in informing your excellency that a Russian courier brought yesterday morning to General van Suchtelen[1] the intelligence that the French army had crossed the Russian frontier on the night of the 24th.

[1] Jan Pieter van Suchtelen (1751–1836) was resident in Sweden as envoy extraordinary of the tsar; personal representative of the tsar at the Swedish crown prince's headquarters, 1813–14; ambassador to the kingdom of Sweden-Norway, 1814–36; count of the Russian empire, 1822.

and 25th. ult. at Kovno, and have thereby commenced hostilities against His Imperial Majesty. No other details have yet reached this place, but the intelligence itself is of the utmost importance.

As every part of the squadron under the command of your excellency, which can be spared from other essential services, will be of great importance along the southern coast of the Baltic, particularly from Danzig to Memel, and even along the coast of Courland, I trust your excellency will give such orders as may be necessary. At the same time, I am not without hopes of being able in the course of a few days to pay a short visit to Wingo Sound for the purpose of communicating many circumstances of great consequence which I cannot by letter. I have etc.

218. *Saumarez to Martin*

Victory, in Wingo Sound,

10 July 1812.

Sir, I have received your letters of the undermentioned dates with their respective enclosures: 30 June stating the information you had secured from Captain Ross of the *Ariel* of the state of the trade at Libau and that the governor had applied to you for vessels to take off the remainder of the corn and of your intention to proceed off that port; 2nd. July informing me of your having had communications with Libau and that all but 13 ships were beyond the reach of the enemy, seven of which were loaded and the others would be completed the next day and that the governor had given you assurances that all the corn should be destroyed if the enemy advance; 2nd. July enclosing a letter from Captain Ross of the *Briseis* reporting a very gallant and successful attack made by Lieutenant Jones[1] and Mr. Palmer[2] midshipman in the boats of that sloop on a large merchantship off Pillau in possession of the enemy, which they recaptured; 2nd. July transmitting a letter from Captain Acklom with two from General Essen,[3] governor of Riga, and informing me that in consequence of his wish you had proposed to proceed off that port and use every exertion to equip a strong division of gunboats, also stating information you had received from an English gentleman at Riga, in whose means of intelligence and strict veracity you had the utmost confidence.[4]

---

[1] Thomas Jones (1786–1845) entered the navy, 1798; lieutenant, 1808; unemployed after 1813; retired commander, 1845.
[2] George Palmer entered the navy in 1805; lieutenant, Nov. 1812; commander, 1840.
[3] Ivan Nikolayevitch, Count Essen (1759–1813) was appointed governor of Riga and chief administrator of Estonia, Courland and Latvia in succession to Bukshevdan in 1810.
[4] Patrick Cumming, a British agent who died shortly after this letter was written.

I particularly approve of the manner you adopted for removing the merchantships laden with corn from Libau and also your intentions to proceed off Riga for the purpose of giving assistance to the equipment of the gunboats or any other service that may be required.

I have to desire you will convey to Captain Ross of the *Briseis* my approval of his exertions and that of Lieutenant Jones and the officers and men under his command in cutting out the *Uriana* merchantship off Pillau.

I place the fullest reliance upon your zeal and exertions in rendering every aid and co-operation in your power to the Russian government against the common enemy; and if they should require an officer of higher rank than a lieutenant to superintend the equipment of the gunboats, I recommend Captain Ross of the *Briseis* being appointed to that service; but I do not approve of the gunboats being manned by British seamen beyond a proportion of ten men to each of the lieutenants who may be appointed. I have etc.

219. *Saumarez to Martin*

Victory, Wingo Sound,

10 July 1812.

My dear Sir, I had great satisfaction on receiving at a late hour yesterday evening your letter of the 2nd. instant, and was very happy to find that your overture to the governor of Riga had met with so favourable a reception. There can be no doubt of the pacific intentions of the Russian government; but, as I stated in my last letter, some obstacle was thrown in the way of the signature to the articles of peace, but which, it is to be hoped, will soon have been removed by the reference to the respective governments. Nothing can more strongly demonstrate the wishes of the Russian government than the application made by Count Essen to Captain Acklom for his assistance in the equipment of the gunboats etc.

I sincerely thank you for your attention in not appointing any officer to this service till after having consulted me upon the subject. At the same time I must request you will not be actuated by motives of delicacy but use your own discretion in what you consider best for the public service. In the event of Riga or any other part of the coast being attacked we cannot be too strenuous in giving every possible assistance and co-operating with the forces of Russia against the French.

I have every reason to expect Mr. Thornton will be here next Saturday, when I expect soon after to proceed to Hanö Bay. You will be glad to receive the account of the destruction of the Danish frigate and the three sloops being totally disabled.[1] They will require all the summer months to be put in a state for service, if ever they can be repaired.

I thank you for the perusal of Mr. Cumming's letter which I return. He may be assured his name will not be mentioned or affixed to any intelligence he may communicate. Be assured that the whole of your proceedings are perfectly consonant to my wishes, and your going to Riga will, I trust, be attended with the best effect in inspiring the Russian officers and the country with confidence in an intention for the good of the common cause. I sincerely hope that Russia will have the firmness to resist the first onset of the enemy and that with the aid of the Almighty we shall ultimately triumph over the ambitionate tyrant who has been so long the scourge of mankind.

With my fervent wishes for your health and every success I remain etc.

220. *Martin to Saumarez*

12 July 1812.

My dear Sir, The report of Marshal Macdonald[2] being in full march for Riga occasioned the greatest consternation and called forth the utmost exertions in preparing the bomb-vessels and gunboats, as well as the works in the garrisons where seven thousand peasants are constantly employed. The continuance of Macdonald in so menacing a position admits of no relaxation of these exertions; nor is the terror of the inhabitants diminished, though they are profiting by the delay to remove themselves and their valuables to a more safe place. General Essen thinks the French corps is waiting the other side of Mittau until the cannon and supplies are brought up over the sandy roads of Courland; and he seems to hope that the Russian corps under General Louis[3] will be able to check their progress.

I very much wished to be spared the mortification of doing any act that could have the least appearance of intruding on your patronage, but the belief that the enemy were close at hand made it indispensably necessary to have a head and chief to the division of gunboats. I feel, however, assured that if I have done wrong, you will judge of my motive with that candour and kindness which I have ever experienced from you.

---

[1] The *Naiad, Kiel* (18), *Lolland* (18) and *Samsø* (18) were defeated near Arendal on 6 July; the British force being led by the *Dictator* (64) commanded by James Pattison Stewart, lieutenant, 1805; captain, January 1812; C.B., 1815.
[2] Etienne Jacques Joseph Alexandre Macdonald (1765–1840) served in the royal and revolutionary armies; promoted general, 1795; created marshal of France and duke of Tarentum, 1809; commanded the left wing of the French army in East Prussia, 1812; negotiated with the allies, 1814.
[3] General Friedrich von Löwis (1767–1824) belonged to a Scottish family which had settled in Russia in the time of Peter the Great; commanded an army corps under Essen, 1812.

All the good maps of the country are brought up. Those which I send are in the Polish language, and scarcely intelligible; and when I refer to them, it must be with the names of the places in the English and Polish languages. A gentleman of the town gives me reason to hope he will be able to get two maps of a better sort from a friend.

A report is in circulation today which, if true, is highly important. It states that the French army has fallen back fifteen miles in consequence of the Cossacks under General Platov[1] and the light cavalry under General Ouvarov[2] having threatened the rear of the enemy; and it is added that these active generals are now at Vilna. I mention this as a mere report to which I do not myself attach much credit.

We are supplied with excellent beef at 5d. per pound, which also covers the expense of half pound of vegetables to every pound of meat. The contractor stood out some time for 6d. a pound, but I would not give more than 5d. and then leave him to benefit by any fall in the price, which is expected as the cattle are driving in from the country very fast. Riga is to be supplied with four months provisions, and the churches are already nearly full of corn. I am in great hopes of the better maps, but lest they should not be sent in time I will put up [with] those I first bought. I am etc.

221. *Saumarez to Martin*

Victory, Wingo Sound,

15 July 1812.

My dear Sir, Your highly important dispatches dated the 7th. instant have just reached me, and I am truly happy to find the cordial reception you met with on your arrival at Riga and the favourable impression your zealous exertions for the defence of that important city must make upon His Imperial Majesty and the whole of the Russian army, who must derive fresh spirits in seeing a nation, with whom they were so recently in hostility, exerting themselves in giving every support to their cause.

I hope Admiral Morris will have hastened the *Orion* to join you as the assistance of her carpenters will be of great service in fitting the bomb vessels and gunboats. If you find two or three small vessels adapted for carrying your dispatches, I have no doubt but General Essen would readily furnish them for that purpose, and you could put an officer with a proper crew from the ships under your orders to man them.

Your former dispatches were transmitted very soon after their arrival,

---

[1] Matthew Ivanovitch, Count Platov (1757–1818) was attaman of the Don cossacks and a general of cavalry.
[2] Lieutenant-General Fedor Petrovitch Ouvarov, a former aide-de-camp to Tsar Paul I.

but the strong westerly winds we experience will occasion some delay to those I have now received. I hope it may give time for the arrival of your next accounts, and that they will convey a favourable result of the battle you expected at the time you sent off your letters.

Mr. Thornton came down from Örebro last Thursday and stayed with me until Monday morning. We both dined with Count Rosen. There can be no doubt of the peace with Russia and Sweden being very soon settled. Two packets have arrived this day, and possibly Mr. T's. letters by them may enable him to sign and to put the finishing hand to the articles. The war will then be carried on upon a more extensive sector, but I regret the tardiness and the delays in so advanced a state of the season. I hope your apprehensions respecting Turkey[1] will prove groundless and that Bonaparte will not have the assistance of the porte in the present contest.

You must allow me to recommend your paying due attention to your health, and not run the risk to impair it by over-fatigue or too much exertion. Believe me etc.

222. *Saumarez to Martin*

Victory, Wingo Sound,
21 July 1812.

My dear Sir, You will be happy to find by my public dispatch that the peace with Russia and Sweden has been happily signed by the plenipotentiaries at Örebro. This important event has been communicated to me by Mr. Thornton in his letter of the 18th., enclosed with his dispatches to government which I immediately transmitted to England by the *Sheldrake* in charge of my flag lieutenant.[2] This blessed event will, I trust, hasten the downfall of Bonaparte and restore tranquillity to Europe. The utmost exertions are making in the different ports of Sweden in fitting large vessels as transports for the conveyance of troops, and before the middle of next month two powerful armies will be in readiness to proceed to their respective destinations. Wherever these expeditions may be intended, they cannot but tend to distract the French in their operations against Russia and promote a great diversion in favour of that country, even if they had no other object.

I expect Lord Cathcart[3] here very soon on his way to Russia as the am-

[1] Peace between Russia and Turkey had been signed at Bucharest on 28 May, but the ratifications were not exchanged until 20 July.

[2] Nicholas Charles Dobrée, lieutenant, 1810; commander, Nov. 1812; nephew to the commander-in-chief.

[3] William Schaw Cathcart, 10th Baron Cathcart, 1st Viscount Cathcart (1765–1843) served in the army in the wars of the American and French revolutions; lieutenant-general, 1801; commanded the army at Copenhagen, 1807; ambassador and military commissioner with the Russian army, 1812–14; created Earl Cathcart, 1814; ambassador at St Petersburg, 1814–21.

bassador to the court of His Imperial Majesty. I hope on his arrival to have it in my power to communicate to his lordship accounts of important advantages obtained over the French, which I am in daily expectation to receive from you.

Two packets are hourly looked for, which I hope will arrive in time to send by the messenger that conveys the dispatches to Hanö Bay.

Pray excuse this scrawl, being much hurried; and believe me etc.

223. *Saumarez to Martin*

Victory, Wingo Sound,

23 July 1812.

My dear Sir, I have this moment received your letter accompanied with the maps you have had the goodness to send me, for which I return you my sincere thanks. I am very much pleased with your appointment of Captain Stewart[1] to the command of the flotilla upon the Duna [Dvina]. He is not the first upon Lord Melville's[2] list for post rank, but I hope the services he will render in that important situation will induce his lordship to confirm him. I have appointed Lieutenant Brine[3] to the *Reynard*, and placed two active young men under the orders of Captain Stewart who happened to be the next on the Admiralty list.

I sincerely hope, notwithstanding the formidable force under Macdonald, that Riga will be enabled to hold out. I am fully aware of the impression to be expected from the first attacks of the enemy's troops. At the same time, if they are opposed with vigour and made to pay dearly for any success they may acquire in so strong a country as they have to go through, from its natural and military defences, their army must soon be greatly reduced in numbers, added to the difficulty of procuring provisions and forage for their cavalry. It is most fortunate you arrived so early at Riga and to be able to give such timely assistance in the defence of the place.

The letters which I have transmitted, containing your correspondence with General von Essen, were acknowledged by the packet which arrived yesterday morning; and I hope those of subsequent date have been received before this time. How much it is to be regretted that the exertions now making in the ports of Sweden were not taken in hand some weeks sooner. It is stated

[1] Hew Stewart (or Steuart) entered the navy from the Naval Academy, 1795; midshipman of the *Bedford* (74) at Camperdown; lieutenant, 1799; commander, 1806; captain, Nov. 1812; knight of the order of St. Vladimir, 1812; dismissed his ship by sentence of a court-martial on the East Indies station, 1814.

[2] Robert Saunders Dundas, 2nd Viscount Melville (1771–1851) was first lord of the admiralty, 1812–27 and again from 1828–30.

[3] George Brine was the son of Admiral James Brine; lieutenant, 1803; a lieutenant of the *Victory*, 1808–12; commander of the *Reynard* sloop, 1812; captain, 1818; retired, 1846.

that the embarkation of the troops in the different ports of the coast will take place about the 15th. of August; but we know too well the delays usual upon such occasions to expect it even at that period. I assure you it has not been for want of my constant representations that measures have not been sooner adopted, for from the time of your sailing for the Belt it has been the subject of my unremitted correspondence to Örebro and other communications. The peace that has now happily taken place will probably accelerate the plans of operations. The crown prince is most zealous in the cause, and to his own personal exertions much is expected. I truly hope they will succeed for the advancement of the good cause and the annihilation of the enemy. With my most sincere wishes for your health and every success, I have etc.

224. *Saumarez to Martin*

Victory, Wingo Sound,
23 July 1812.

Sir, I have this evening received your letter of the 12th. inst. detailing the intelligence you had received of the force, movements and operations of the Russian and French armies, and enclosing maps of the seat of war, and informing me of the application you had received from several merchants to know if the existing understanding between Russia and England would admit of property being shipped in Russian vessels for conveyance to Great Britain; and as there was an immense quantity of corn, hemp, flax, masts and iron laying at Riga you had granted a certificate (a copy of which you have enclosed) permitting the shipment of such articles direct to Great Britain; which I much approve of, as well as the pass you have given for colonial produce, most belonging to British merchants, to be sent to Petersburg to prevent its falling into the hands of the enemy, and the exertions you have used to get all the ships out with British licences under Danish and Prussian flags. I also approve of your having given your opinion to Rear-Admiral Morris that light vessels may go to Riga without risk, but that it would be wrong and very hazardous to bring cargoes.

The peace that has now so happily been signed between Russia and England renders it adviseable that every encouragement should be given to the trade between the two nations; and you will be pleased to take an early opportunity of signifying to His Excellency General von Essen for the information of the Russian government that I have complied with the applications of several merchants to allow their vessels to proceed to the ports of Russia laden with English colonial produce and merchandize without being furnished with licences; and you will please to facilitate as much as in your power the trade between the respective countries. I have etc.

P.S. As flour may be procured in the ports of Russia at a moderate price, you are at liberty to purchase some for the use of the ships under your orders, to bring as much as they can stow conveniently as also for the ships under the orders of Rear-Admiral Morris.

225. *Melville to Saumarez*

Admiralty,

25 July 1812.

Sir, I have received today your letters of the 13th. and 16th. inst. and I am happy to find that you have determined on remaining for the present in Wingo Sound where, it is probable, your presence will be more necessary than in the Baltic.

You will learn by an official letter that it is proposed to cut off, if possible, all communication between the island of Zealand and the neighbouring Danish territories, for which purpose an additional force is sent to you. With that reinforcement and the vessels already under your command, I should hope you may be able to accomplish the object; and I conclude that as you will now have no enemy to fear in Russia or Sweden you may withdraw from the Baltic the greater number of your ships-of-the-line and apply them to the blockade of Zealand, where they will also be of use passing your convoys through the Belt. There are two bomb-vessels now at Spithead ready for sea, which will be sent to you immediately to be employed at Riga or wherever you may have occasion for them.

Lord Cathcart will proceed in the *Aquilon* in a few days hence from Yarmouth and will go direct to Gothenburg where he will have an opportunity of communicating with you.

It is proposed to withdraw the marine battalion from Anholt and to employ them elsewhere, in which case they will be replaced in that island by a corps of the line. I have etc.

226. *Saumarez to Martin*

Victory, Hawke Road,

5 Aug. 1812.

Sir, Accept, I pray you, my most sincere thanks for your friendly letter of the 25th. which I have this moment received. It has dissipated the apprehensions I had formed in reading those dated the day preceding for the fate of the Russian army. But the bulletin you enclosed with that of the 25th. proves some dependence may be placed upon the emperor's troops and that, when they have the opportunity afforded them, they can show that the French are not invincible.

The too precipitate destruction of the suburbs of Riga, and the barbarous manner in which it was effected, fills the mind with horror; and I fear we shall have many more such scenes to deplore. I sincerely wish that with the confidence General Essen so justly places in you he would also profit of your opinion on many points wherein he could derive the most essential benefit.

I have always understood the Russian army to be the worst provided with any medical staff and that when a soldier is wounded he is generally left to his fate. In the event of Riga being invested spacious buildings adapted for the reception of wounded, independent of the hospitals, might be the means of preserving many lives and of encouraging the soldiers, when they know in case of being wounded they will be attended with care and humanity.

I have stated to government your suggestion of enlisting men for the German legion; and I expect that General Dörnberg, who is at present at Gothenburg, will very soon be ordered to Russia and possibly to endeavour to raise a corps from among his countrymen who are serving with the enemy.

I am grieved that I cannot give you any encouragement of immediate co-operation from Sweden. I have urged all in my power to promote the object; and I have lately sent extracts of your letters to Mr. Thornton, wherein you so earnestly recommend the subject. But I fear it will be September before any embarkation and, between ourselves, I am at present very doubtful whether the destination of the Swedish troops may not be differently directed.

I have no doubt of Captain Steuart's zealous exertions in forwarding the service he is upon; and I hope Mr. Bointon and the other officers are by this time under his orders. I was happy in giving you an opportunity of nomination any two young men from your quarter deck you might consider deserving; and I hope Lord Melville will confirm the different appointments.

We are in daily expectation of two packets, but the wind continues unfavourable and it also retards the arrival of Lord Cathcart who was expected to embark this day week from Yarmouth. I shall not fail to mention to his lordship what you point out for his route. You will be surprized when I mention that I expect Mr. Thornton tomorrow on his way to England where he is going to make necessary arrangements and expects to return immediately. My son left me last week on a short visit to him; and he writes me he was to accompany Admiral Bentinck[1] to Stockholm. This last was on his way to the emperor with letters from the crown prince.

[1] William Bentinck, lieutenant, 1782; captain, 1783; rear-admiral, 1805; vice-admiral, 1810; was received by the tsar and the crown prince in a private capacity during a tour of the north in 1812.

Captain Dumaresq and Champion desire best remembrances, and I remain etc.

P.S. I usually send copies of the original letters I receive from you on service, which I have always marked *most secret*.

227. *Morris to Saumarez*

Vigo, Hanö Bay,

7 Aug. 1812.

Sir, I have to acknowledge the receipt of your letter of the 2nd. instant marked most secret and shall communicate its contents to Captain Dashwood[1] in the cautionary manner therein indicated. I have also received its accompanying letters marked secret directing me, in consequence of the Lords Commissioners of the Admiralty having signified their direction to use every endeavour to cut off every communication between the island of Zealand and the other Danish territory, to instruct Captain Wilkinson of the *Courageux* after delivering the charge of the Baltic convoy to Captain Lloyd[2] of the *Plantagenet* and seen one from Wingo Sound in safety off the south end of Langeland to repair with the *Courageux* and *Mars* off Sproe, using his best endeavours to cut off all communication between Zealand and the other islands in the Belt, taking the captain of the *Dictator* and commander of the *Acteon* under his orders pursuant to the orders he will receive from you by the *Plantagenet* directing Captain Pater in the *Cressy* with the *Woodlark* to proceed to Hanö Bay with the trade under their protection; and further directing me to detach Captain Pater (when the *Cressy* is complete with water after her return to join me) with one of the sloops or gunbrigs to cruise between Dars Head and Femeren using his utmost endeavours to cut off all communication between Zealand and the opposite coast, and signifying the same to Captain Serrell of the *Helder* and keeping the *Crescent* off Hanö for the next convoy that may arrive there.

The *Courageux* having sailed with the convoy on the 4th. instant, I conclude Captain Wilkinson will receive your orders by the *Plantagenet* before I can have any communication with him. And I shall lose no time in completing and detaching the *Cressy* with a sloop (after her arrival here) between Dars Head and the island of Femeren, instructing Captain Pater according to your orders and sending by him the same instructions for Captain Serrell of the *Helder*.

[1] Dashwood was ordered to command a detachment posted between the south end of Langeland and Fehmärn for the purpose of observing the use made by enemy shipping of the Kiel Canal.

[2] Robert Lloyd, lieutenant, 1790; captain, 1799.

I will also direct Captain Dashwood to send the *Crescent* here in readiness for the next convoy and, if I can possibly spare a small vessel, send one in her place to be under Captain Dashwood's orders. I will direct the *Cressy* to supply the *Helder* and *Bellette* as they may require it. I have etc.

228. *Saumarez to Martin*

Victory, Hawke Road,

12 Aug. 1812.

Sir, I yesterday received your letters of the 4th. and 5th. inst. informing me of the arrival at Riga of the flotilla of gunboats so long expected, also detailing your proceedings and the intelligence you had received of a severe action between Count Wittgenstein's[1] corps and Marshal Oudinot[2] in which the latter was defeated with the loss of three thousand men taken prisoners and some cannon.[3]

As by the time you will receive this letter the season of the year will be too far advanced for the *Aboukir* to remain at the insecure anchorage off Riga, I have to desire you will repair in her to Hanö Bay leaving Captain Acklom in the *Ranger*, with such small vessels as you may judge necessary to place under his command, to co-operate against the enemy upon the Dvina and also leaving Captain Steuart with such officers and men under his orders as you may judge adviseable for the service entrusted to him. But in the event of your considering it inexpedient to leave the *Ranger* off Riga, I have to desire you will please to give orders to Captain Acklom to repair with her off Revel, placing such small vessels as you can spare under his command for the purpose of keeping up a communication from the Russian headquarters, directing him to transmit his letters to me to Dalarö under cover to Mr. George Foy at Stockholm and also communicating to His Excellency Edward Thornton Esq. at Stockholm any intelligence he may consider of importance for my information. I have etc.

[1] Ludwig Adolf Peter, prince of Sayn-Wittgenstein-Ludwigsburg (1769–1843) began his military career in the army of Prussia in the campaign of 1793; transferred to Russian service; fought against Napoleon, 1807 and 1812; named commander-in-chief of Russian and Prussian forces, 1813; relieved of his command after battles of Lutzen and Bautzen; retired, 1815.

[2] Charles Nicolas Oudinot (1767–1847) fought in Flanders and Italy during the revolutionary war; present at Austerlitz, Friedland and Wagram; created marshal of France and duke of Reggio, 1809; remained loyal to the monarchy in 1815; later a minister of state and governor of the Invalides.

[3] Wittgenstein, whose army covered the road to St. Petersburg, defeated Oudinot at Zakubuwo on 31 July.

229. *Chetwynd to Croker*

Council Office, Whitehall,

13 Aug. 1812.

Sir, Having laid before the Lords of His Majesty's Most Honourable Privy Council the copy of a letter from Sir James Saumarez, dated the 5th. instant, with its enclosure (transmitted in your letter of yesterday) on the subject of the difficulties experienced by Admiral Martin with respect to Prussian and Danish vessels furnished with British licences, I am directed to desire you will acquaint the Lords Commissioners of the Admiralty that it appears to the Lords of the Council from Admiral Martin's statement that he has acted with great judgement on the subject to which it refers. I am further directed to transmit you a note of the description of licences that have been granted for vessels trading to the ports of Russia within the Baltic; which the Lords Commissioners of the Admiralty may perhaps think it may be useful to forward to Admiral Martin for the purpose of assisting him in preventing, as far as may depend upon him, any abuse of such licences. I am etc.

Enclosure:

229a. *Description of Licences*

To export to a certain amount and to import return cargoes.

To export generally goods allowed by law.

To import goods allowed by law in return for cargoes exported in the previous year.

To import grain meat or flour on certain conditions as to the course of their voyage etc.

To import goods allowed by law from Riga or ports of Russia within the Baltic or Gulf of Finland to the north of Riga, without a previous export.

In all these licences the name and character of the vessel, the tonnage and master and the ports of import and export were named.

They were granted to Prussian or Danish vessels, as well as to American or other vessels.

These were granted in blank for any vessel not French in order to facilitate the importation of grain into this kingdom.

These were granted in blank to any vessels but French, and were first issued on the 14 July 1812 when, from the intelligence received, it was presumed that British property in those ports might be in danger.

To import hemp and other naval stores for the use of the dockyards.

These were granted in blank for any vessel not French, but were only granted to persons who had actually contracted to bring home stores.

Since the 1st. of August, the day after the news arrived of the signature of peace with Russia, no licences have been granted for foreign vessels not Russians to trade between Russia and Great Britain.

230. *Cathcart to Saumarez*

Örebro,
18 Aug. 1812.

Dear Sir, I have to thank you for your letter of the 11th. instant. I undertook either to return to you or to send you a confidential communication concerning military operations, if any plan for this campaign in which you might be concerned should be determined. I find that there are circumstances which necessarily retard this decision and that the season will still be more exhausted before anything can be finally arranged. In as far as any project may depend upon the quarter to which I am going, as well as upon the government of this country, I will not fail to give you the earliest information I can thro' Mr. Thornton of anything of importance in addition to the communications you will receive from him.

The government of His Swedish Majesty is particularly desirous that the measures taken to prevent intercourse to and from the island of Zealand, either in regard to the other Danish islands, Jutland, Norway or the north of Germany, may be continued; and there is great jealousy of a communication between Norway and Jutland or the Belt. An imagination has got about that the Danish royal family might meditate an excursion to Norway which, if it were to be attempted, this government are very anxious should be prevented.

Were operations to be put in practice such as we talked of, I apprehend that Wingo Sound and Hanö Island or Carlscrona would be convenient points of assembly for such parts of the naval force as are not stationed in the Belt; and I should imagine the places last named would be the most advantageous for the more considerable reserve and the most handy either for demonstration or actual operation.

I mean to set out early tomorrow morning for Stockholm, and soon afterwards I hope to arrive at the residence of the court of Russia. I have etc.

P.S. The prince royal promised me he would give orders that every assistance in their power should be given by the Swedish gunboats and armed vessels in the Sound and in the Malmö passage to our trade or to any of His Majesty's ships or vessels.

231. *Saumarez to Martin*

Victory, Hawke Road,

21 Aug. 1812.

My dear Sir, I beg you will accept my most sincere congratulations on the change of your flag,[1] which I hope will prove a happy presage of continued success to the important service entrusted to you. I place such implicit reliance on your skill and known judgement that I leave it to you to make any variation in the arrangements pointed out in my former dispatch, and which was in consequence of what you suggested as to the insecure anchorage off Riga for the *Aboukir*.

I have been obliged to station in the Belt another line-of-battle ship more closely to watch the canal of Kiel, where you will find by the enclosed intelligence the enemy are endeavouring to push a large force, most probably intended for Zealand. I received a letter yesterday from Lord Cathcart who left Örebro three days since on his way to the emperor after having seen the crown prince. It grieves me to find that the season is likely to be still more advanced before anything is finally arranged for the intended operations. It is, however, satisfactory to know that the delay does not proceed from want of the best disposition from all parties. And you will be happy to find that the ratification of the peace with Sweden was transmitted yesterday by an extra packet; by which conveyance your different letters were also transmitted.

The omission you allude to in Captain Steuart's order was, I assure you, not meant to give less title to rank of post, but was owing to the difficulty of giving rank where no ship could be named to which he was appointed. But in my public and private communications to the Admiralty I took care to claim the rank of post-captain for him; and (in) a letter which I have received from Lord Melville, he says, 'I perceive that you have appointed Captain Steuart of the *Reynard* and other officers to act in the gunboats in conjunction with the Russians, but of course it must depend upon circumstances as to how far it may be deemed expedient to confirm those appointments'. I shall, however, make the addition you wish in the order Mr. Champion will inclose to Captain Steuart. I have received no account of the promotion that is understood to have taken place except in a letter from Admiral G. Hope, who says there are to be twenty from the post list and a proportion of commanders and lieutenants. The next packet, which I hope will arrive before the messenger for Hanö sets off, will doubtless bring the gazette with the

[1] Martin's promotion from rear-admiral of the blue to rear-admiral of the white was dated 12 Aug. 1812.

promotions and, what is of greater importance, the details of Earl Wellington's glorious victory.

Lord Walpole,[1] who is appointed secretary to the embassy in Russia, arrived here yesterday in the *Calypso* and proceeded thro' the Belt with a convoy under the protection of the *Zealous*. I hope your health is perfectly restored. Be assured of the sincere and unvaried attachment etc.

232. *Thornton to Morris*

Stockholm,

25 Aug. 1812.

Sir, I have received this evening from Mr. W. D. Wilkinson, who is at the head of our establishment on the island of Hanö, the enclosed letter which I send you in the original (having no time to make a copy of it) for your information; and I beg you will have the goodness to inform him of any answer in conformity to a reference which I have taken the liberty of giving him to you.

I confess I am a little surprized that so long after the period of the signature of the peace between Great Britain and this country, of which I think it impossible that he should not have received some intimation, he should have imagined that any state of things, whether commercial or political, founded on a state of war and established within the dominions of Sweden under the avowed protection of a hostile force, could have continued to exist for a moment on the return of peace without the permission of the Swedish government; and that he had not immediately adopted such precautions for the protection of the property entrusted to his care as have been taken in other places and as were rendered necessary for the restoration to the Swedish government of all their territorial rights. Without entering at all into the question whether the depot of British goods in the island of Hanö were intended for a contraband introduction in the dominions of Sweden (an introduction perfectly justified by a state of war, as was the island itself) or solely for the purpose of introducing them into the enemy's dominions on the south side of the Baltic, it is perfectly clear that this use can no longer be made of the island without the consent of the Swedish government, and that the most innocent depot cannot be established there without their permission or without an agreement on that point with the British government.

If I had been at all aware of this use of the island of Hanö, I should have taken the liberty of writing to you, as I did that of speaking to His Excellency Sir James Saumarez on the subject of similar establishments in Wingo

---

[1] Horatio, Lord Walpole (1783–1858), M.P. for King's Lynn, 1809–22; secretary to the British embassy at St. Petersburg, 1812–15; 8th earl of Orford, 1822.

Sound a short time before the signature of the treaty of peace, and I should have urged the immediate removal to a place of safety, and under the legitimate protection of His Majesty's ships of war, of all such merchandize and British goods as were in depot upon the island for any purposes whatever.

As it is, I must beg you, sir, to have the goodness to recommend to Mr. Wilkinson without a moment's loss of time to remove all the goods entrusted to his care into such vessels as he may have at his disposal and to prevent all other goods from being disembarked without the permission of the Swedish authorities, as it will be utterly out of my power to afford any sort of protection to them consistently not only with the principles uniformly adopted by His Majesty's government, but with the established usages of all nations returning to a state of peace and amicable relations. In the meantime I shall use all the means in my power for obtaining for His Majesty's subjects the privilege of depot for their merchandize intended to be exported to other parts of the Baltic; but it cannot under any circumstances be expected to be obtained except in such ports or places as are under the complete control and superintendance of the Swedish government, and subject to such regulations and charges as may be established by law in Sweden or by an understanding with the government of His Majesty.

May I beg the favour of you to return me the enclosed letter and to inform me as soon as possible that the entire depot of British goods has been removed on board of ship or has been permitted by Swedish authorities to remain on the island. I have etc.

Enclosure:

232a. *Wilkinson to Thornton*

Hanö,

20 Aug. 1812.

Sir, Having received repeated information from Carlshamn that the Swedish government has premeditated some very severe measures against our establishment on this island involving the safety of the property under our care, I hope you will excuse the liberty I have taken in appealing to you on the occasion.

I think it necessary that I should state for your information that this establishment was decided upon and undertaken by me with a direct view to the promotion of the interests of the British merchants engaged in the Baltic trade. It was carried into execution in the spring of the last year under great difficulties of all kinds and at a period when unprecedented obstacles were opposed to the trade between Great Britain and Russia. The sequestration of the cargoes at Carlshamn and the decrees by which all intercourse with their vessels was interdicted along the Swedish coast left the British merchants without the means of obtaining any information regarding their property on its way home or of protecting it in case of emergency, at the same time that the more immediate channel of communication with Russia was thereby cut off and no other left open for their correspondence but the circuitous and tardy route over Stockholm, exposing their letters to interception on the Russian frontier. Under those circumstances it appeared to me that an establishment on this intermediate station would prove of natural utility; and having submitted my ideas concerning it to Sir James Saumarez and obtained his sanction, so far as regarded himself individually, I carried it into effect. And the commercial body at home, as well as in Russia, interested in the Baltic trade have borne ample testimony that I was [not] mistaken in my original idea of its utility by concerting the requisite arrangements as well by packet boats as a regular intercourse by way of messengers with Gothenburg. The communication between Great Britain and Russia was not only restored, but a degree of safety and celerity given to it that had never before been attained; whilst the early intelligence transmitted from hence to England of the arrival of the vessels very frequently produced a considerable reduction in the premium of insurance, from the knowledge of the vessel having left her port of lading and reached in safety this rendezvous.

Having troubled you, sir, with this detail explanatory of the nature and leading object of our establishment, I beg leave to add that, although the circular letter by which it was announced was placed by the French minister under the observation of His Royal Highness the prince regent at Stockholm, no intimation was then, or have at any subsequent period, been given to us that the Swedish government objected to the establishment; and whatever may be their present disposition in regard to it, I presume it was not usual in treaties of alliance to adopt measures of a retrospective object. The property in merchandize now in our possession may amount to £20,000. and something further is now on its way, but should it be the intention of the Swedish government to interfere in regard to this island, which I am pursuaded can only arise from aggravating misrepresentations (which jealousy in a neighbouring port may have dictated) I shall cheerfully conform to any regulations of a future tendency. These misrepresentations, I am led to think, are circulated to induce a belief on the part of the Swedish government that the island has been rendered a depot for smuggling goods into Sweden; but I can assure you that we have never regarded Sweden as a market for the description of goods which we have brought out and that the chief, if not indeed the sole, quarter to which we look for a *debouche* is the coast of Prussia west of Rugenwalde, but exclusive even of Swedish Pomerania. Whatever may have been surreptitiously introduced into Carlshamn has been effected by the merchants there from their own peculiar sources, but assuredly not from this establishment.

Having so fully expatiated on the subject, I have only to repeat that it is not our wish to seek a protection in defiance of the spirit of the Swedish laws, at the same time that I confidently rely upon the principles of common justice and universal equity in flattering myself that you will take that considerable interest in our cause as effectually to prevent any measures of a retrospective nature militating against the property of our own and of the other British subjects committed to our care.

I feel it peculiarly painful at a juncture like the present to bend to the necessity of this appeal, in the anticipation of one of the first consequences of the reconciliation of the two countries against the subjects of the others. But such have been the jealous insinuations at Carlshamn that, although divested of anything immediately official, I should consider ourselves betraying the confidence of our friends did I permit them to pass wholly unnoticed or longer to delay this attempt to place their property and our own beyond the reach of danger. I have etc.

233. *Morris to Saumarez*

Vigo, Hanö Bay,

28 Aug. 1812.

Sir, On the 26th. instant I had the honour to receive your letter of the 22nd. with the *Gazette Extraordinary* giving the account of the Earl of Wellington's victory[1] over Marmont,[2] on which I beg leave to offer you my congratulations. I dispatched the *Devastation* for Riga immediately with the gazette and packets for Rear-Admiral Martin agreeably to your directions.

The *Orion* and *Steady* sailed on the 26th. to take the station between Dars Head and Femeren; and the *Cressy*, *Rose* and *Woodlark* sailed yesterday afternoon with 118 sail of convoy. The *Anne* victualler having discharged her cargo sailed with the convoy, as also the three American vessels detained by the *Vigo*, the part of their crews that have been taken out being put on board the *Cressy* for passage to Wingo.

With the convoy list I enclose copies of the orders I have given to Sir A. C. Dickson and a general memorandum for permitting vessels laden with timber to proceed from the port of Danzig to this anchorage for convoy, which I hope you will approve of, and of my letter to Mr. Steffens,

1 Wellington's victory over Marmont at Salamanca, 22 July.
2 Auguste Fréderic Louis Viesse de Marmont (1774–1852) distinguished himself at the battles of Lodi and Marengo; created duke of Ragusa, 1807; commander-in-chief in Spain, 1811–12; swore allegiance to the Bourbons, 1815; ambassador to Russia, 1826–28.

Mr. Pickering's[1] correspondent, on the subject, which I had an opportunity of forwarding on the 26th. and will probably reach Danzig earlier than he expected.

I also forward reports of survey on two lieutenants of Royal Marines and two seamen. I have etc.

234. *Cathcart to Saumarez*

Åbo,
31 Aug. 1812.

Sir, The conferences which have been held at this place ended last night, when the emperor and the prince royal took their departure for Petersburg and Stockholm respectively. H.M.S. *Aquilon* is on her passage to Cronstadt from this port; and I am setting out to follow the emperor by land.

A reinforcement of 20,000 men has been added by the emperor to the Russian force in preparation to act under the prince royal with the Swedish army; but this reinforcement, judged to be necessary for the attainment of the objects of this campaign, cannot be even partially ready for service for several weeks. Meanwhile the Russian force, now at Helsingförs, will be borrowed for an expedition to be undertaken from Riga. It is to be returned and sent to its original destination as soon as the first half of the reinforcement shall be embarked.

It is requested that you will be pleased to continue the demonstrations and other services in which His Majesty's ships and vessels are at present employed under your orders as long as the season, and your instructions from His Majesty's government, may warrant the same.

I have written by this conveyance to Lord Castlereagh that it was my intention to make a communication to you to this effect. Should you continue with the whole or any part of your force in these seas and straits when active operations commence, H.R.H. the prince royal will, either himself or thro' Mr. Thornton, communicate to you the nature of the operation he proposes and the extent and detail of the concert and assistance he wishes to obtain from you. I have etc.

235. *Saumarez to Martin*

Victory, in Hawke Road,
6 Sept. 1812.

Sir, I have received your letter of the 27th. ultimo with its several inclosures, and informing me of your having sailed from Riga on the 21st. with

---

[1] Pickering was a British merchant engaged in the purchase of timber from Danzig.

the squadron under your orders accompanied by the Russian frigate *Amphitrite* and two sloops-of-war together with a detachment of four hundred and thirty soldiers for the purpose of making a diversion at the Heel of Danzig in order to distract the enemy and retard their operations against Riga. I have to inform you that I approve of your proceedings and the measures you have adopted with a view of drawing the enemy's attention from an attack upon Riga. I have etc.

236. *Saumarez to Martin*

Victory,

9 Sept. 1812.

My dear Sir, Lord Cathcart's messenger arrived at Gothenburg late yesterday evening, by when I have received a dispatch from his lordship the purport of which you will read in my public letter. It appears that until the reinforcement of 20,000 troops can be collected it is intended to send those at Helsingförs [Helsinki] to Riga, when they will be returned in time to join the expedition from Sweden. I am as yet unapprized of its real object, but expect it will be communicated to me from Stockholm when it has been finally determined upon.

In the meantime should you find that your presence at Riga is no longer required, I would wish you to repair to Hanö Bay with such part of the force as can be spared from the services at Riga or on that part of the coast. The services of Captain Steuart and the officers under him may be particularly useful at Riga, but you will of course follow the wishes of General Essen respecting them. I hope soon to receive accounts of the favourable results of your expedition.

Mr. Thornton will not arrive at Stockholm before tomorrow. His slow journey on account of Mrs. T.[1] occasions great murmuring among the Swedes. It is certainly unfortunate he should be so tardy at this important crisis. I remain etc.

237. *Morris to Saumarez*

Vigo, Hanö Bay,

13 Sept. 1812.

Sir, I had yesterday the honour to receive your letter of the 6th. instant directing me to send the *Pyramus* with the first convoy to Wingo Sound and have in consequence written to Sir Archibald Dickson (a copy of which letter

---

[1] Mrs. Thornton was pregnant. She gave birth to a son in Dec.

I enclose) to endeavour to call her in to relieve the *Ethalion* in charge of the convoy, when the latter frigate is to return to Hanö.

I have also to acknowledge by the same conveyance the receipt of your letter of the 9th. (most secret and confidential) directing me to keep H.M. ships and vessels under my command in readiness for an expected service, but without drawing them at present from the services on which they are respectively employed; and requiring me in the event of any application being made to me for assistance, either in fitting out the Swedish transports or embarkation of troops or in any other measures in which the service can be promoted, to comply therewith; also informing me you had been pleased to direct that Rear-Admiral Martin in the event of the *Meteor* and *Devastation* bomb vessels being no longer required to order them to Hanö Bay to be under my command. The two accompanying letters bearing Rear-Admiral Martin's address I dispatched the *Furious* with immediately they arrived.

I enclose herewith the disposition of all the ships and vessels that have received the orders they are acting upon through me; also an abstract of the last weekly accounts I have received from them.

I have sent by all vessels likely to fall in with the *Raleigh* orders to Captain Hooper[1] to join me immediately, and have requested Admiral Martin to return the *Censor* to me; when I expect (in six days time) to have those brigs together with the *Earnest* and *Furious* here ready to proceed with any orders you are pleased to direct me to send to any of the other ships. I have recalled the *Raleigh* as she must want refreshments; and in a letter of the 9th. Captain Hooper has sent by a merchant vessel, he complains of not having seen a sail upon his station. As soon as the *Meteor* and *Devastation* shall arrive, should their late service have occasioned defects, I will lose no time in refitting them for service as far as the means I have will allow; and have only to regret the assistance I shall be able to afford the Swedes, if called on at present, will be so trivial.

I have received reports of several small privateers being at sea and have kept the *Earnest*, (as much as the service of carrying your dispatches to Riga would admit) and the *Centinel* cruising between Öland and the Eartholms for the protection of the passing trade. But I fear one or two vessels have been taken. It is reported that Admiral Puke has sailed in a frigate for Dalarö; and Swedish armed vessels have been moving in all directions these two days. I have etc.

[1] George Wastell Hooper, lieutenant, 1800; commander, 1808; appointed to the *Raleigh* gunbrig, 1810; captain, 1817.

238. *Morris to Saumarez*

Vigo, Hanö Bay,
23 Sept. 1812.

Sir, I have the honour to acknowledge the receipt of your letter of the 19th. directing me, should I find it necessary to go into Matvik Harbour either with the *Vigo* or with other ships for their greater security, to occupy that anchorage; and informing me that it having been signified to the merchants that the latest period for the last convoy to sail from Hanö was fixed for the first favourable wind after the 1st of October and requiring me to regulate myself accordingly; at the same time instructing me, as the occupation of the Belt by the line-of-battle ships will afford security to the trade, it may be advisable to allow them to proceed with convoy so long as the favourable state of the wind will admit.

And I have in consequence directed Captain Heywood,[1] who had been obliged to return again on the 20th. to this anchorage with the convoy under his charge from the wind backing to the W.S.W., to inform the masters of the vessels that they are at liberty to proceed to Matvik Harbour for their better security, directing them to hold themselves in momentary readiness for sailing the instant there shall be a favourable shift of wind.

I had this morning prior to receiving your letter sent the *Ranger*, with the master of the *Vigo* and pilots of the bombs and vessels who were not acquainted, to Matvik to inform themselves of the pilotage in. I have etc.

239. *Cathcart to Saumarez*

St. Petersburg,
24 Sept./6 Oct. 1812.

Sir, In addition to my letter of 21 Sept./3 Oct. sent by the *Sheldrake* to be forwarded to you from Hanö by an officer from Admiral Morris overland, with a duplicate by messenger to Stockholm, I send this by a *feldtjäger* in the service of His Imperial Majesty. Lest by any accident this messenger should be the first who reaches you, I will shortly recapitulate the subjects.

The emperor having from many causes judged it expedient to desire that his fleet in the north should winter in Great Britain, I have taken it upon me to accede to the proposal subject to the arrangement and conditions, which it may be found necessary to be made by His Majesty's government, for regulating and distributing this force.

I have written in duplicate to Lord Castlereagh to request him to send the

---

[1] Edmund Heywood, commander of the *Ethalion* (36); lieutenant, 1797; captain, 1806; died, 1822.

instructions of government to you at Gothenburg in order to save time. I have written to you to request that you will be pleased to remain at Gothenburg until you receive these instructions, disposing in the meanwhile of the ships and vessels under your own command according to orders from home or as you may judge best for His Majesty's service.

I have forwarded in quadruplicate the emperor's mandate to Admiral Crown[1] to remain in Wingo Sound and to place himself under your command with the Archangel squadron under his orders. I have concerted with the Russian government that the fleet shall proceed to England in four succeeding divisions, *viz.* the Archangel squadron to sail in two divisions and the squadron from the Gulf of Finland to sail in two divisions. Two copies of the emperor's order to Admiral Crown are sent to Admiral Morris to be sent by him on board his cruisers to meet that admiral in case he should have proceeded to the eastward; and I have notified to Admiral Morris that it is probable he may hear of two squadrons of Russian sail-of-the-line sailing towards the Belt.

Enclosed you will find the most exact statement of the ships and vessels intended for England and of their several departures that I have as yet been able to ascertain. It will be sufficient for your purpose. My object in recommending four divisions is for the facility of distribution in our ports and to attract the less attention. The fleet from the Gulf of Finland will be commanded by Admiral Tate[2] who will have the emperor's orders to conform himself to the instructions which he will receive thro' you.

The object of this dispatch, you will see, is most interesting and immediate, namely, the pilotage of His Imperial Majesty's ships thro' the Belt and Cattegat. The Russian ships have hitherto invariably been in the practice of passing thro' the Sound. It is now judged expedient that they should proceed by the Belt. It is not impossible that they may receive pilots, but it is also possible that this aid may be denied under existing circumstances by Denmark; and it is extremely doubtful whether any number of pilots capable of taking charge of three-deckers and other large ships can be found on this side. I am therefore to request that you will immediately turn your thoughts to this subject and that you will have the goodness to state, by the *immediate* return of this courier, for the emperor's information what assistance you can

---

[1] Roman Crown (1754–1841), a native of Scotland who joined the Russian navy, after service in the British navy, in 1788; captain, 1795; rear-admiral, 1799; vice-admiral, 1804; in retirement, 1808–12 because of the war with Great Britain; commander-in-chief of the Archangel squadron, 1812; served in the North Sea, 1813–14; admiral, 1818.

[2] George Tate (1745–1821) was the third son of George Tate who also served for a time in the Russian navy; captain, 1784; commanded ships-of-the-line in the war of 1788–90; rear-admiral, 1793; vice-admiral, 1798; admiral and commander-in-chief of the Baltic fleet, 1802; in retirement, 1808–12; led the Cronstadt fleet to Britain, 1812 and back to Russia, 1814.

give or procure and what suggestions you can recommend towards carrying the service into effect.

The minister of marine is as much impressed as I am with the expediency of sending off all these ships as early as may be practicable; and I am not without hopes that considerably the largest division may move, wind permitting, sooner than the day named. The last and smallest division includes a 64 recently launched which, it is feared, cannot be got ready much before the close of the month of October new style. It is between the camels[1] and was to reach Cronstadt this day; and every exertion will be used.

The expedients which occurred here were that you might send some pilots overland to Hanö or to wait at the entrance of the Belt, but most of all that you might be enabled to continue a chain of vessels in the Belt if that can be done without too great hazard.

You will judge how impatiently your answer stating what you intend to do and what you can recommend will be expected; and I have therefore to request that you will not only dispatch the *feldtjäger* without delay by way of Stockholm, but also that you will send a duplicate of your answer by an officer to Hanö overland with an instruction to the officer commanding His Majesty's ships in that road to forward the same to Cronstadt by sea, which the prevailing westerly winds may render the most expeditious conveyance.

I inclose in the same packet a letter for Lord Castlereagh to acquaint His Majesty's government with the request above stated to you.

No change is known here to have taken place in the position of the troops near Moscow since my last. I have etc.

240. *Saumarez to Martin*

Victory, Hawke Road,

25 Sept. 1812.

My dear Sir, I have had the pleasure to receive your letters of the 12th. 13th. and 15th. and I am happy to find the diversion you have made in the Gulf of Danzig has been attended with all the good effect that was to have been expected. I have no doubt of its having tended to distract the enemy in some of their operations and drawn a considerable part of their force from the army in Courland, and possibly from the corps opposed to Count Wittgenstein of, at least, preventing reinforcements from joining those divisions of the enemy's army.

The accounts you have transmitted of the actions near Smolensk cannot

---

[1] Camels were flat-bottomed floats in which warships built at St. Petersburg were passed over the sand banks of the Neva river on their way down to Cronstadt. Once beyond the banks the camel was sunk beneath the warship which immediately floated in deep water.

fail being well received at home, for except the mutilated accounts contained in the French bulletins there appear to have [been] no other details of those actions received in England; at least none have been transmitted before yesterday from Sweden. It is rather surprizing that no bulletins have been received from Petersburg and—what will astonish you—no dispatches have reached this place from Lord Cathcart since his departure from Åbo. I had a few lines dated the 18th. instant from Mr. Thornton, but they contained nothing of importance. I expect to hear from him tomorrow on the subject of the expedition, but I am truly concerned to find that the Russian troops that were expected to form a part have not yet joined; and it is even doubted whether they can be spared by the emperor, which will entirely set aside all our expectations of the great benefit to have been derived from a powerful diversion being made in the lower part of the Baltic.

I yet hope it will not be given up, but without the powerful co-operation of the troops from Russia, Sweden will not act. Thus, my dear sir, the whole of the summer has been thrown away, when the troops alone that were so long idle at Helsingförs would have been sufficient to decide the fate of Macdonald's and Marshal Oudinot's corps and afforded permanent security to Riga. Admiral Cederström arrived at Gothenburg last Saturday; and the whole of the troops that were meant to embark from that place have been coming in since Monday and were intended to have embarked this day, the whole consisting of 7,500 men. You may therefore judge the great disappointment this has given me. I yet hope the timely arrival of a Russian force (even 15,000 troops) the expedition will yet go on. [sic]

I expect this letter may find you in Hanö Bay and that I shall be enabled after receiving my next dispatch to direct you to repair to this anchorage in the *Aboukir*, which is what I know will be agreeable to you. I forget whether I have written to you respecting Captain Thicknesse[1] who has solicited me to recommend him for your flag captain. I can only say that I believe him to be a very deserving character.

Dumaresq and Mr. Champion desire their best compliments. I am etc.

241. *Morris to Saumarez*

Vigo, Hanö Bay,
6 Oct. 1812.

Sir, I received last night your letter of the 29th. acquainting me you had directed Rear-Admiral Martin to repair in the *Aboukir* with the *Ariel*,

---

[1] John Thicknesse, lieutenant, 1795; commander, 1800.

Sheldrake, and *Reynard* to join you at Wingo; and directing me to signify to the trade that they are on no account to expect a convoy after the 10th. inst., it being ten days later than the arrangements made with the merchants in London, and to govern myself accordingly.

The rear-admiral having sailed on the 30th ult. with the *Daphne*, I have directed Captain Ross of the *Ariel* to proceed to Wingo with the *Ethalion*'s convoy and shall likewise direct Captains Brine and St. Clair[1] to do the same if the *Reynard* and *Sheldrake* arrive before it sails; and I have signified to the establishments at Hanö and Carlshamn, for the information of the trade, the time of the last convoy's sailing from the Baltic as directed.

The packets addressed under your cover to Rear-Admiral Martin I shall keep until I receive your next dispatch; and as you have been pleased to signify the orders you have sent to him, shall not open it unless I receive orders to send again to Riga in which case I shall see if either of the enclosures are for Captain Steuart.

The weather has been extremely baffling these two days, the wind varying from S.E. by E. to S.S.E. and the swell coming in from the southward, that this anchorage became hazardous for the merchant vessels to ride at. Therefore I have sent those that remained here with the *Ethalion* to Matvik that they may start together, the moment the winds favours and weather is sufficiently settled for so large a convoy of all classes of vessels to proceed.

I have completed the *Raleigh*'s provisions and hold her in readiness to go out to meet and proceed with the transports laden with arms for Cronstadt the moment they appear off. 2 p.m. The *Aquilon* and *Calypso* have just anchored; and I avail myself of Mr. Saumarez's obliging offer, who is charged with His Excellency Lord Viscount Cathcart's dispatches, to send my reports instead of the post which I was preparing them to go by. I have etc.

242. *Morris to Saumarez*

Vigo, Hanö Bay,

10 Oct. 1812.

Sir, I have to acknowledge the receipt of your letter of the 4th. inst., marked most secret, directing me in the event of the Russian troops from Finland not having arrived in Hanö Bay or *my receiving intelligence* of their being on their way to any port in Sweden to repair without delay in H.M. ship *Vigo* to Hawke Road, taking with me H.M. ships and vessels named in the margin [*Raleigh, Ariel, Reynard, Sheldrake, Meteor, Devastation, Censor,*

---

[1] David Latimer St. Clair, lieutenant, 1802; commander, 1812.

Earnest]; and to place under the orders of Captain Chetham[1] of the *Hama-dryad* Captain Acklom of the *Ranger* and the other ships and vessels remaining in the Baltic, directing Captain Chetham to remain in Hanö Bay or Matvik Harbour for the protection of the trade that may assemble at that anchorage and for the purpose of carrying on such services as may be required, and to furnish him with any intelligence I may deem proper for his knowledge and also giving him such further orders, as from my local experience, circumstances may render necessary; and to cause them to be completed with such provisions and stores as may be wanted.

In my letter of yesterday's date I had the honour to acquaint you that the *Ariel* and *Reynard* had sailed with the convoy under the *Ethalion* for Wingo and that the *Aquilon*, *Raleigh* and *Briseis* were to accompany them until clear of Bornholm and to afford assistance to the *Hamadryad*'s convoy in the event of falling in with them

I expect the *Ranger* to return this evening from cruising off the Eartholms, and shall leave with Captain Acklom the orders, of which the enclosed is a copy, for Captain Chetham, which I hope will meet your approbation; and proceed immediately for Wingo Sound. I have etc.

243. *Gyllensköld*[2] *to Saumarez*

Stockholm,
15 Oct. 1812.

Admiral, I have had the honour to lay before the prince royal the respectful sentiments of your excellency towards his august person. His Royal Highness, who is most sensible thereof, has directed me to make the following communication to you, sir, on his behalf.

His Royal Highness, observing with the utmost regret that the advanced season of the year precludes the idea of an expedition being undertaken the present campaign with the slightest possibility of success, has decided to launch it as soon as the navigation is open next year. Being convinced that His Britannic Majesty's ships-of-the-line, which must necessarily co-operate in this expedition, can arrive in sufficient time for it from the ports of England, His Royal Highness has already declined the offer, of which he is duly appreciative, made by your excellency through Mr. Thornton to leave four such vessels in this quarter throughout the winter; but he desires that your excellency will give orders for all the light craft of the fleet, that can be

---

[1] Edward Chetham, lieutenant, 1794; served on board the *Agamemnon*, Captain Horatio Nelson, 1794–95; captain, 1807; C.B., 1815; commanded the *Leander* (60) at the bombardment of Algiers, 1816.
[2] Carl Edvard Gyllensköld, naval aide-de-camp to Bernadotte.

spared, to remain in the Kattegat and Baltic throughout the winter; resorting, should the need arise, to the ports of His Swedish Majesty where they will be granted every aid and afforded a reception appropriate to the ships of a friendly and allied power. Not only will the appearance of English men-of-war off the German and Danish coasts from time to time cause alarm in those quarters, it will also arouse anxieties calculated to further the good cause and restrict the privateers within their own harbours.

The prince royal has, furthermore, recently learned by very reliable channels of the acute apprehension in Copenhagen that if communications between the island of Zealand and the province of Holstein are cut for any length of time there will be a shortage there during the winter of provisions and firewood; and that the king of Denmark, fearful of our late military preparations, has requested the aid from France of twelve thousand troops which are to be crossed into Zealand in the winter months: a step he has hitherto always refused to take. His purpose is to strengthen the military means of resistance which he anticipates will be required next spring. Your excellency will see from the foregoing the benefits to be derived from, and the disadvantages to be avoided by, the presence of an English flotilla in the Kattegat and Belt this winter, quite apart from the pressing need to sever communications between Jutland and Norway. His Royal Highness also intends to order various light craft of our fleet to cruise in the Belt. The sight of these cruisers, acting in collaboration with those of the Britannic Majesty, will alarm and irritate the Danish government perhaps to the point of taking an ill-considered step which will invite and provide public justification for a retaliatory measure on our part: a punishment long deserved by Denmark at the hands of Sweden and England on account of her blind and servile attachment to the power which is the sworn enemy of the welfare and independence of all nations.

As a solemn proof, admiral, of his confidence in your professional talents, esteem for your steadfastness of character and ardent desire to observe you co-operating with him on active service, His Royal Highness has ordered Mr. Rehausen,[1] the Swedish envoy to your king, to request positively in his name that the command of His Britannic Majesty's fleet in the Baltic should continue to be entrusted to your excellency.

The prince royal believes that in the present state of affairs every effort should be devoted to the aid and immediate liberation of Russia. When that great object has been achieved, there will still be many noble tasks to complete, many unfortunate and distraught peoples to deliver. Providence will

---

[1] Gotthard Mauritz, Baron von Rehausen lived at Broadstairs during the state of war between Britain and Sweden and acted as the unofficial representative of the Swedish court. He was appointed ambassador on the resumption of peaceful relations.

favour the arms employed in the sacred cause of humanity and the rights that have been denied it. Be pleased to accept etc.

244. *Melville to Saumarez*

Admiralty,
17 Oct. 1812.

Sir, You will probably before you receive this letter have learnt from Mr. Thornton or from the officers employed under the Swedish government that, in the event of the Russian troops from Finland being detained in the neighbourhood of Riga till the season is too far advanced to admit of operations against Zealand (of which there can be now little doubt), it is proposed by the king and prince royal of Sweden to make an attempt upon Norway. In a dispatch from Lord Castlereagh to Mr. Thornton of the 10th. instant, the latter was instructed to apprize the Swedish government that we shall not oppose any obstacle to such an attempt by withdrawing the support of such part of our fleet as the advanced season of the year may permit us to leave in the Baltic for that purpose. The instructions which you have already received from the admiralty appear sufficiently to warrant your assisting the Swedes in that enterprize, but I presume you will not deem it necessary to employ any of your line-of-battle ships in the operation and that a few frigates and smaller vessels will be sufficient. I trust that you will soon be enabled to send home all the ships under your command which will not be required to continue for this service or the other objects pointed out in the instructions which have already be sent to you. I have etc.

245. *Melville to Saumarez*

Admiralty,
22 Oct. 1812.

Dear Sir, We have received today your dispatch of the 13th. inst. with the important enclosures from Lord Cathcart respecting the intention to send the Russian fleet to winter in British ports. This intelligence is very satisfactory and his lordship's proceedings on that subject will accordingly be approved. I regret very much the calamity[1] which has occurred in your family, more especially as it has naturally produced an anxiety in your mind to return to this country. Participating in the feeling which dictates that wish on your part, I have not felt myself at liberty to withhold my sanction to your immediate return; and you will accordingly receive an order to that effect.

[1] The death in September of the commander-in-chief's eldest daughter, Mary Dobrée Saumarez (1792–1812).

As it is extremely necessary, however, that an officer should be sent to relieve you in Wingo Sound and as Admiral Morris may be detained in Hanö Bay, I have been induced to propose to Admiral George Hope to proceed forthwith on that service; and he will accordingly set out for Deal tomorrow where he will hoist his flag and sail without delay. A great deal of arrangement will be necessary in assisting the Russian ships; and from Admiral Hope's local knowledge I have no doubt that the most adviseable measures for that purpose will be adopted.

In my letter to you of the 17th. inst. I adverted to the enterprize which the Swedes had in view against Norway. It now appears, however, by a communication made yesterday by Mr. Rehausen, the Swedish minister in this country, that the scheme is abandoned for the present. I have etc.

246. *Saumarez to Wilkinson*

Victory, In Hawke Road,

24 Oct. 1812.

Sir, Since my letter to you of the 22nd. inst., having received information from Captain Ommaney[1] of H.M. ship *Vigo*, senior officer in Hanö Bay, that the Russian squadron under Vice-Admiral Crown has passed that anchorage without the vice-admiral having received the letter addressed to him from his government directing him to repair to Wingo Sound; but as it is very probable he may receive the said orders before he reaches the Gulf of Finland, I have to desire, in addition to the *Helder* and *Bellette*, that you also detach Captain Lloyd of the *Plantagenet* to Wingo Sound and that you take under your orders the remainder of H.M. ships and vessels stationed in the Belt, complying with the directions you have already received for their accompanying the two divisions of Russian ships expected from Cronstadt, and to consider their safety thro' the Belt as the chief and primary object of your attention. I am etc.

247. *Hope to Saumarez*

Egmont, in Hawke Road,

30 Oct. 1812.

Sir, Having this day received an order from you 'to put myself under your command and to follow such orders and instructions as I shall from time to time receive from you for His Majesty's service', I have to request you will be

[1] Henry Manaton Ommaney, the third son of Rear-Admiral Cornthwaite Ommaney; lieutenant, 1794; commander, 1802; captain, 1806; appointed to the command of the *Vigo* (74), 1812; rear-admiral, 1840.

10

pleased to explain to me whether I am to consider this order as superseding the instructions I have received from my Lords Commissioners of the Admiralty which direct me 'to proceed with all possible dispatch to Wingo Sound and having taken under my orders Rear-Admiral Morris together with the whole of the ships and vessels belonging to the Baltic squadron which Vice-Admiral Sir James Saumarez has been directed to deliver over to my command etc.', or whether it is your intention to authorize me, agreeable to those instructions from the admiralty, to take under my command the said rear-admiral together with the ships and vessels of the Baltic squadron. As I conceive it will be attended with much benefit to His Majesty's service at this late season of the year if before Rear-Admiral Morris leaves this place I am authorized to make such arrangements with him and give him such orders and instructions as I may judge necessary for executing the service with which it has pleased their lordships to entrust me. I have etc.

248. *Saumarez to Hope*

Pyramus, in Hawke Road,
31 Oct. 1812.

Sir, I have received your letter of yesterday's date signifying that you had received your order 'to put yourself under my command and to follow such orders and instructions as you shall from time to time receive from me for His Majesty's service' and requesting I should explain to you whether you are to consider this order as superseding the instructions you have received from the Lords Commissioners of the admiralty. In reply I have to acquaint you that the order you have received from me is not intended to supersede the instructions you have received from the Lords Commissioners of the Admiralty, but that until I have received dispatches from the Right Honourable Lord Cathcart, His Majesty's ambassador at St. Petersburg, which I hourly expect, I do not feel myself authorized to leave the station; and as your arrival here renders it expedient that Admiral Morris should return to Hanö Bay without delay, he has received my orders to that effect. I have etc.

249. *Saumarez to Martin*

Oxford,
29 Nov. 1812.

My dear Sir, I received with the greatest pleasure your letter of the 25th. yesterday morning. As I will owe to you, anxious as I ever have been to preserve your esteem and favourable opinion, it was a disappointment to me not to hear from you upon your arrival in England and since my return from the station. It has made me happy to find that you are in good health; and I trust Mrs. Martin is much recovered from her late indisposition.

You will probably have heard that my late command has ceased. The order to strike my flag was accompanied by a letter from the admiralty marked in the strongest terms of the approval of the board as also of His Majesty's government for my conduct in the various points connected with the station.

It has also afforded me the highest gratification to find that your services have been so highly appreciated by Lord Melville and that they have been so justly considered by the emperor of Russia, as the official letter I transmitted to you from Lord Cathcart so amply testifies. I can truly say that I have ever felt happy in doing justification to the zealous exertions and to your abilities and judgement upon all occasions, but particularly in the defence of Riga when closely invested by the enemy. And it will ever be to me a source of the highest satisfaction that I had it in my power to select you for that important service.

The *Victory* is ordered to be paid off. Our friend Dumaresq informs me he is desirous to pass some months with his family before he is again employed. I know no one more truly deserving than he is, and I hope his merits will be justly appreciated at the admiralty. I am here on my way to Cheltenham where I propose to remain till January. Lady Saumarez writes her best compliments to Mrs. Martin and yourself. I remain etc.

250. *Thornton to Saumarez*

Stockholm,

18 Dec. 1812.

My dear Sir James, I was not willing to mix politics with the tenderness of a domestic subject, such as is that of my letter of this day.[1]

You will see by the public papers the surprizing and most happy turn which affairs in Russia have taken and the series of great and brilliant successes which have distinguished the Russian arms. The packet which carries this letter conveys other most signal advantages gained by their generals, particularly Count Wittgenstein over the corps of Victor[2] and Oudinot, now joined to the wreck of Bonaparte's army. I am afraid, however, it carries with it the disappointment of the hopes of all of us, that the Great Enemy

[1] Thornton invited Saumarez to be godfather to his newly born son.
[2] Claude Perrin Victor (1764–1841) entered army 1781; promoted general, 1793; created marshal of France and duke of Belluno, 1807; accepted the Bourbon restoration; minister of war, 1821–23.

would, if he escaped at all, have reached the frontier almost alone and the survivor of his companions in arms and of his former glory. It appears that in the passage of the Beresegna [Beresina], a little above Borrisaw [Borisov], he has eluded the army of Tchitchagoff;[1] and that this army must now only be regarded as joining in the pursuit instead of encountering him in front and arresting his flight. It is possible that this disappointment may be recovered by increased activity and that he may be cut off before he reaches the Niemen, proceeding as he seems to be on the Vilna road; but this I think is at least doubtful. Certainly he will be harassed in every step of his retreat by his enemy, by famine and by cold. He will probably lose the little remains of his artillery as he has already lost the whole, or nearly so, of his equipages and plunder; but I think he has effected his personal escape and may carry back with him an army, if it can be called so, of forty or fifty thousand men.

There will therefore be another campaign, depend upon it. There *must* be, rest assured of it. And I trust you will have a part in it in these seas, for the scene *must* shift to the shores of the Baltic and to Germany. It is there that the denouement must take place, even if the great tyrant of the tragedy had fallen in the fourth act. So much for politics, my dear Sir James, ever your most faithful etc.

[1] Admiral Paul Vassilievitch Tchitchagov (1762–1849) was Russian minister of marine, 1802–09; assumed command of the army in Moldavia, 1812. The Moldavian army left Bucharest on 31 July and joined that of Tormasov near Lourdsk. Tchitchagov seized Minsk on 16 November and the bridgehead of Borisov on the Beresina on 21 November, but failed to prevent the French retreat across the river.

LIST OF DOCUMENTS AND SOURCES

I

II

INDEX

References in italics give biographical details of persons.
Ranks and titles are those at the time of reference.

operation with Swedish navy, 19–21, 38;
requests additional flag-officer, 22–3;
reaction towards detention of Sir John
Moore, 26–7, 29, 31–3; attention drawn
to Spanish troops in Danish territory,
25, 29–31; rescue of Spanish troops,
36–40; operations off Baltic Port, 41–4,
46–50, 52, 54–6; defence of his conduct
(1808) 52–9; private letter to tsar of
Russia, 56 and *n.*, 57, 59, 215; arrives
of Gothenburg (1809), 76; informed of
critical situation of Sweden, 77–9;
arrangements for maritime defence of
Sweden, xviii, 79–81, 84–6; occupies
Anholt, 80–2; proceeds to Gulf of Finland, 90–2, 97; offer of Swedish decoration, 91, 99, 100; operations in Porkala
Sound, 94, 97–8, 102; reflections upon
consequences of Russo-Swedish peace,
104, 111; caution on supply of arms to
Prussia (1809), 109; arrives off Gothenburg (1810); ordered to blockade
Elsinore, 122; lenient policy towards
Swedish trade, 128, 129–32, 134–6, 138,
142, 152, 159; appoints Hanö Bay rendezvous for trade, 129, 133; attitude
towards naval patronage, 139, 239, 247;
reports loss of convoy in Skagerak, 141;
requested to send home part of the fleet,
144–4; recommends compensation for
Schröder, 145–6; reports election of
Bernadotte as crown prince of Sweden,
146–8; anxiety concerning trade with
Mecklenburg and Prussia, 148–50, 154;
instructions to Captain Barrett, 157–8;
states advantages of holding Anholt,
158–9; reaction to the election of
Bernadotte, 159–60; reports Swedish
declaration of war, 161–2; sympathetic
interpretation of Swedish motives, 162–
5; arrangements for secret correspondence (1811), 171; transmits intelligence
concerning Scheldt fleet, 172–3; his
orders (1811), 173–4; receives assurances from Krusenstjerna about Swedish
policy, 176–7; learns of detention of
vessels at Karlshamn, 177–8; admiralty
instructions thereon, 178–9; comments
upon Swedish policy towards Norway,
179–80; reaction to detentions at Karlshamn, 182–3, 185, 187; requests instructions for conduct in event of Franco-
Prussian war, 188–89; requested by
Gneisenau to aid Prussia, 189–90;
ordered to assist Prussia in event of war,
190–1; prepares to assist Prussia, xxiii–
iv, 191–4, 197–203; ignorant of intentions of Prussian government, 203–5,
207; reports defects of *St. George*, 206;
attempt to aid Prussia abandoned, 206;
reports loss of *St. George* and *Defence*,

208–9; gives orders for defence of
Anholt (1812), 216–17, 226; orders to
isolate Norway, 217; arrival off Gothenburg, 219; informed of Anglo-Swedish
peace negotiations at Örebro, xxiv, 223,
230, 238; complains of passage of Swedish convoy to Kiel, 228–30; learns of
French invasion of Russia, 233–4;
approves Martin's resolve to assist the
defence of Riga, 234–7, 239; hopes of
Swedish military co-operation, xxiv,
238–40, 242, 246–7, 252–3, 258; block-
ades Zealand, 241, 243, 246–7; advises
Martin to proceed to Hanö Bay, 244,
247, 253; approves Martin's diversion
off Danzig, 252–3, 257; arrangements
for Russian fleet to winter in Britain,
xxiv, 255–7, 262–4; expectations of
Swedish co-operation disappointed,
260–2; granted leave to return to
Britain, 262
Saumarez, Mary Dobrée, 262*n.*
Saumarez, Matthew, xi
Saumarez, Captain Philip, R.N., xi
Saumarez, Captain Thomas, R.N., xi
Sausmarez, Matthew de, xi
Sayn-Wittgenstein-Ludwigsburg, Ludwig
Adolf Peter, prince of, *244*, 257, 265
Scania, 12, 20, 48, 87, 106*n.*, 123, 175*n.*,
177, 186
Scaw, the, 143, 208
Schaeffer, August, 83; see Schröder, E. F.
Schaw, diplomatic messenger, 14
Scheldt fleet, 105, 142–3, 145, 160 and *n.*,
161, 172–3 and *n.*, 174, 181, 183, 197,
207, 229
Schill, Colonel Ferdinand Baptista, *90*
Schmidt, Franz; see Mills, George Galway
Schmidt, Messrs. and Co., 158
Schönbrunn, treaty of (1809), 105*n.*
Schröder, E. F., 65, *83*–4, 96, 112, 115, 137
and *n.*, 140–1, 145–6, 171, 192–4, 199;
and see Colberg
Schulenberg, Captain John, 188
Schwartz, Captain Gottfried, 137 and *n.*
Sekleider, Mr., 127
Selby, Oswell and Co., 232
Selby, Captain William, R.N., *81*
Serrell, Captain John, R.N., *229*, 243
Seyer [Sejerø], island of, 58
Sheridan, Lieutenant John, R.N., *97*, 102
Shipwrecks:
  Defence, 169, 206, 208–10
  Hero, 169, 206 and *n.*, 210–11
  Magnet, 60
  Minotaur, 114*n.*, 119
  St. George, 125*n.*, 139*n.*, 169, 206, 208–10
Sierach, Captain, 219
Silver Pits, the, 210
Skagerak, xix, xx, 142*n.*; see Sleeve, the
Skekel, Lieutenant John, R.N., *97*, 102

QUEEN MARY COLLEGE LIBRARY

Navy Records Society

(FOUNDED 1893)

THE Navy Records Society was established for the purpose of printing rare or unpublished works of naval interest. The Society is open to all who are interested in naval history and any person wishing to become a member should apply to the Hon. Secretary, c/o The Royal Naval College, Greenwich, London, S.E.10. The annual subscription is two guineas, the payment of which entitles the member to receive one copy of each work issued by the Society for that year.

The annual subscription for members under thirty years of age is one guinea.

MEMBERS or NON-MEMBERS requiring copies of any volume should apply to the Hon. Secretary.

The price of volumes published before 1950 (*i.e.* Vols. I–LXXXVII inclusive) is 30/– to members and 40/– to non-members. Volumes published after that date are available at 42/– to members and 50/– to non-members. As postage is charged extra, please pay on receipt of invoice, and not on ordering.

The Society has already issued:—

Vols. I. and II. *State Papers relating to the Defeat of the Spanish Armada, Anno* 1588. Edited by Professor J. K. Laughton. (Vols. I and II). (*Out of Print.*)

Vol. III. *Letters of Lord Hood,* 1781–82. Edited by Mr. David Hannay. (*Out of Print.*)

Vol. IV. *Index to James's Naval History,* by Mr. C. G. Toogood. Edited by the Hon. T. A. Brassey. (*Out of Print.*)

Vol. V. *Life of Captain Stephen Martin,* 1666–1740. Edited by Sir Clements R. Markham. (*Out of Print.*)

Vol. VI. *Journal of Rear-Admiral Bartholomew James,* 1752–1828. Edited by Professor J. K. Laughton and Commander J. Y. F. Sulivan.

Vol. VII. *Hollond's Discourses of the Navy,* 1638 and 1658. Edited by J. R. Tanner.

Vol. VIII. *Naval Accounts and Inventories in the Reign of Henry VII.* Edited by Mr. M. Oppenheim.

Vol. IX. *Journal of Sir George Rooke.* Edited by Mr. Oscar Browning. (*Out of Print.*)

Vol. X. *Letters and Papers relating to the War with France,* 1512–13. Edited by M. Alfred Spont.

Vol. XXXI. *The Recollections of Commander James Anthony Gardner*, 1775–1814. Edited by Admiral Sir R. Vesey Hamilton and Professor J. K. Laughton. (*Out of Print.*)

Vol. XXXII. *Letters and Papers of Charles, Lord Barham*, 1758–1813 (Vol. I.). Edited by Sir J. K. Laughton. (*Out of Print.*)

Vol. XXXIII. *Naval Songs and Ballads.* Edited by Professor C. H. Firth. (*Out of Print.*)

Vol. XXXIV. *Views of the Battles of the Third Dutch War.* Edited by Mr. Julian S. Corbett. (*Out of Print.*)

Vol. XXXV. *Signals and Instructions*, 1776–94. Edited by Mr. Julian S. Corbett. (*Out of Print.*)

Vol. XXXVI. *A Descriptive Catalogue of the Naval MSS. in the Pepysian Library* (Vol. III.). Edited by Dr. J. R. Tanner.

Vol. XXXVII. *Papers relating to the First Dutch War*, 1652–1654 (Vol. IV.). Edited by Mr. C. T. Atkinson.

Vol. XXXVIII. *Letters and Papers of Charles, Lord Barham*, 1758–1813 (Vol. II.). Edited by Sir J. K. Laughton.

Vol. XXXIX. *Letters and Papers of Charles, Lord Barham*, 1758–1813 (Vol. III.). Edited by Sir J. K. Laughton.

Vol. XL. *The Naval Miscellany* (Vol. II.). Edited by Sir J. K. Laughton.

Vol. XLI. *Papers relating to the First Dutch War*, 1652–54 (Vol. V.). Edited by Mr. C. T. Atkinson.

Vol. XLII. *Papers relating to the Loss of Minorca in* 1756. Edited by Capt. H. W. Richmond, R.N.

Vol. XLIII. *The Naval Tracts of Sir William Monson* (Vol. III.). Edited by Mr. M. Oppenheim.

Vol. XLIV. *The Old Scots Navy*, 1689–1710. Edited by Mr. James Grant.

Vol. XLV. *The Naval Tracts of Sir William Monson* (Vol. IV.). Edited by Mr. M. Oppenheim.

Vol. XLVI. *The Private Papers of George, second Earl Spencer* (Vol. I.). Edited by Mr. Julian S. Corbett.

Vol. XLVII. *The Naval Tracts of Sir William Monson* (Vol. V.). Edited by Mr. M. Oppenheim.

Vol. XLVIII. *The Private Papers of George, second Earl Spencer* (Vol. II.). Edited by Mr. Julian S. Corbett.

Vol. XLIX. *Documents relating to Law and Custom of the Sea* (Vol. I.). Edited by Mr. R. G. Marsden.

Vol. XCI. *Five Naval Journals*, 1789–1817. Edited by Rear-Admiral H. G. Thursfield.

Vol. XCII. *The Naval Miscellany* (Vol. IV.). Edited by Mr. C. C. Lloyd.

Vol. XCIII. *Sir William Dillon's Narrative of Professional Adventures (1790–1839)* (Vol. I. 1790–1802). Edited by Professor Michael A. Lewis.

Vol. XCIV (additional volume for 1953). *The Walker Expedition to Quebec, 1711.* Edited by Professor Gerald S. Graham. (*Out of Print.*)

Vol. XCV. *The Second China War*, 1856–60. Edited by Mr. D. Bonner-Smith and Mr. E. W. R. Lumby. (*Out of Print*)

Vol. XCVI. *The Keith Papers*, 1803–1815 (Vol. III.). Edited by Professor C. C. Lloyd.

Vol. XCVII. *Sir William Dillon's Narrative of Professional Adventures (1790–1839)* (Vol. II. 1802–1839). Edited by Professor Michael A. Lewis.

Vol. XCVIII. *The Private Correspondence of Admiral Lord Collingwood.* Edited by Professor Edward Hughes.

Vol. XCIX. *The Vernon Papers* (1739–1745). Edited by Mr. B. McL. Ranft.

Vol. C. *Nelson's Letters to his Wife and Other Documents.* Edited by Lieut.-Commander G. P. B. Naish, R.N.V.R.

Vol. CI. *A Memoir of James Trevenen* (1760–1790). Edited by Professor C. C. Lloyd and Dr. R. C. Anderson.

Vol. CII. *The Papers of Admiral Sir John Fisher* (Vol. I.). Edited by Lieut.-Commander P. K. Kemp., R.N.

Vol. CIII. *Queen Anne's Navy.* Edited by Commander R. D. Merriman, R.I.N.

Vol. CIV. *The Navy and South America*, 1807–1823. Edited by Professor G. S. Graham and Professor R. A. Humphreys.

Vol. CV. *Documents relating to the Civil War*, 1642–1648. Edited by the Rev. J. R. Powell and Mr. E. K. Timings. (*Out of Print.*)

Vol. CVI. *The Papers of Admiral Sir John Fisher* (Vol. II.). Edited by Lieut.-Commander P. K. Kemp., R.N.

Vol. CVII. *The Health of Seamen.* Edited by Professor C. C. Lloyd.

Vol. CVIII. *The Jellicoe Papers* (Vol. I: 1893–1916). Edited by Mr. A. Temple Patterson.

Vol. CIX. *Documents relating to Anson's Voyage round the World*, 1740–1744. Edited by Dr. Glyndwr Williams.

Vol. CX. *The Saumarez Papers: The Baltic*, 1808–1812. Edited by Mr. A. N. Ryan.

Vol. CXI. *The Jellicoe Papers* (Vol. II: 1916–1935). Edited by Professor A. Temple Patterson.

WITHDRAWN
FROM STOCK
QMUL LIBRARY